150.19
Machan

The pseudo-science of B.F. Skinner

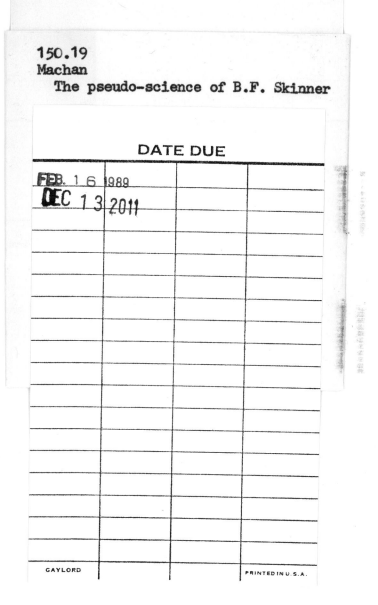

DATE DUE

FEB. 1 6 1989			
DEC 1 3 2011			
GAYLORD			PRINTED IN U.S.A.

the Pseudo-Science of B.F. Skinner

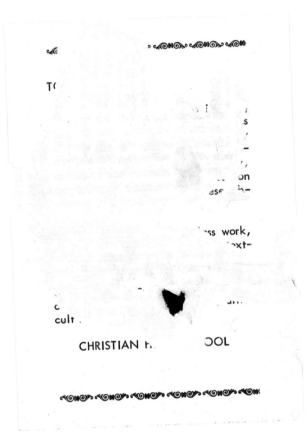

T(

s

on
ese

ss work,
xt-

c
cult .

CHRISTIAN F.   OOL

the Pseudo-Science of B.F. Skinner

Tibor R. Machan

ARLINGTON HOUSE·PUBLISHERS
NEW ROCHELLE, N. Y.

Manufactured in the United States of America

Library of Congress Cataloging in Publication Data

Machan, Tibor R
   The pseudo-science of B. F. Skinner.

   Bibliography: p.
   Includes index.
   1. Skinner, Burrhus Frederic, 1904-   2. Operant conditioning. 3. Free will and determinism.
I. Title.
BF319.5.06M32   150'.19'434   74-23742
ISBN 0-87000-236-8

The ultimate result of shielding men from the effects of folly is to fill the world with fools.

—Herbert Spencer

By convention sweet is sweet, by convention bitter is bitter, by convention hot is hot, by convention cold is cold, by convention color is color. But in truth there are atoms and the void.

—Democritus

If there is anyone who holds that the study of the animal is an unworthy pursuit, he ought to go farther and hold the same opinion about the study of himself.

—Aristotle

TO MY FRIENDS

Acknowledgments

Thanks must go to all those who have helped with this work and commented on different segments in its preparatory stages. I have benefited from many conversations with my colleagues Professors Ken Lucey and Mort Schagrin, and with my friends and associates in other projects—J. Roger Lee, R. A. Childs, Jr., James Chesher, Ned Dwelle, and others too numerous to list. Professor Meredith Watts offered many valuable comments on parts of this book. Professor Patsy Sampson helped me grasp Skinner's views. Dr. Nathaniel Branden's influence is evident in various areas. Among other commentaries on Skinner to which I am indebted are those by Arnold Toynbee, Noam Chomsky, Ayn Rand, John Platt, and Max Black. I have tried to follow Ms. Edith Efron's suggestions on style; but probably did little justice to them in the end—although without them I would have been lost on this, my first, book. My wife, Marty Zupan, has practically co-authored the work with her invaluable critical support, editing, and companionship. And I must thank the taxpayers of New York State who helped, albeit mostly unknowingly, to support my writing with a SUNY Summer Research grant. How I have made use of all this help, of course, is my own responsibility—even if a good Skinnerian will dispute that fact.

—Tibor R. Machan

Fredonia, New York, 1974

Contents

Text References

Following is a list of text references. These are placed in parentheses at appropriate points in the text and give the sources of quotes and material cited. Names of authors and editors are listed in the bibliography. This method is used to reduce the number of footnotes, and to make the work easier to read. All text references concern works by or about Skinner (and his point of view).

I   *Beyond Freedom and Dignity,* New York: Bantam Books, 1972 (Skinner).

II   *Science and Human Behavior,* New York: Macmillan, 1953 (Skinner).

III   *Verbal Behavior,* New York: Appleton-Century-Crofts, 1957 (Skinner).

IV   *Cumulative Record,* New York: Appleton-Century-Crofts, 1961 (Skinner).

V   *American Scholar,* Vol. 25, 1955 (Skinner).

VI   *The Man and His Ideas,* New York: E. P. Dutton & Co., 1968 (Evans/Skinner).

VII   *Beyond the Punitive Society,* San Francisco: W. H. Freeman & Co., 1973 (Wheeler/Skinner).

VIII   *Behaviorism and Phenomenology,* Chicago: University of Chicago Press, 1964 (Wann/Skinner).

IX   *The Virtue of Selfishness,* New York: Signet Books, 1965 (Rand).

X   *Readings in the Philosophy of Science,* New York: Appleton-Century-Crofts, 1953 (Feigl & Brodbeck/Skinner).

XI   *Explanation in the Behavioural Sciences,* New York: Cambridge University Press, 1970 (Borger & Cioffi/Bannister, et al.).

XII   *A Treatise of Human Nature,* Garden City, N.Y.: Dolphin Books, 1961 (Hume).

XIII   *The Review of Metaphysics,* Vol. XXVI, No. 1, Sept. 1972 (Boyle, et al.).

XIV   *A History of Philosophy,* New York: Harper Torchbooks, 1958 (Windelband).

XV   *The Science of Behavior and the Image of Man,* New York: Basic Books, 1972 (Chein).

XVI   *Knowing and Being,* Chicago: University of Chicago Press, 1969 (Polanyi).

XVII   *American Philosophical Quarterly,* Vol. 8, No. 1, Jan. 1971 (Ziedins).

XVIII   *The Ways of Paradox,* New York: Random House, 1966 (Quine).

XIX   *The Structure of Scientific Thought,* Boston: Houghton Mifflin, 1960 (Jeffres/Farber).

XX   *Perspectives in Biology and Medicine,* Vol. 11, No. 1, Autumn 1967 (Efron).

XXI   *The Uses of Argument,* New York: Cambridge University Press, 1958 (Toulmin).

XXII   *Reason,* Vol. 5, No. 8, Dec. 1973 (De Mille).

XXIII   *Metaphysics,* Bloomington, Ind.: Indiana University Press, 1966 (Aristotle).

XXIV   *The New York Review of Books,* Dec. 30, 1971 (Chomsky).

XXV   *New Views of the Nature of Man,* Chicago: University of Chicago Press, 1965 (Platt/Sperry).

XXVI   *Invictus,* No. 10, Nov/Dec. 1970 (Bissell).

XXVII   *Journal of Philosophy,* Vol. 63, No. 1, Jan. 6, 1966 (Feinberg).

XXVIII   *Cerebral Mechanism in Behavior,* London: Chapman Hall, 1951 (Lashley).

XXIX   Unpublished paper (to appear, revised, in *Reason Papers,* No. 1, Fall 1974), (Bissell).

XXX   *An Introduction to Logic,* New York: Oxford University Press, 1961 (Joseph).

XXXI   *The Psychology of Self-Esteem,* New York: Bantam Books, 1969 (Branden).

XXXII   *Studium Generale,* Vol. 23, 1970 (Efron).

XXXIII   *Logical Positivism,* New York: Macmillan, 1959 (Ayer/Carhap).

XXXIV   *Boston Studies in the Philosophy of Science,* New York: Humanities Press, 1969 (Cohen & Wartofsky/Efron).

XXXV   *Explanation and Human Action,* Berkeley: University of California Press, 1966 (Louch).

XXXVI   *The American Political Science Review,* Vol. 62, No. 3, Sept. 1968 (Ashcraft/Locke).

XXXVII   *Natural Right and History,* Chicago: University of Chicago Press, 1953 (Strauss).

XXXVIII   *American Philosophical Quarterly,* Vol. 10, No. 2, April 1973 (Epstein).

XXXIX   *The Monist,* Vol. 52, No. 4, October 1968 (Nielsen, et al.)

XL   *Wittgenstein,* Garden City, N.Y.: Anchor Books, 1969 (Pitcher/Stroud).

Introduction:
Science vs. Liberty

Human freedom and dignity have been, and to some measure still are, basic to the point of view upon which America's culture is built. Politically, America began with the explicit belief that freedom from interference of other people's actions is everyone's right; that every individual should be free to decide and act within the limits of his own justifiable sphere of interest. Borrowing heavily from the tradition of natural-right theory and its most astute intellectual architect, John Locke, the belief in human rights is founded on a moral position: each person possesses the capacity to reason and to choose what he will and should do for the greater part of his life, therefore each person should be free to act in accordance with his best or worst judgment where his own life is concerned. For better or for worse, these ideas are integral to American culture—albeit not fully consonant with America's history.

Dignity refers to what every human being can achieve if he chooses to live by the moral principles suited to man's life. Each person possesses *moral dignity* in the eyes of the law, or should, because he has the capacity to make a morally decent life for himself. The idea, naturally, is that as people with the option to do right or wrong, we are all equally important in a human community and must be treated as ends, *not* means to other people's goals and aims. A political system founded on such beliefs considers individuals in most respects to be autonomous and capable of independent thought and action, self-control, and self-improvement. As long as each person is allowed to exercise his personal choices, his life should be his own to govern and direct.

While the American political tradition does not universally accord with all that is implied by the above, it has done better than others. And among those who accept this tradition (as basically right and suited to human community life) many are not ready to defend its ideas in identical ways. Some have managed to degrade this tradition by using it to shield contradictory actions. But America's culture still may be strongly identified with the values of freedom and dignity.

A problem that continues to confront those defending the merits of a free society is that the ideas and arguments supporting it have not satisfied many of the scientists in our society. Admittedly, the term "scientist" carries too many meanings, often depending on one's own outlook. For the most part, however, people understand it to mean someone who insists on a firm theoretical and factual foundation for what he says and the statements attributed to him—especially if these statements are to be taken seriously. For several centuries many theoretically minded people, e.g., philosophers, psychologists, economists, historians—in short, the bulk of the intellectual community—denied that moral and political ideals could be rationally reconciled with the scientist's high standard of truth. Two centuries ago David Hume, the British empiricist and skeptical philosopher, argued against a certain type of reasoned approach to values, namely rationalism. He held that conclusions about what one ought to do, how communities ought to be organized, and other matters of right or wrong have no basis in pure reason. Since Hume's time, and in consequence of taking him to have undermined all rational ethics, time, morality and politics have been divorced by many influential thinkers from all that may be scientifically or rationally respectable. To this day the situation has not changed to any appreciable degree.

The few defenders of human freedom and dignity are left in a bind. With all sorts of advances within the sciences and technology, the attraction of certain modes of thinking has grown enormously. Methods of physics and chemistry have been transported into biology, psychology, sociology, and political science. By an eager adoption of these methods, students of the second group have aimed at success and, most of all, respectability. The motto has become, for practically any field of study: "to be scientific is to mimic the hard sciences, whatever our subject matter." The bulk of scholars in the social and humane sciences now insist on research and analytic methods that were originally part and parcel only to some of the hard sciences. Not that no opposition to this trend can be found. But if there are victories about such matters, the advocates of making all fields of inquiry copy what physicists or chemists do—by now it would be more accurate to say "did"—have thus far won the battles. Their model of what it is to be scientific reigns in popularity, respectability—if not so *obviously* in truth value.

By all such counts freedom and dignity seem to many of us to be clearly unscientific. High schools, colleges and universities abound with eminent professors who teach that moral and political values such as freedom and

14

dignity can be viewed in our sophisticated age only as myths, albeit convenient ones, of the past. The public at large, increasingly exposed to academia in classrooms and through news media, cannot be expected to lag far behind this kind of development. We shall not prejudge if it be progress or regress, for that remains to be seen. The general conception of the scientific trend has been that we must either embrace it fully or reject it in favor of some antiscientific alternative. To name just a few countertrends, both Existentialism and Eastern mysticism consider current efforts to put everything on a scientific basis to be a typical manifestation of Western civilization's alleged one-sidedness. As many have expressed this, the emphases on objectivity and categorization are mere extensions of our unfortunate Greek heritage. What we need instead, say the antiscientists, is closer attention to our "subjective worlds." Most recently the so-called counterculture has entered its cry of protest against the scientific/technological viewpoint. Here again many make references to "higher consciousness," turning inward toward "subjective experiences," and developing intuitive forms of awareness. (Often the tone becomes elitist when these prescriptions are announced—surely troubles abounded in the Orient despite unity with the universe.)

So to many people the choice appears to be, to put it bluntly, between the scientific (ergo: rational, factual, meaningful, objective, manageable by common criteria of understanding) and the humane (ergo: emotional, personal, elusive, private, mysterious, and not appropriately dealt with intellectually but only intuitively). This dichotomization between two allegedly separate ways of coping with the world has been in evidence throughout human history. Certainly however the philosophies of the West have given expression to it over and over again. One need only recall that Plato argued for two worlds, as did Descartes, Kant, and virtually all the major thinkers who have commented on man's relationship to the universe. The specific terms of the dichotomy may differ—after all, this is the point of constructing different philosophical systems by which to explain it. But we find traces of it everywhere. People either accept two worlds or reduce what is thought by some to be part of one world into components of the other, or else they advocate that the world has many different, consistent (but often baffling) facets to it.

Today the most emphatic and publicized expression given to the second option, thought by many to be required by science, is the social philosophy of Burrhus Frederic Skinner. Skinner's is *not* the most theoretically coherent or "clean" rendition of the view that tries to reduce all of what exists in the universe, especially in human affairs, to material substance in motion. Karl Marx, and subsequent Marxists, certainly made a valiant attempt to develop a scientific philosophy they called "dialectical materialism." Earlier, Hobbes and others wanted to become scientists of human behavior by way of reductionism. And even today there are philosophers called materialists (or physicalists) who advocate pretty much what Skinner's ideas of man and nature amount to—but they do not usually produce political recommendations on the side.

Skinner's incursions into political theory illustrate a disturbing, sometimes frightening fact of modern life. This is the unwillingness on the part of intellectuals to develop philosophical systems, leaving it to specialists to make the attempt. Under the impact of Hume's ideas, many outstanding minds have refused to embark on the development of grand, systematic theories of man and his world. The few who have tried have been rebuked by official, academic philosophy—or at least the bulk in the class. Why exactly this has occurred is not at issue here. We must admit that people require some way to make sense of things, some framework in terms of which they can understand the myriad facts, events, problems, conditions, pains, and pleasures they encounter in life. When only inklings of good sense emerge from the divergent products of scholars working in their respective special fields, the grand synthesizer tends to appeal to the population at large. He will very likely influence the specialists as well, even when he fails to notice or admit it. Since the specialist feels need at times to attend to matters outside his own field, he will rely on concepts, ideas, clichés, slogans, or whatever in his attempt to organize his common, everyday experiences.

The evidence for this kind of practice is overwhelming. The thousands of outpourings from specialists concerning matters only peripheral to their fields borrow heavily from prevailing popular fads and pseudophilosophies. For example, the hundreds of books by those writing on ecology, conservation, the quality of life, and so on, can be backed up by knowledge derived from investigations conducted within their own fields—biology, zoology, and the like. Nonetheless, many attempt to exploit their findings in their special fields by making contributions in areas where they have only shallow knowledge—such as political theory, ethics, or economics. In such instances they simply adopt ideas they have barely checked out or rarely put to the test of appropriate standards of inquiry. (It is notorious how many ecologists happen to blame "big business," the scientific revolution, capitalism, and other factors for what ails us. Surely this lies outside the field of biology.) Sociologists, computer scientists, psychologists, and all— their recourse to the most readily available world view is understandable, if perhaps not entirely admirable. Yet what is to be expected in an intellectual, philosophical vacuum in which philosophers—that is, those of the profession supposedly dedicated to the integration and synthesis of basic knowledge—deal with miniscule problems, talk to each other in "scholarly" journals, and generally deny that philosophy can do anything to contribute to the solution of human problems?

Today B. F. Skinner's language, generated within that small branch of psychology called "animal behavior study," is riding prominently and gaining acceptance in wide-ranging areas of concern. Concepts such as "conditioning," "stimulus," "response," "reinforcement," "operant," and "control" crop up all around us. Skinner's central idea—that man does not act or choose to act but merely "exhibits behavior" for which the environment is "responsible"—has influenced not only psychologists but others who are impatient about the conditions of contemporary human affairs.

But all this is no mystery. Most people want and need to be able to cope with what happens in areas in which they are incompetent outside their expertise. Even if they borrow from one field at one turn and another at the next, this seems understandable when we appreciate their perfectly sensible willingness to make the world, or at least segments of it, intelligible.

According to Skinner, the ideas of human freedom, dignity, human rights, a free society, and similar "mysterious" notions make little sense: they are indefensible; they are inconsistent with certain important domains of human interest; they are clearly prescientific. And if that is what science and technology demand, many people will acquiesce. Did not scientists, that is those who work in labs, research centers, and the like, facilitate many of the wonderful and delightful experiences we have in our lives? How could we travel, entertain ourselves, enjoy the arts, and do other exciting things without the props of technology? True enough, there are problems we associate with the growth of science, but this is easily accounted for by reference to human ignorance—and now, with Skinner's thesis, to the lack of scientific analysis and treatment of human behavior. Many people consider Skinner an enemy of humanity. These people charge him with dehumanizing man. Yet, to be perfectly fair, what other alternative has so much going for it? What promises success with what appears to be such solid evidence to back it up? At a time when most of us expect our politicians to set our lives in order, when high prices, dirty air, unfriendly neighbors, bad readers, dropouts, pornography, X-rated movies, and whatever annoys anyone are all supposed to be set right by congressmen, senators, district attorneys, the White House, and all the other proven angels of our culture—at such a time it cannot be surprising that Skinner's "help" from outside, for which no effort need be exerted, is welcome. And if by science we can send men to the moon, change our wrinkled faces to look young, and perform other fantastic feats, why not allow the Skinnerian experiment—a scientifically based behavioral technology—its turn at the wheel?

Many of us firmly believe however that there is something very wrong with that line of reasoning. But what? Just to feel ill at ease with it does not matter—all novelties are strange at first. Some of us lash out against Skinner, charge him with inhumanity, demoralization, and other sins, but what have we to offer as an alternative? What are we to say to those who insist that freedom and dignity are unscientific, divisive, a constant source of controversy, and should be given up as we gave up the idea of phlogiston two centuries ago in chemistry?

In fact, there is far more than feeling to go on. While not many people may be aware of it, alternatives to Skinnerian utopianism do exist. Again Skinner seems to know well where these lie, since his attack is focused on the source—the literature of freedom and dignity. Of course he has distorted that literature, chosen its weakest elements to ridicule, and smeared its contributors with emotional and psychologistic labels. But that itself is a clue to what he knows well. Skinner proposes an inadequate, unsupported, fanciful theory of man and human action. And he knows that a well-put defense of freedom and dignity could easily overcome the false promises and outright threats from his theoretical contributions. Given, however, that almost any shortcut to universal happiness is received by many with open arms (consider the hundreds of fads in vogue) and given our frequent substitution of the label "science" for actual scientific education and thinking, we can understand why he gains not just fame but widespread respect and a following by way of his books and articles of not more than a series of flat assertions, hints, hunches, and dubious extrapolations. It is evident that all of his works rely on a sophisticated form of faddism, via the term "science," in order to create a myth of promise for his unsupported doctrines.

Close inspection of his works shows that Skinner is wrong on many more fronts than he is right. But it must be realized that some of what he has done—promoting the application of what he and others now in the field call "operant conditioning in prisons" (token economies, treatment of "behavioral disorders" in adults and children)—has been valuable, even successful, by standards any rational person can employ in an evaluation of his work. But not all these successes can be linked to his overall outlook. After all, plain animal-training occurred long before Skinner came upon the scene, as did training in sports, acrobatics, and child-rearing. But because of Skinner, certain techniques have gained importance in areas that theretofore had been left to common sense or simple rule of thumb.

Still, most of what he has done—especially in the two major works I shall examine—is wrongheaded. He has overstepped the bounds of wisdom and good sense, not to mention science, with his grandiose proposals. But to feel uncomfortable about Skinner is not enough. And we cannot simply *believe firmly* that he is wrong when the issues are as wide-ranging in significance and potential applicability as those that he discusses. Thus I will argue the case *against* Skinner and *for* freedom and dignity.

My argument is not directed to Skinnerians; most of them are firmly set on accepting his views. And even if they question him on some counts, their basic assumptions are Skinnerian and these they are reluctant to give up—after all, it could mean renouncing their entire careers to do so. (But does that guarantee that they cannot be swayed by criticism?—even if a different approach might have to be taken.) Skinner has said that he considers the English language to be "prescientific" and therefore incapable of conveying what is true about human affairs. So I would like to challenge this view and submit a competing framework.

This does not mean that this book is a polemical attack on Skinnerism. While judgments of the quality of Skinner's work—and thus, at least by implication of the person himself—will emerge, the focus is on his ideas, arguments, theories, and proposals. My purpose is to reject Skinner's point of view—mainly his analysis of human affairs as such—and suggest instead that the ideas of human freedom and dignity are sound as well as supported by relevant scientific work. As with all works that attempt to reach a wide audience, mine invites questions that will need further inquiry. My aim here is to defend that a human being can *choose* what he will do, that he is better off living in a *free* society, and that his dignity can be his highest achievement in such freedom. Rejecting these facts is to reject the crucial features of one's personal and community life. It is to court disaster, as disaster is courted whenever reality is rejected in favor of myth and pseudoscience.

Initially I will examine the ideas and contentions that have led Skinner to conclude that human freedom and dignity are "mythical" or "meaningless" concepts. We shall see that his grounds, as stated or implied in his books (especially in *Beyond Freedom and Dignity*) are shaky at best, and often completely confused and illogical. Secondly, I will argue for an alternative approach to show that man can be free, should live in political freedom, and should strive for dignity in his life. I consider these facts to be consistent with a sensible, rational, and nondogmatic conception of the nature of science. Although my central goal in this book has been to criticize Skinnerism, I thought it best to at least outline an alternate position. No criticism is without its framework. And while mine could not be provided full support here, the direction of the argument is clearly indicated, so the reader will have no trouble seeing how a comprehensive justification would have to develop.

Despite its obvious limitations, the present work should provide what so many commentators on Skinner and his critics asked for: a counter-thesis to Skinnerism.

PART I

1

Skinner vs. Freedom, Dignity, and Liberty

THE CONTENTION THAT human beings are free to initiate some of their actions, that they can actually choose some of what they do in their lives, has been attacked and defended throughout mankind's intellectual history. B. F. Skinner is among those who are thoroughly hostile to the idea—he believes that human freedom does not exist. He thinks that believing in human freedom is on par with believing in myths, demons, mysteries. "The hypothesis that man is not free is essential to the application of scientific method to the study of human behavior. The free inner man who is held responsible for the behavior of the external biological organism is only a prescientific substitute for the kinds of causes which are discovered in the course of a scientific analysis." (II/447)[1]

Skinner starts his most popular book by claiming supreme virtue for science and technology: "We play from strength, and our strength is science and technology." (I/1) He literally denounces the idea of human freedom, although he says that science calls for its rejection. He says freedom is outmoded, unscientific, and reactionary. The modern age with its developments in physics and biology should not be cajoled into accepting what, after all, is an ancient human superstition. He simply views the tradition of libertarian ideas—into which he lumps any doctrine that invokes notions of choice, liberty, responsibility—as outmoded and prescientific, while claiming advancement, modernity and, of course, truth for his "scientific analysis."

To see if Skinner has any kind of a case we need to consider several of his assertions. To begin with, are the basic ideas of Skinnerism novel while the doctrine of human freedom is ancient?

Free choice—ancient or novel?

If any ideas have some claim to novelty in intellectual history those of human freedom and dignity have a far better chance than what Skinner offers. But in fact germs of both kinds of ideas have been with us since ancient times. While the general belief that demons or other humanly uncontrollable forces governed behavior is ancient, so are the ideas of freedom and responsibility about conducting oneself traceable to practically any age. Indeed we get a mixture of freedom and what is generally called (somewhat misleadingly) determinism in the views of most noted thinkers throughout history. As far as a consensus is concerned, few people would credit anyone for having shown conclusively either the basic independence of human conduct or its full dependence on factors outside of one's own control.

What is more important is not whether there have been germs of doctrines of liberty and thoroughgoing determinism throughout the ages, but that the latter idea was prominent in the very age Skinner condemns as prescientific. Ancient philosophers such as Democritus and Leucippus argued that everything in the world constitutes an interrelated collection of atoms that must by necessity move along predetermined lines. This is not the complicated and modern determinism of Skinner. But the germs of his idea of human nature are clearly there. Throughout the religious eras when human conduct was tied directly to noble or vicious supernatural forces, the doctrine of determinism, separate from scientific theory, had prominent influence. A sort of "devil made me do it" approach to a great deal of misbehavior lurked behind even the more sophisticated theologies. True, these views did not prevent violent responses to human misbehavior. But it was often accepted, in some very influential circles, that punishment would cleanse the evildoer of his bad influences. The idea of original sin is clearly part of the many suggested explanations for the evil that people do. And original sin means just that all men are moved to do wrong by their inheritance of the characteristics of their ancestors.

So the concept of personal responsibility is not in itself an ancient one—if by this is meant that the notion was prominent throughout premodern times. Quite the contrary, even today the notion is circumvented in most intellectual circles. Instead what people *do* is often attributed to their inherited characteristics, the conditions of their environments, social influences, intervention from the will of supernatural entities, or certain biological conditions which are considered to be a malignant aspect of the entire species.

There are significant exceptions to what these beliefs express. The fundamentals of contemporary criminal law, in most civilized societies, attribute to people in general (unless otherwise shown) the capacity for choice. And it does so without relying on any univocal idea of an "inner agent"—the bane of Skinner's scientific psychology—to account for what

Skinner so disparagingly calls "autonomous man." According to the legal frameworks of most societies where the rule of law is at least approximated, a person is responsible to learn what is right, and to differentiate right from wrong—at least by law. Exceptions are of course admitted, and some people are identified, subsequent to close examination, as incapable of making choices in accordance with standards of good conduct. Within the law—i.e., in court—the explanation of a person's behavior, especially when he has harmed another, involves reference occasionally not to what he has chosen to do but to influences which he could not control. But this is done to serve justice by specifying cases where it would be incorrect to attribute to someone the consequences of his behavior. This serves to *contrast* such cases with others where such attribution is quite right.

Freedom and the social sciences

For Skinner and many others in the social sciences there is no difference between the kinds of cases contrasted above. Skinner maintains that people cannot help what they do, how they behave—not just sometimes but under all circumstances. There are no criminals, he contends, just people whose behavior deviates from some written generalization, norm, or preference. There are no wrongdoers, simply people we label as such (due to our ignorance of the factors which caused their behavior). Wars, riots, crimes, personal disasters, pain, misery, injustice, and the like are *never* caused by people but by their history of reinforcement. Good and bad people alike cannot help being what they are. A recent example: Watergate had nothing to do with wrongdoing, impropriety, negligence, bad judgment, injustice ("obstruction of justice"), or the violation of human rights—the affair simply *had* to come about and was caused by the inevitable chain of events that constitutes the evolution of the universe, the human species, and each individual.

Before getting to Skinner's views on freedom and dignity it must be stressed that such notions as the above are clearly not unique to a handful of Skinnerians. With variations, this is how most of today's social scientists, philosophers, and intellectuals—including laymen in some of the reflective moments of their lives—conceive of the situation. Most of those who study and theorize about history, economics, culture, social affairs, education, government, international relations, and the like propound, if only implicitly, a deterministic concept of human nature. Their particular versions may differ. The "causes" of behavior and consequences fall into different categories, but man's efficacy is systematically denied.

We are interested in Skinner's ideas on this issue. And an examination of them will take us through a number of areas of his position.

First of all, we need to understand Skinner's denial of the proposition that human beings are capable of choice. By choice we mean the capacity to initiate some action, mental and/or physical, all on one's own. Most of

25

us know this to be the traditional problem of free will versus determinism. It is important to see how Skinner deals with this problem and what if any difficulties he faces.

Next, his dismissal of human dignity will come under scrutiny. This topic is directly related to the first one, and it will be useful to keep the two in focus. By dignity Skinner means the characteristic of achieving worthwhile goals for which personal moral credit is deserved. That this notion relates to human freedom of choice is quite evident. Skinner certainly finds linking the two ideas to be unexceptionable; that is why he insists on attacking both under the same roof.

Finally, we will consider his concomitant attack on the idea of political liberty. He does not always make clear whether he is attacking freedom of choice or political freedom—the term "freedom" is left unqualified in most of Skinner's discussions. But from specifying the context it will be possible to delineate which freedom he has in mind.

Reductionism vs. free choice

Later we will see that Skinner's determinism is not a conclusion that can rest on scientific investigations that yield the denial of human liberty. Skinner has not made a scientific discovery to the effect that human beings cannot cause their actions, that they have no choice about what they are doing, that their entire behavior is (must be) caused by factors over which they can exercise no control. Neither has he carried out scientific experiments *with human beings* from which the most sensible generalization has to be that people simply respond to their environment—or even that their response is always, although in complex ways, caused by something over which they have no control.

At best Skinner has demonstrated that *some* animals behave with no evident options on their own part; that they act without the capacity to originate behavior, to make active, creative contributions without being prodded, molded, or stimulated to do so by factors within their environments. Even this is not borne out conclusively by his laboratory experiments without certain unproven assumptions concerning the states of deprivation of various selected members of the animal species under inspection and strict experimental control.

As Dr. Richard de Mille explains:

> The furor in the popular press over B. F. Skinner's *Beyond Freedom and Dignity* is the more disconcerting because, when not indulging his grandiose fancies, Skinner remains a notable scientist. Unfortunately, the public has no way to distinguish plausible, limited applications of operant conditioning from utopian schemes and science fiction. But the limits are inherent; by definition, an "operant" is an emitted act, which can be reinforced/conditioned/shaped only *after* it has spontaneously appeared. We have to ask, then, what makes the act appear for the *first* time. . . . (XXII/29)

26

Skinner's own, often useful, contributions to behavioral *science* actually leave room for what could turn out to be human freedom. His concept of the "operant," introduced to supplant the idea of purposive behavior and voluntary activity, does *not* require determinism for all of the affairs and activities of human beings. Operant behavior *could* be free, even if with simple behavior we can identify some cases as stemming from drives, instincts or other fixed and humanly unalterable causes.

Despite this, Skinner demands the requirement of a thoroughgoing determinism that allows for no genuine choice in human affairs. "The hypothesis that man is not free is essential to the application of scientific method to the study of human behavior." But there is no attempt to prove this claim anywhere in Skinner's works. What with the questionable conception of science he offers it can be appreciated why this is so, even if the certainty of the position is severely undercut as a result. The emerging idea then cannot be linked either with what science itself dictates or to the scientific contributions Skinner himself produces. Instead, the prejudice against human freedom arises out of a philosophical commitment that we examine in chapters 2 and 3. The position to which Skinner clings, mostly by implication but here and there quite explicitly, is most usefully (and in accordance with philosophical parlance) characterized as reductive materialism.

The main tenet of this doctrine is that there exists only one kind of entity for science to investigate, appearances to the contrary notwithstanding. And a corollary tenet is that the laws governing the behavior or motion of this kind of entity are those we call laws of mechanics. Because Skinner does not bother to detail this position, one can quarrel with the label given it here. Especially since Skinner's reference to his agreement with Whitehead's philosophy (I/15) departs from many materialist philosophies. Whitehead himself was not a determinist. But Skinner seems to borrow only the reference to "processes" as the metaphysically basic elements of reality, not the rest of Whitehead's teachings. (It is doubtful, as well, that he knew of Whitehead when he began his own work.)

There are powerful objections to the reductionist point of view that should caution a student of human affairs about its adoption and advocacy. Some scientists who accept it admit that it is a faith (perhaps it is based on some desire) and not a stricture based on a rational assessment of the results of scientific investigation. The reductionist position is not the requirement of scientific simplicity, parsimony, or economy. Matters get more rather than less confusing by imposing the reductionist framework on everything. The fact of numerous branches of knowledge and science gives evidence for a hierarchy of not just the kinds of things there are in nature but the laws and principles appropriate to understanding and explaining their behavior. The laws of mechanics are unsuited for purposes of understanding what we find in various areas or realms of reality—not even physics is happy with them in our times.

And these are only some of the reasons why reductionism must be rejected as unproven and inappropriate within a science of human behavior. However much one would like to have a science of human behavior that leads to the kind of prediction and control possible in laboratory experiments with small animals, a scientific approach simply does not permit the faith Skinner and many others propagate. Nor can this faith be adequately supported from a philosophical perspective.

On denying free choice

But the faith in determinism itself, be it reductionist or not, has other problems aside from its lack of scientific and philosophical support from within the Skinnerian framework. To Skinner, determinism means that nothing human beings do is up to them; that they are in no actual or possible circumstances the causes of anything, including their own behavior. "The mistake . . . is to put the responsibility anywhere, to suppose that somewhere a causal sequence is initiated." (I/72)

We must distinguish this kind of determinism from the kind used, for example, in the statement, "He was all along determined to become a doctor." In such a case it is an open issue whether the determination was the person's own or had another source. But usually we would assume that the person had taken it upon himself, firmly and with resolve, to become a doctor by strong commitment to a choice. This kind of determinism is the sort that Skinner rejects. (II/448) He has no patience with theories of self-determination. (Although this does not square with his advocacy that people take it upon themselves to design a culture.)

What then are the flaws in Skinner's universal judgment that nothing we do is up to us, that in whatever activities we are involved, in whatever behavior we are engaged, we cannot help ourselves? First, this claim must be applied to Skinner himself; how could he avoid its application?

Now a person who utters something he cannot help uttering is quite imaginable: people talk in their sleep, for example. And what they say could be taken to be true or false by those who hear them, although the person asleep is hardly in the position to judge.

If we make the condition of the sleep-talker a universal one, such that *by our nature as human beings* we cannot help saying the things we say, could there still be a distinction between true and false statements? Perhaps if some other species of beings existed with the capacity to learn and understand our language as well as to know about the world, this could be the case. Thus, although parakeets can repeat sentences, including the sentence "Human beings are not free," they are not capable of understanding statements or of establishing whether they are true or false. But Skinner is not a member of a different species, nor are we all parakeets.

The Skinnerian position, however, places us in the camp of constant sleep-talkers or parakeets, claiming that what we say we cannot help saying. Under such circumstances no one can tell what is or is not true. When disagreement occurs and some say "p" while others "not-p," both parties have to have said what they said. To then inquire into whether "p" or "not-p" is true can only result in the further problem of everyone having to say what he will about that. And so forth, *ad infinitum*.

Therefore by the tenets and requirements of determinism, it is impossible ever to render a decision as to whether determinism is a true doctrine—a correct theory of human behavior. The requirement is that nothing we do can be free of outside or inherited control. Thus the articulation of determinism must also be an unfree act. When a deterministic analysis emerges from the lips of the determinist, by that view nothing else could have emerged. By the same token nothing else could have come from the lips of anyone who denies the truth of determinism. From the point of view of the determinist neither position could be held by choice.

To ascertain what is being said as true or false requires, however, that one be capable of objective, unbiased judgment. If the mind can only go in one direction, the person is unable to render an objective judgment. The minimum requirement to establish whether some claim is true is that one be *capable* of objectivity, unhampered judgment, and absence of prejudice. Other factors may also be needed, such as the willingness to attend carefully, without bias and prejudice. But if even the *capacity* to judge is missing, there can be no distinction between truth and falsehood, objective judgment and bias, and considered opinion and prejudice. Someone might accidentally say what others could consider to be true, but in line with determinism we are *all* talking in our sleep—unable to focus our minds, to make sure what we say is indeed true to the facts. We have no way of being either right or wrong since that would mean that we can choose between one or the other.

This objection has had some rebuttal from determinists, although Skinner himself never takes up the issue. There is profit in dealing with one formidable objection however. We need to clear the road leading up to Skinner so that the positive analysis coming up further on can have a smoother prospect than what could be achieved by simply refuting him. For example, the philosopher Adolf Gruenbaum has objected to the present argument by saying that when a determinist accepts his own position as it applies to himself "determinism is not jeopardized by this fact: if anything, it is made credible . . ." and tells us that truth and falsehood must be ascertained by finding out "the particular character of the psychological causal factors which issued in the entertaining of the belief [in question] . . . ." (X/775)

But the response is inadequate because what is at issue is whether the truth of some belief can be *established*, not whether some belief is actually true. That issue is secondary to the former; it is statements that are true, but their truth needs establishing. To the determinist, independent, objective appraisal of any position (including determinism) would be impossible because no such activity as discovery, establishment, or appraisal could ensue; only predetermined, *imposed* beliefs, states of mind, or patterns of behavior could be possible. Being right or wrong in the way we come about these beliefs makes no sense by the doctrine of the determinist.

Several philosophers have answered the Gruenbaum challenge. In the end the main problem with Skinnerian and other kinds of all-encompassing determinism is that the position actually must assume what it flatly denies. Some philosophers have put it thus: "Every determinist makes the claim that his account of the data is superior to his opponent's, and therefore *ought* to be accepted in preference to the alternative position." (XIII/24) But as it is seen in Skinner, what can the phrase "ought to" mean to a determinist? Only those who admit that people can make choices can ask of them that they ought to do something; determinists can only predict that they will or will not. The idea that one ought to do something assumes that he could do it or refrain from doing it. And by advocating determinism the Skinnerians *(et al.)* presuppose what they deny—that others are free to appraise and eventually judge as correct a position such as determinism.

Determinism, then, has a major flaw: it is inconsistent. While Skinner believes that his form of behaviorism does not have to yield to logic (X/594), for those who insist that philosophy and science conform to the principles of logic—which are after all grounded on the nature of reality itself—this is not at all satisfactory.

What must be remembered, however, is that the above objections are not sufficient to prove that human beings *are* free. This is crucial. Thus far we have only argued against Skinner and have not proposed an alternative view; what we have so far shown is that Skinner's theory cannot be proved. Perhaps people never are free—some, I am sure, never exercise their capacity for choice, others do so very infrequently. What we aim to prove is that people *can* be free, that determinism is false.

Actually Skinner spends very little time on the idea of human freedom; he flatly denies that he discusses the problem. (VII/261). Since he believes that science must exclude human freedom, he does not seem to think that any independent argument for determinism is needed. I have dealt with the issue at some length because Skinner largely rests his position about man, society, and the future on his constantly reiterated denial of free will.

Why does he do this? Why does he feel he must reject even the possibility of human freedom? He does so in preparation for his denial of human dignity, of the fact that people can be better or worse, that they can achieve or fail, not just at some tasks but at living a successful life—at being morally excellent. All these notions, including the appropriateness of punishment in cases where persons do certain irresponsible things, depend on the fact that people are usually free to choose between alternative courses of conduct. And to pave the way toward the rejection of these facts and corresponding ideas about human affairs, Skinner has to attack the very possibility of human freedom of choice.

Skinner vs. human dignity

In everyday affairs as well as in critical situations human dignity plays an important role. The fact that everyone possesses the dignity of human life enables them to act in ways that they otherwise would not. For instance, although most of us know only a few persons intimately enough to have a personal regard for them, we are certainly acquainted with many other people. Our capacity for moral worth, that is, our human dignity answers the question of how these people, without any close relationship to us, ought to be treated. Perhaps not everyone needs to know that human beings possess dignity, that they are capable of moral achievement and should be understood in that light. But in many circumstances our emotions, immediate concerns, fears, or related factors can obliterate the empathy or natural feeling of community people can have for each other. This is especially so in cities with large populations where we know only a few people among those encountered each day. The feelings of kinship, friendship, and fraternity can be superseded by other, more hostile emotions.

Yet even then other people are due at least a minimal degree of respect, simply by virtue of their humanity, however remotely that touches one at the moment. The idea that people are capable of freedom and can have moral aspirations of their own can be a lifesaver. Those who think before acting under emotional strains and other pressures certainly have a firmer than *ad hoc* guideline on how to deal with others. Not that we must view human dignity as some kind of useful myth. Without a basis, our belief in it could lead only to error—quite as Skinner would contend. Yet keeping in mind man's essential dignity, the fact that each person is capable of moral growth, is both in accordance with good judgment and fruitful conduct.

Human dignity is the link between the fact that people are capable of free choice and the value of political liberty for their social existence. Skinner knows this. If man has dignity, then violating his rights so as to secure some "nobler" aim—e.g., the survival of the culture—can be objected to on powerful grounds. Should it be proven, however, that dignity is a myth, that no man is worth the trouble in the face of such a "glorious" goal as the survival of a culture (whatever that means—for that notion belongs with such other vague ones as "society," "civilization," "race," "the people," and so on), then resistance to any social engineering cannot but be intellectually unfounded and based on irrational fears, just as Skinner suggests. The advocates and defenders of liberty are then simply unstable and emotionally disturbed. If one accepts that human dignity is a myth, this suggestion doubtless has a great deal of force. Skinner would seem to have every reason to combat the ideas of freedom and dignity, to marshal science, technology, and the art of rhetoric in his behalf. They are his major obstacles on the road to a world of behavior technologists who would induce everyone to promote the survival of the culture.

31

What then is Skinner's substantive objection to the idea of human dignity? Basically he argues *ad hominem*. He tries to show that whenever people refer to human dignity, they are really after some dubious goal—they are deceitful, sneaky, and altogether underhanded. Consider what he says: "We attempt to gain credit by disguising or concealing control. We try to gain credit by inventing less compelling reasons for our conduct." (I/55)

Dignity for Skinner is what merits credit, so we claim dignity to gain credit. "We recognize a person's dignity or worth when we give him credit for what he has done . . . What we may call the literature of dignity is concerned with due credit. . . ." (I/55) The reason we cling to dignity or worth is that "We are not inclined to give a person credit for achievements which are in fact due to forces over which he has no control." (I/41) So we go to extremes of denying, cheating, concealing, and so on the truth Skinner brings to light:

> We try to avoid discredit for objectionable behavior by claiming irresistible reasons. . . . We magnify the credit due us by exposing ourselves to conditions which ordinarily generate unworthy behavior while refraining from acting in unworthy ways. . . . We seek out conditions under which behavior has been positively reinforced and then refuse to engage in the behavior; we court temptation . . . (I/46, 7)

We go through all this because "Any evidence that a person's behavior may be attributed to external circumstances seems to threaten his dignity or worth." (I/41)

Beyond assaulting the motives of those who stand up for it and those who refer to it in their own or someone else's case, Skinner has nothing to say in criticism of human dignity. He does note that the idea of dignity is often used to justify punishment—after all, he rather simplistically maintains, if credit is due for achievement, punishment must be due for failure. He cites no one who defends such a crass view of punishment—but then he cites no one extensively enough to give himself some kind of challenge.

Dignity, free choice, and Skinner's strategy

Yet Skinner's procedure cannot be chalked up to ignorance. He seems to be well aware of the problems and mentions them here and there, without, however, coming to grips with any of them. Supposedly, his being aware of the problems provides the reader with evidence that he must have dealt with them somewhere, if only in his "private mental life." For example, he is well aware of the practical connection between human dignity or worth and free choice. He observes that

> Goodness, like other aspects of dignity or worth, eases as visible control wanes, and so, of course, does freedom. Hence goodness and freedom tend to be associated. . . . (I/66)

One hopes in vain to see this issue taken up. Indeed, Skinner seems to recognize the fact that if human freedom is denied, no sense can be made of the idea that something or someone is good or bad, including the idea that the survival of the culture is good and should be promoted. But he leaves the matter untouched. All he adds is the observation, again hardly sufficient concerning its brevity *and* the significance of its topic in intellectual history, that

> John Stuart Mill held that the only goodness worthy of the name was displayed by a person who behaved well although it was possible to behave badly and that only such a person was free. . . . (I/66)

Beyond this the topic is dropped.

What is so puzzling is that Skinner's indictment of those who hide behind phony claims to credit, based on mythical notions about dignity or worth, cannot make sense within his frame of reference. But he does not bother to explain these inconsistencies. To disguise, conceal, invent, refrain, refuse, avoid, or court temptation all presuppose the ability to choose freely. Other than his original disclaimer about consistency, attributed to the prescientific character of the English language, Skinner says nothing to justify his exposition.

A point to be noticed here, easily obliterated in the search for arguments not forthcoming, is Skinner's approach to his readers. He counts on people's acceptance of humility as a cardinal virtue. He trades on this by discrediting any admission of self-worth, of the very possibility that one may indeed have earned some credit, or that any of the values one has come by are really through one's own achievements. Most people consider excessive pride a fault. It is generally called conceit or vanity. And overemphasizing one's achievements, especially in public, is an example. Should one respond to Skinner and Co. by protesting that, yes, he has achieved some goals and is due credit for them, it may appear that he "doth protest too loudly." Because to talk that way means *taking* credit and doing it in public. Just imagine someone standing up, after Skinner has finished speaking on the subject of how no one deserves credit for anything, and announcing that he feels he *does* deserve credit for what he has accomplished! In contemporary circles, however, most people would disdain to do this. And Skinner is trading on this fact when he attacks dignity. He convinces more by browbeating than by argument: "You have no dignity because you cannot achieve anything worthwhile"! To argue with this takes a good deal of self-confidence and unabashed pride in oneself, so most people will withdraw from the fight. Yet clearly, if man can be free (and to insist otherwise is inconsistent), he can also achieve dignity. One need not get involved in personal demands for credit to establish that much.

The virtues Skinner attacks are, significantly, those that can lead to personal pride. He never talks down at humility or modesty. Those human character traits he needs. But we must see in what light Skinner sees virtues. In all cases he finds them at the feet of autonomous man. It is in this respect (i.e., autonomous, free man, human beings as conceived by most defenders of the claim that people can do some [things] on their own) that human dignity is related to freedom. Only free beings can achieve what is valuable. And only free beings are capable of making of themselves morally worthy individuals.

Man and moral values

Rocks do not achieve values for themselves. Rocks break apart or dissolve, but they do nothing wrong. Nothing bad has thus happened by any standard of being or existing as a rock. It makes no sense to say that as far as rocks are concerned, breaking is bad. Some rather way-out mystical doctrine might wish to argue this, but the philosophy of human life which may flow from this is intolerable. (It would be the philosophy of death, for then we could never manage to avoid doing evil, at every stage of life, in all aspects—for life always involves changing the being of something into another thing, therefore contributing to the nonexistence of some [things]).

Animals do gain from some things and lose by others. We can identify water as necessary to fish in order to live. But in the case of the bulk of the animal kingdom these values seem to be sought automatically. Little ones may be *trained* by older ones, but then they proceed to sustain their own lives. And they are deterred by inadvertent circumstances—matters they cannot plan for and cope with—quite often. There may be some cases where an animal approaches a stage of its life and experiences and, as some say, "having developed its cognitive capacities," begins to make choices about what it will do, i.e., select brand new alternatives. But the only evidence for this is in laboratory cases, or in instances involving a minute level of cognitive expansion from generation to generation. Most animals do not change from generation to generation; chicks and kittens and puppies and calves and colts and cubs learn no new tricks, as it were. And on what we call the lower level of evolutionary development, the issue of training does not arise—the relationship between conditions of birth and maturation are accounted for in purely chemical terms.

It is only with human beings that we must account for differences and changes in life styles, occupations, locations, economic conditions, partnerships, and all of the variations we find at the level of individual life. And it is here that we must cope not just with errors (animals make "errors," misperceive some things) but with gross, sustained, often fatal failures that have not been even faintly attributed to factors outside one's control. It is here that achievements can occur, also.

Dignity, too, is an attainment that man can be worthy of. But dignity does not come with the achievement of just any sort of goal. It is only in a facetious and parasitical sense that a cruel or dishonest man gains dignity by achieving his goal of insulting or deceiving others; by self-deception *he* may consider this dignified. But this is trading on a different meaning

34

of that idea. Dignity is earned by the achievement of goals that a human being *ought* to achieve.

In a way Skinner has a keen understanding of what he is doing. He may seem careless and sloppy and he is at times, but he has rationalized that fact very carefully. It fits in well with his program—to abolish rational man. "To man *qua* man we readily say good riddance." (I/191) In bringing about this eviction it would be odd for Skinner to exhibit a great deal of care, precision, logic, and the host of other traits that we usually consider the virtues of man *qua* man (at least in the sense of the Greeks who started from these virtues and then came up with the rest of them). But Skinner sees clearly what he must do in order to establish his case. He must destroy all respect for human virtues, at least those associated with individualism, and for the condition that can be achieved by being virtuous—human dignity. Without human freedom there can be no dignity. And without dignity, why would anyone have reason to protest when his freedom is ignored by others? A totally dejected human being, convinced of his own impotence in the face of the world, will yield to whatever urges or pushes him the most—his own fears, others' criticism, the authority of some, or whatever. Psychologists see enough variations of this condition to have produced many books, each claiming that a different manifestation is the central one.

Skinner and political liberty

Free will and the possibility of human dignity demand a system that protects and preserves political liberty. What is Skinner's attitude toward political liberty and what role would it play in a Skinnerian world?

We need not imagine that Skinner evades altogether the differences between a society where political liberty is respected and one where arbitrary state power reigns. Skinner associates the conditions of political liberty with the absence of harmful, painful control, that is, aversive conditions. What is meant by the latter is tied up with Skinner's notion of negative reinforcement, "Negative reinforcers are called aversive in the sense that they are the things organisms 'turn away from.'" (I/25) *Why* any organism would turn away from certain stimuli is not *explained*.

It is impossible that man's genetic endowment supports this kind of struggle for freedom: when treated aversively people tend to act aggressively or to be reinforced by signs of having aggressive damage. Both tendencies should have had evolutionary advantages, and they can easily be demonstrated. If two organisms which have been coexisting peacefully receive painful shocks, they immediately exhibit characteristic patterns of aggression toward each other. The aggressive behavior is not necessarily directed toward the actual source of stimulation; it may be "displaced" toward any convenient person or object. Vandalism and riots are often forms of undirected or misdirected aggression. . . . (I/27)

When the aversive treatment is intentional (i.e., when people act aversively toward each other to gain certain ends) people may do a number of different things.

> For example, they may simply move out of range. A person may escape from slavery, emigrate or defect from a government, desert from an army, become an apostate from religion, play truant, leave home, or drop out of a culture as a hobo, hermit or hippie. Such behavior is as much a product of the aversive conditions as the behavior the conditions were designed to evoke. (I/26)

But people can turn against their controllers, "attack those who arrange aversive conditions and weaken or destroy their power."

> We may attack those who crowd us or annoy us, as we attack the weeds in our garden, but again the struggle for freedom is mainly directed toward intentional controllers—toward those who treat others aversively in order to induce them to behave in particular ways. (I/27)

What Skinner is trying to say is that resistance to control makes sense only if the control is exercised unwisely—by way of aversive stimulation. That is to say, as long as people use harmful, annoying, painful means by which to make other people do something, it is likely that there will be very powerful resistance. In spite of the "probable" genetic source of this resistance, the literature of freedom has been important because "Without help or guidance people submit to aversive conditions in the most surprising way." (I/29) Skinner mentions that some people even fail to ward off bad weather conditions, that is "aversive conditions [that] are part of the natural environment." Thus he concedes that "The literature of freedom has made an essential contribution to the elimination of many aversive practices in government, religion, education, family life, and the production of goods." (I/29)

The literature of political liberty

But Skinner does not like the literature of freedom despite these accomplishments which he claims are worthwhile. This is because (a) the literature has emphasized how the absence of aversive control *feels*, and (b) while it has "overlooked control which does not have aversive consequences at any time, it has encouraged escape from or attack upon all controllers." (I/38). In short, Skinner considers the literature of freedom harmful because it has renounced not only aversive control, but the kind of positive reinforcing control that he believes should be employed to effect the survival of a culture.

One may imagine that Skinner may be thinking of a rather small and relatively harmless faction of that literature—hardly to be compared with what has been produced by John Locke, John Stuart Mill, and others who have advocated political liberty. That is, he may be thinking of the "humanistic" intellectuals, or some of them, who consider technology itself dangerous. Much is made these days of the horrible effects of computers, the impersonality of assigned numbers in various bureaucratic situations, the omnipresence of machinery and gadgets. There are technophobes in virtually every age—people who denigrated the locomotive, the airplane, the atomic power generator—and they often argue their "humanism" in terms of the *feelings* of dehumanization engendered by all the machines around them. One may imagine also that this is why Skinner focuses on Joseph Wood Krutch, Feodor Dostoevsky, Arthur Koestler, C. S. Lewis, Abraham H. Maslow, *et al.* as the *major* exponents of the literature of freedom. But they should be more properly considered humanists because they focus on the value of man *vis-à-vis* machines. However, their approach is relatively free of specific political recommendations. Among the people Skinner mentions, only Mill, Popper, and de Jouvenel offer comprehensive political theses—actually, Mill is the only well-known political theorist in the lot, and Skinner has mentioned him just once.

But imagining all this is to miss Skinner's purpose. He must know, as anyone else in our cultural and academic arenas must, that there have been very lengthy, prominent expositions on the nature of a free society. Skinner tells us that

> A person escapes from or destroys the power of a controller in order to feel free, and once he feels free and can do what he desires, no further action is recommended and none is prescribed by the literature of freedom, except perhaps eternal vigilance lest control be resumed. (I/30)

But this is not true. Many philosophers concerned with the nature of a free society write about the kind of life that will gain a person happiness. Among the free society's recent defenders H. B. Acton, Leo Strauss, and Ayn Rand have been the most articulate about matters of personal conduct and morality in connection with political liberty.

"Further action is recommended" also by sources outside the community of political philosophers who advocate a free society; and this is only natural in an intellectual environment where a division of labor must prevail. Not everyone can worry about all aspects of human life. So some recommend the best political circumstances, others talk about various personal aspects of man's life, and still others consider occupation, health, and recreation. So from within positions advocating a free society there has been a great deal of valuable discussion about how people might make the best of their freedom.

What Skinner seems to dislike is that most of those who consider the free society a good social organization for human beings, in spite of their concern with themselves, are willing to leave the conduct of a person's life in his own hands. These people recognize that no matter how diligently they write books, offer advice, or teach children (barring coercion and the power of the state) it is ultimately they themselves who must choose to select what is good and exciting about life. At least they will have this chance secured for them. Then, of course, the individuals in the community can engage in the voluntary exchange of advice, recommendation, education, religion, and other forms of "Skinnerian control."

Skinner's political ideals

It is this basic trust in the capacity of individual human beings to conduct their lives with reasonable success that Skinner considers unwise. He agrees that controlling people with the result that they feel hurt, angry, or annoyed is imprudent—mainly because it gets people angry at control itself. Instead, the technology of behavior, with its emphasis on positive reinforcement (nonaversive control), must be employed. With the science of behavior "The feeling of freedom becomes an unreliable guide to action as soon as would-be controllers turn to nonaversive measures, as they are likely to avoid the problems raised when the controlee escapes or attacks. Nonaversive measures are not as conspicuous as aversive and are likely to be acquired more slowly, but they have obvious advantages which promote their use." (I/30) So the opposition to controlling human beings evidenced by the literature of freedom stands in the way of potential controllers who will use more subtle means by which to achieve the ends desired by cruder and less genteel precursors.

The problem is that at first Skinner's opposition to political liberty seems to amount to a dislike for some of its rhetoric. Indeed, the technophobia which emanates from some humanist circles, including the "back to nature" faction of the counter-culture, may pose obstacles to progress in, for example, the technology of teaching. Teaching machines, even though *machines*, have proven to be helpful to many children precisely because they can be adjusted to the child's individual needs. Skinner's own contribution to the field seems to promote attention to individuals and to cut down the need for directing educational measures to a hypothesized lowest common denominator.

In this respect Skinner poses no threat to the libertarian. He joins hands with those who consider it wrong to impose restrictions on making technology work in man's behalf to its fullest capacities. And that is often opposed by humanists, ecologists, and conservationists. On top of this, the libertarian—the current advocate of political liberty and producer of the literature of freedom—would protect the rights of Skinner and others to offer and trade their services wherever they can and without interference from any political agent. (The latter qualification is a response to the kind of control advocated by Skinner.)

Skinner, who understands that the characteristics of the society advocated by libertarians (laissez-faire capitalism, with the function of government specified as the protection of the rights to life, liberty, and the pursuit of happiness—including property) should know that his own techniques can best be employed where freedom is protected. This would enable those who want to "feel free" and reject contact with technology to live their lives; while Skinner and all those interested in employing rigorous methods for improving the performances of people in various professions, crafts, and arts can charge ahead free of coercive controls, prohibitions, and restrictions—so long as they respect the rights of those involved.

But strangely enough this is not what Skinner is after. Some people have claimed that he actually is not committed to any particular political philosophy. Chomsky tells us that

> As to its social implications, Skinner's science of human behavior, being quite vacuous, is as congenial to the libertarian as to the fascist. If certain of his remarks suggest one or another interpretation, these, it must be stressed, do not follow from his "science" any more than their opposites do.

Yet in the very same paragraph of his devastating review of *Beyond Freedom and Dignity*, Chomsky admits that

> . . . There is little doubt that a theory of human malleability might be put to the service of totalitarian doctrine. If, indeed, freedom and dignity are merely the relics of outdated mystical beliefs, then what objection can there be to narrow effective controls instituted to ensure "the survival of a culture"? (XXIV/18)

Indeed, Skinner's "science" implies no political principles whatever. But what he *claims* is science, and what he claims follows from a "scientific" view of man, accommodate theories that support totalitarian regimes: people are fully malleable, albeit more by means of positive reinforcement rather than aversive control.

In the final analysis, Chomsky is right. No science can support such systems. There has never been a successful attempt to show that in a human community (not in a nursery!) some people ought to run the lives of others; and, all claims to the contrary, such efforts require force, not persuasion, for their popularization. Any philosophy or scientific theory is always an attempt to give rational support for certain beliefs or suggestions. But the one belief or suggestion that cannot be given rational support—and we can know this because it makes the very idea of such an undertaking unintelligible—is that agreement and cooperation should be achieved by abandoning rational efforts. Agreement and cooperation are but frauds once they are the result of force, the wholesale rejection of reason. There cannot be rational justification for irrationality. This is so even while we admit that when irrationality is introduced into the human sphere by some, others may need and are rationally justified to protect themselves by using physical force—as in plain self-defense, as well as incredibly more complex circumstances, involving as a result violence and war. But the initiation, i.e., unprovoked introduction, of force in human relationships cannot be given rational foundation. The two cancel each other out by their very nature.

The deceptive attractiveness of Skinner's thesis is that we can readily admit to a place for his technology of behavior in various aspects of human life. Skinner has contributed to the improvement of such training. He has shown how some kinds of activities can be perfected, made smoother, speeded up, and, most importantly, adjusted to the capacities of the individual.

It is only when he introduces the idea that all this must be directed toward securing the survival of a culture that we must consider to what use his technology is limited. It is not necessary for Skinner to *advocate* totalitarianism. He need only show that he wants his techniques to be used for the *kind of* purposes that could only be served systematically by centralized control of a culture from above—a state or government. By counting on the direction of expert behavioral technologists, in the role of designers, he is necessitating what amounts to a totalitarian state. Never mind that the expertise must manifest itself in positive reinforcement only. The idea of benevolent dictatorship is always the announced intention of designers of cultures who wish to invest power to exercise control only in selected personnel. Even if confusedly, Skinner explicitly rejects political freedom, granted, however, that he may not have intended to do so with full knowledge of what a free society could offer as a competing alternative to his utopian vision.

Skinner's utopianism

Is it fair to call Skinner's view utopian? The word is derived from the Greek term for "no place" and it characterizes societies that are distinguished by one central feature—impossibility. In ancient political philosophy a utopia or "ideal state," as described by Socrates in Plato's *Republic*, meant a condition which, though impossible to implement on earth, should still be used to evaluate worldly approximations. But that is not what Thomas Moore's vision of the perfect state meant to achieve, nor was it what the Utopian Socialists or Karl Marx aimed at (vaguely and without specification) in what they promised to the world. And Skinner falls within this last class of utopians.

> . . .It is hard to imagine a world in which people live together without quarreling, maintain themselves by producing the food, shelter, and clothing they need, enjoy themselves and contribute to the enjoyment of others in art, music, literature, and games, consume only a reasonable part of the resources of the world and add as little as possible to its pollution, bear no more children than can be raised decently, continue to explore the world around them and discover better ways of dealing with it, and come to know themselves accurately and, therefore, manage themselves effectively. Yet all this is possible, and even the slightest sign of progress should bring a kind of change

which in traditional terms would be said to assuage wounded vanity, offset a sense of hopelessness or nostalgia . . . (I/204-5)

. . . there is no reason why progress toward a world in which people may be automatically good should be impeded. . . . (I/63)

One might object that calling him utopian is to misunderstand Skinner; for he says only that such a state of affairs is "possible." And he promises only that "people *may* be automatically good." The trouble is that he hardly ever says that something *will* be the case if we do this or that. Even his most "scientific" findings are combined with numerous qualifications and uses of "may" and "might." So there really is no saving clause where there appears to be one. It is a matter of style that Skinner does not commit himself to any of the promises he makes. If we took his "mays" and "mights" seriously, we would say that he is unsure of what he is saying, that most of his claims are empty speculations that might or might not be true. It is therefore fairer both to his reader and to Skinner himself to take him to be more affirmative about his ideas than such an interpretation would allow.

The idea of being "automatically good" is perhaps the most problematic. In any meaningful sense of the term a good person cannot be good automatically. This is a contradiction in terms. Skinner himself seems to notice this when he adds: "The problem is to induce people not to be good but to behave well." Unfortunately the term "induce" cannot be juggled into Skinnerism; for Skinner there is only "control." And "behave well" may be appropriate to describing dogs and little children, not adult human beings. When we make reference to someone who is well- or ill-behaved we are not talking about his general moral character but about some specific aspect of his life, some task where there is question about his following rules or strictures. Moreover, the idea calls to mind a nursery or training ground for studio (movie, television) animals, not adult human beings.

Freedom vs. survival of a culture

Skinner's politics seems at first to be harmless. But with the insistence on generalizing the practice of behavior technology to a top-to-bottom regulation of the lives of people in a culture, it amounts to an advocacy of some benevolent dictatorship. The specific principles of manipulation are not provided, but the goal is unambiguous: the survival of the culture.

Clearly, the ideas of freedom and dignity (the former in both of its meanings) vis-a-vis man's capacity for choice and the political value of protecting his right to choose, violate the Skinnerian goal. If a person is free to exercise his choice of goals in life, he may elect to weave tapestry, compose songs for children, carve statues, play football, raise pigs, or perform any of the infinite array of activities that infringe on no one's liberty but may have nothing to do *per se* with the survival of the culture or of the species. If he knows that he has achieved his goals, any person may possess dignity without having added anything to Skinner's noble purpose. So both freedom and dignity must go in order to make room for the massive effort that would be needed for everyone to follow the Skinnerian goals in life.

There are admittedly too many of us who care very little about the survival of the culture. Most of us hope that our culture will not survive as it exists today, that·a far better one will develop, which will subsequently give rise to better ones. But that is a hope and relates rather remotely to what our worries are and should be. As to enabling the species to survive, it is again a goal that interests only academicians—for how can one reasonably ask a person to concern himself with whether ten thousand or even two hundred years from now mankind will still inhabit this universe or live in any manner we can envision? How else but through some massive guidance, submitting all of us to the omniscience of some race of behavioral technologists, could we go to work on the preservation of mankind? Skinner seems to be well aware of this. So his advocates would have to be very good at making it appear that we are benefiting *ourselves* while actually making sure that the species itself survives.

The idea is impossible and we hope to bear this out. Simply put, it is because human beings are free, capable of dignity, and can merit it only to the extent that their liberties are protected or left unviolated. For those interested in the survival of the species, it is the only hope; to leave individuals free to improve on their lives as best they can, with mutual aid, cooperation, and the continual risk that things could turn out worse than they would like because they are free to do worse than they should in the conduct of their lives.

Before ending this summary of Skinner's assault on freedom, we need to consider some of the technical obstacles to his grand program.

Skinner's God's-eye view

An important characteristic of Skinner's treatment of nearly every issue deserves special attention, even though he shares it with a hundred others who write on human affairs. Skinner takes what is called the "God's-eye view" of his subject matter. The twist is to assume that one is no longer a member of the human race, then proceed to talk about people and draw any conclusions as though they did not apply to oneself. If this can be done, objectivity par excellence has been achieved.

In *Science and Human Behavior* Skinner comes closest to admitting openly what he is doing. He says:

> Operant conditioning shapes behavior as a sculptor shapes a lump of clay. Although at some point the sculptor seems to have produced an entirely novel object, we can always follow the process back to the original undifferentiated lump, and we can make the successive stages by which we return to this condition as small as we wish. (II/91)

After he outlines the experiment he has in mind, Skinner goes on to explain his activities:

> . . . we reinforce only slightly exceptional values of the behavior observed. . . . We succeed in shifting the whole range of heights of the pigeon's head at which the head is held. . . . (II/91)

The picture Skinner paints must be taken seriously because he is, in the end, proposing the sort of totalitarian society he offers in *Walden II* where experts "shape behavior as a sculptor shapes a lump of clay." The behavioral technologists are these experts. One shouldn't take it lightly when, without kidding, Skinner makes use of such phrases as "we reinforce," and "we succeed." This entire section abounds in such expressions "we wait," "we may detect," "we first give," and so on and so on. Indeed, there is every reason to accept Skinner's claims about what "we do" with pigeons on the analogy of what sculptors do with clay—at least to a point. (II/91-93). Clay simply lies there to be molded, whereas pigeons do not—they have to be caught and kept confined in order to be available for experiments. Moreover, pigeons, unlike clay, do not lose the characteristics they were trained to possess by a simple act of leaving them in the rain to melt away. But to a point the analogy is fine.

The problem is that while there is the sculptor for the clay and the Skinnerian for the pigeon, there is no comparably positioned Skinnerism for Skinnerians. Skinner does not believe in divine intervention, so there is no way for him to escape the fact that if human behavior is like pigeon behavior, he cannot appeal to some intelligent external molder of man as he can with clay and pigeons. For the crucial thing about the clay is that it materializes according to the sculptor's plans. Throwing clay around at random is not the work of sculptors—at least not while we have some sane notion of art. Nor is a pigeon going about its pigeon business (as all good pigeons do) a *trained* pigeon.

To be trained requires a trainer with intelligence and the capacity for conceptual thought. And with Skinner's examples we have just that relationship before us: sculptor/clay—Skinner/untrained pigeon. But no such relationship is available for Skinner in his explanation of human behavior. What he does in this case is to claim that man "plays two roles: one as a controller, as the designer of a controlling culture, and another as the controlled, as the product of a culture." He quickly adds that "there is nothing inconsistent about this; it follows from the nature of the evolution of a culture, with or without intentional control." (I/197)

But this simply won't do. A sculptor shapes the clay—and by this we assume that he will design it with some idea of how it will turn out, with some *purpose*. Skinner trains the pigeon for some purpose—unless he himself randomly moves around in the pigeon's vicinity, something that certainly *cannot* be considered subjecting the pigeon to *schedules* of reinforcement, the antithesis of randomness. A schedule requires intelligent, calculated design. We take this for granted as long as we retain the view that people are capable of rational thought and action. So they have the option of moving around in the pigeon's vicinity (or throwing clay around at random) or making rational effort to train the pigeon (or producing a meaningful statue). Even Skinner would have to admit that the experimental training could not have been done randomly.

Now when it comes to controlling human behavior, designing schedules of reinforcement that will produce intelligible behavior, what can we appeal to in the environment as the guiding intelligence? God won't do, especially for Skinner. (God's ways, whatever that means, are mysterious, so we cannot begin to make sense of that idea in a context where the issue is whether man is part of nature yet not quite passive "clay.") We can appeal to man himself. But Skinner denies that man is an agent of control because "the autonomous agent to which behavior has traditionally been attributed is replaced by the environment—the environment in which the species evolved and in which the behavior of the individual is shaped and maintained." This Skinner claims is the viewpoint of "a science of behavior" and adds "that a man's behavior owes something to antecedent events and that the environment is a more promising point of attack than man himself has long been recognized." (I/175)

Notwithstanding all the pleas about harmless inconsistency, Skinner cannot escape his dilemma. Yes, sculptors shape clay, Skinner trains pigeons, but what makes a man as he is? The environment? If so, the analogy fails. For the environment has no capacity comparable to sculptors and Skinnerian pigeon trainers. And Skinner knows this; why else would he require the entirely illogical admission, from *his* framework at least, that a man does play the role of "a controller, as the designer of a controlling culture." (Or is Skinner a Marxist, with some notion of historical purpose?)

Skinner gets into the race denying that man has the capacity to determine what *he will do,* but finishes claiming that he does possess it after all. But note where this admission of capacity creeps into Skinner's schema: just where does the human engineering start, where do the designers of the culture—the good Skinnerian behavioral scientists—come into focus? Not that Skinner has very much to say about what these people would do—he is curiously obscure on that, even if he has made allusions to his preference for Red Chinese techniques for controlling members of the culture in the service of its survival. Nevertheless he does show totalitarian inclinations when he brings designers onto center stage. Curiously, also, with their emergence, man all of a sudden possesses the capacity to exert control upon his own life!

Note, however, that Skinner grants this kind of capacity or power only to mankind, culture or the species in general, not to individual human beings. As he puts it, "It appears . . . that society is responsible for the larger part of the behavior of self-control. If this is correct, little ultimate control remains with the individual." He spells it out further:

A man may spend a great deal of time designing his own life—he may choose the circumstances in which he is to live with great care, and he may manipulate his daily environment on an extensive scale. Such activity appears to exemplify a high order of self-determination. But it is also behavior, and we account for it in terms of other variables in the environment and history of the individual. It is these variables which provide the ultimate control. (II/240)

By accounting for all human behavior in terms of "other variables," Skinner denies himself the logical claim of being able to reinforce behavior, to condition anything, and the possibility of intentionally designing a culture. He and we, by his account, cannot do such things—we are powerless and incapable of exercising control. Trying to do such things, then, would be a rejection of Skinner's own ideas.

The moral of the Skinnerian maze is that any theorist—considering the nature of human behavior—must leave room for understanding his own actions. If a theory is to prove adequate, it must be capable of accounting for human affairs even at the time when the author is doing the theorizing. There is no God's-eye view possible to any human being, not even to B. F. Skinner. (It is not even clear what this view would be for God, since it would have to encompass everything, including God's own viewing.) So if Skinner claims any God's-eye view for himself; if that capacity is required for what he proposes, but the powers he wishes to claim for himself and his helpers are not permitted by his own theory, then he is caught in an impossible situation. He may as well forget his entire project vis-a-vis human affairs.

Man's role in culture

The blatancy of this error is greater in Skinner than others. Marx, at least, claimed only to have a special view of the world, unknown to others. This allowed him to dodge the charge that dialectical materialism falls prey to the fallacy of self-exclusion (although in the end he too succumbed to the problem). Skinner has no such clever dodge to invoke, although his special position as a behavioral scientist and analyst might serve him as such. But we have no grounds to assume that Skinnerians, as cultural designers, would be empowered in ways that other, more common, folk are not.

For Skinner "an analysis which appeals to external variables makes the assumption of an inner originating and determining agent unnecessary." (II/241) And here is a classic self-description:

In the present analysis we cannot distinguish between involuntary and voluntary behavior by raising the issue of who is in control. It does not matter whether behavior is due to a willing individual or a psychic usurper if we dismiss all inner agents of whatever sort. Nor can we make the distinction on the basis of control or lack of control, since we assume that no behavior is free. If we have no reason to distinguish between being able to do something and doing it, such expressions as "not being able to do something" or "not being able to help doing something" must be interpreted in some other way. When all relevant variables have been arranged [by whom?], an organism will or will not respond. If it does not, it cannot. If it can, it will. (I/112)

Again, one need only replace the "we's" with "I's" and quite a comic reading develops. Oh, the cloak of impersonality, the "editorial we," hides many responsibilities and revelations!

The problem is that we do have reason to distinguish between being able to do something and doing it. Just think that being able to drive a car is surely something one relies on in considering doing so. If one did not know that he is able to drive a car, he would be a fool to attempt it. But since he can, then he has the option of doing it. Anything else is unintelligible.

But if Skinner is taken seriously, his own advocacy of employing cultural designers makes absolutely no sense. If we will employ them, then we will; if we will not, then we will not. What's the point of writing a book about it? Of course from Skinner's perspective he had to write the book, reinforced by the National Institute of Mental Health, Grant number k6-MH21, 775-01. And whether what he said is right or wrong is beside the point. He simply said it.

Yet with this admission Skinner makes it impossible to make sense of his admonition that we forget freedom and dignity, autonomous man and man *qua* man; this will either happen or not happen, and there is nothing anyone can do about it. The environment will be responsible. To say, in response, that *we* make our environment, cannot be taken as anything but a feeble attempt to escape the force of logic and reason. Some might think that Skinner has simply come up with a paradoxical-sounding idea which he, in his expertise, can understand even though we cannot. But there is no chance of resolving this paradox—it is a flat-out contradiction.

Skinnerism vs. freedom and dignity

Skinner denies human freedom, one's capacity to choose, but his denial leads to contradiction. Man *does* have the capacity to choose—although few people may actually exercise this capacity.

Skinner denies human dignity, but only choice can explain some of what human beings have accomplished—the environment has neither will nor purpose to create symphonies, tract houses, Skinner boxes, and so on. (And Skinner has not defended some claims about a purposive force in history— although *he* talks of evolution as if it exhibited such a force). So if achievement is possible, dignity is also possible.

Finally Skinner confuses political liberty with a feeling people want to have that technology is not taking over their lives. But that is not what liberty means. Skinner does admit that oppression will achieve very little good. But he denounces those who would withhold their consent to massive human engineering, those who have been influenced by the literature of freedom. Why? Because although he never calls outright for such massive engineering, and although he gives no hint of what specific measures controllers ought to employ, he "knows" that the goal of keeping the culture in existence requires the subtle but firm regimentation of people to follow a design not of their own making.

Skinner may not be able to make clear what he means by the survival of the culture. Sometimes, by "culture" he means "species." But that also makes little sense—to work for the survival of the species. It is doubtful that one can actually make the effort to ensure such things. But Skinner believes that this is possible and desirable by way of behavioral technology. And he knows that the ideas of individualism—autonomous, free, dignified, and politically liberated man—simply do not conduce people to devote their lives to such obscure goals as helping along the life of the species or culture, beyond doing the best they are capable of in their own lives.

This is why Skinner attacks freedom and dignity. But his attack fails on so many counts that only stubbornness can keep one believing that Skinner really has contributed much to political theory in his *Beyond Freedom and Dignity*. All his talk about molding and shaping human behavior amounts to a case of the blow-up fallacy—taking the picture of sculptors and clay, or trainers and pigeons, and imposing it on an entirely different relationship, namely human beings vis-à-vis other human beings. As D. Bannister points out,

> Of the requirements which make a concretistic imitation of the natural sciences unprofitable in psychology, probably the most serious is that of reflexivity.
>
> . . . from a reflexive standpoint the psychological experiment is not a logical copy of the natural science experiment. It is inevitably a social situation in which one professional, formally qualified theorizer and predictor tries to predict the behavior of nonformally qualified theorizers and predictors.
>
> . . . if the reflexive argument is accepted the psychologist cannot present a picture of man which patently contradicts his behavior in presenting that picture. (XI/417)

Throughout Skinner's books he is violating this prohibition. He is refusing to acknowledge that if *he* is capable of choosing values, the rest of us are too. And if we come up with different ones from his, the argument must be settled between us at the level at which values are established—logic, reason, and human nature. It is not enough just to say "I am doing science, you are not; so I must be right and you must not." Especially when no science is being done at all in the process of coming up with the value in contention.

47

2

Is Skinnerism
Science?

IF THE CLAIM that one is treating an important topic scientifically is true, one cannot deny that the conclusions which emerge deserve attention. Not that it is always clear what "being scientific" or "scientifically" means. But there is a specifiable meaning to the terms, and even without knowing them fully most people accept them. A scientific approach to some feature of reality involves rigorous analysis, careful reasoning, tests or experimentation, and precision in the application of the appropriate methods. All this is aimed at an accurate, up to date understanding of what is being investigated. The conclusions which emerge would, therefore, have the best chance of being true.

Most of us value truth despite our willingness to distort it here and there, sometimes in the most private aspects of our lives. But even distortions presuppose truth—to know that one is distorting something requires knowledge of at least an inkling of the truth of the matter. Truth, in short, is widely respected and its pursuit a generally accepted, if not always practiced, virtue.

Does not the scientific approach facilitate the search for truth, even if it cannot guarantee the success of that search? So with truth such a highly prized achievement, the claim to treat some topic scientifically, if believed, must carry with it well-deserved initial respectability. As Skinner tells us at the outset of *Beyond Freedom and Dignity*:

In trying to solve the terrifying problems that face us in the world today, we naturally turn to the things we do best. We play from strength, and our strength is science and technology (I/ 1)

48

Skinner's first and central thesis of practically all that he has written is laid down early in his best selling book:

A scientific analysis shifts both the responsibility and the achievement to the environment. (I/23)

It is only by prescientific approach, Skinner argues, that responsibility for some of what occurs in the world is ascribed to human beings: some of the advances in human history identified as achievements of human beings (either individually or in cooperation). But, Skinner tells us, a scientific perspective on the situation forces the conclusion that man is neither responsible for nor capable of achievement—it is the environment that must be accorded these characteristics. Must we accept Skinner's central contention? Does he prove these claims?

The appeal to science

The bare bones of Skinner's argument are as follows: science shows that both responsibility and achievement are aspects of the *environment* in which mankind lives, but human freedom and dignity make sense only if people can be responsible and could indeed achieve some of their goals; therefore, human freedom and dignity simply do not exist—they are, instead, prescientific myths, on a par with the ancient belief that "a falling body accelerates because it grew more jubilant as it found itself near home." (I/6)

Simply, if Skinner's conclusions about freedom and dignity follow directly from a scientific analysis of human affairs, as he claims, then they ought to carry a good deal of weight for us. It would simply be futile and irrational to deny the truth of conclusions that follow from good scientific work. In this book the purpose certainly is not to do that! But before we can tell if we should accept Skinner's conclusions we need to make clear what he means by a "scientific approach" to the "terrifying problems that face us today." There is certainly no clarity about this, not just in connection with Skinner's work but with the work done throughout the social and human sciences.

Skinner tells us of his firmly established place in the scientific tradition in virtually every technical and popular piece that he has written. He also charges "the literature of freedom and dignity" with careless and harmful adherence to myths, trading on people's ignorance, insisting on dealing with mysterious entities and other practices totally unbecoming a responsible truth-seeker and scientist of any age.

The charge Skinner levels against this literature is nothing more than usual polemics—with only some highly selective quotes from one or two advocates of free will or political liberty to back it. Many well-known advocates of political change, the revolutionary revamping of society, or any other programs for the community of human beings at large charge their

49

opponents with being scientifically backward. And they themselves are always true to the most rigorous, the highest strictures of science. Machiavelli, Bacon, Hobbes, Comte, Marx, and, most recently, the positivists (in politics and economics) starting with Max Weber and now represented by David Easton, Henry Manne, and hundreds of others—all these individuals and many others have laid claim to scientific validity where their political analysis and advice were concerned. Skinner is not alone in claiming to have reached his conclusions on the basis of scientific analysis. And since others who offer that claim have arrived at conclusions quite different from Skinner's—some in economics have in fact provided scientific grounds for the very opposite conclusions from Skinner's—it must be considered what scientific approaches amount to to deserve that name.

There is a lot to be gained—at least in superficial circles—from making a claim to being scientific in one's approach to some issue. People whose values do not bar them from seeking fame, fortune, or just widescale acceptance may prefer to hail their work as scientific because the term is an honorific one. (It is a fact of reality that unless we have some grounds for distrusting someone, we have reason to pay him heed: he is a human being who can be trusted. So the claim to being scientific is generally ground enough to command some attention and regard.) Science is a popular commodity, and most people in the Western world admit to its enormous value. In the times of the philosopher Thomas Hobbes, for example, science was beginning to take the form it has today. Most people had but a meager notion of what it was to be scientific. The bulk of the intellectual/academic world had a vested interest in confining science to a narrow area of human concerns. But in today's world, where science surrounds us in our homes, our places of work, where we go for pain or for pleasure—gadgets, instruments, devices, machines, computers, and the lot are everywhere—the values of the scientific approach are evident to all. Even if some of the "humanistic" intellectuals offer their perennial warnings that mankind is being dehumanized by our machine age, that is only a loud but ineffective outcry in the midst of overwhelming (although perhaps only tacit) respect. We recognize, of course, that machines can break down. Our troubles with the television set, the tape recorder, refrigerator, oven, Xerox machine, automobile, supersonic airliner, conveyor belt, and all the things that now make up mankind's ingenious array of scientifically devised tools cannot be evaded. Yet all we need is a competent, expert mechanic, electrician, or other technologist—usually the thing can be fixed and matters put back to normal in a jiffy.

The idea that if it were not for the "human factor" all things would function perfectly is, paradoxically enough, extremely popular. The suggestion, then, that we deal with people's problems scientifically, by turning to expert technologists of behavior who will fix up everyone and "induce people not to be good but to behave well," simply comes naturally to most. The idea no longer has a torture chamber, or even "Brave New World" ring

about it what with Skinner's expressed disavowal of "aversive control," meddling with which does not please us. Judging from the reception the reading public has given *Beyond Freedom and Dignity*, there seems to be widescale favor with the basic message of the book, but perhaps reservations remain, as with almost any ideas no comprehension is there.

Today however we are all well aware that science has paid o... know this better than people know it before. Or at least we think we... it, given that few of us have thought about the issue in great enough detail... to commit himself with a firm "I know." And one may not always manage to, but often does, make an easy sale by announcing much scientific alle... glance, observe the relative audience sizes of such obvious pseudosciences as scientology, yoga, transcendental meditation, and hundreds more. Still, one can certainly entice men to become more tolerant to whatever is put out in the name of science.

Science and scientists

But what is science? What permits us to include some and exclude other ventures from this important realm of human activity? If we cannot identify science as something reasonably specific, we cannot continue to give it our respect—since anything could be called science with no standard of justification in checking out the claim. And what field of study addresses itself to this question? Who studies the nature of science? Who are the "experts" on science, just as scientists may be the experts on stars, the liver, the atom, the constitution of hydrogen, and so on.

Scientists themselves, contrary to what may appear to be the case, are not necessarily the best sources of knowledge of the proper domain of science. Scientists, as politicians or artists, are at home doing their work, not in identifying what constitutes their domain, where the borders should be drawn, what is authentic and inauthentic about the field itself.

A chemist does not concern himself with what chemistry is, but with the subject matter chemists are troubled about at any given time. This at least is the order of the day, even if exceptions, sometimes formidable ones, emerge. Mozart, or Van Gogh, or Dostoevsky had only peripheral concern with what the nature of art is; their central focus of attention was to create works of art—not treatises on art itself. Nor do physicists, on the whole, engage in dissertations about the nature of physics, its relationship to chemistry or literature. That is not what makes for being a physicist, even if some physicists do embark on such tasks now and then.

When the scientist leaves his field to begin to talk about it, he is no longer an expert. He has no reason for being taken more seriously than anyone else, outside his own field but with his attention focused on it in relation to other human activities. While not necessarily so, many who are close to their fields of work tend to be casual about what their specialty can and cannot handle. Thus we find biologists exporting the principles of their subject matter into practically every aspect of reality; we see economists characterize all human relationships in terms of the laws discovered within their own domain; dentists are making teeth the source of all of history's significant events; zoologists are advancing political theories; animal psychologists design systems of university education; physicists get into the business of explaining the true nature of household furniture, and on and on. Perhaps this is the result of the frustration of specialization. We all want a general framework, to formulate a world-view with which to integrate all that we become even vaguely aware of. So we often take entirely different sorts of discoveries, explanations, analyses, and just plain facts and attempt a shortcut to understanding. The shortcut is only apparent and the actual result is that a virtual hand-to-hand combat develops among the various special fields of inquiry, all battling for the position of superscience—economists, psychologists, sociologists, biologists, physicists, and all, each telling us that truth, in the end, must be reached by way of what they are doing.

This shortcut might be called the "blow up" approach. It consists, first, in making diligent inquiries into some aspect of reality and arriving at significant, often true, and, at times, startling conclusions, including principles, by which we can best understand what happens in the area being studied. But then an entirely unjustified turn is taken. The conclusions and principles are lifted out of the special field and imported into some other area. The picture taken in the special domain is *blown up* with the intent to offer us an understanding of much more, and sometimes all, of reality.

The phenomenon is widespread indeed. It is not just professionals who multiply the number of crackpot theories floating about in hopes of solving all of the world's problems. People who have done hardly any specialized study are doing it everywhere. It happens when an individual takes a successful step in some area of his private life, say in dealing with a mother-in-law, and begins to believe that this step is the clue to success in living *for everyone*. Perhaps, when a culture lacks in philosophical productivity, everyone has the urge to spin out grand theories about nature, society, and human relationships—and sects of people with conflicting notions of the world increase. The closer these notions are to scientific respectability, however, the more pompous the claim to universal validity. This is exactly what is encouraged in what we know today as the humane or social sciences. Most often the professionals in these areas conduct their studies by uncritically adopting the methods of more established fields of inquiry; never mind if those methods have never been shown to be appropriate where they are now employed. Presumably, by mere adoption of rigorous quantification, economics will have succeeded in being scientific and, of course, productive of important knowledge. And, by making use of controlled laboratory conditions, psychology must be considered a full-blown science—are not physicists and chemists making their progress in the labs?

All of this can lead to serious setbacks and confusions. When scientists like Skinner begin to talk about issues they have not shown to belong within their field of expertise, they can undermine the consideration they deserve in the special areas in which they are at home. A relatively mature science generally prepares its practitioners, through the educational practices in vogue, to deal coherently and meaningfully with its particular sphere of reality. No spillover effect is guaranteed by this. Because a person is competent to substantiate his claims within one branch of knowledge, it does not follow that he is equally equipped either in another field or in regard to the nature of science itself. It makes no difference how emphatically he cites his credentials from his own field. To become skilled in these different tasks calls for different considerations. One would not be wise to send a dentist to do a tailor's job, or even to send an auto mechanic to check out an airplane. In the applied fields where people's actions are immediately tied to consequences, sometimes life and death, the integrity of each seems to be kept in mind. But in the theoretical realm, where the groundwork but not the actual application of a science occurs, this element of integrity is not so visible, nor so open to public inspection. Here we must rely on the honor system—the personal integrity of the scientist/ theoretician. For those of us not close enough to what these individuals know, we must rely on what they tell us about these matters and their own expertise in them. Provided, of course, that they can demonstrate to us, who are laymen but not mindless, that they are experts. This can be complicated.

The warnings given above should prepare us for what we get from Skinner concerning the nature of science (and his own expertise and its range of applicability). He tells us his idea of science quite explicitly and now we must consider whether, despite all the above, he may not be right. His conception of science should not be dismissed or accepted a priori. What then does he take to be the scientific approach? Once we know that we can examine whether he is right—for here we are at least as proficient as Skinner himself. That is, anyone with a reasonably updated contemporary education.

The nature of science has certainly been investigated fairly continuously throughout human intellectual history. While it is generally believed that science was given its important boosts during the 16th and 17th centuries, in full justice, despite the bad press he has received, Aristotle laid the foundation for virtually all of modern science. (It is the combination of Aristotle's ideas with the dogmatism and idiosyncracies of the Middle Ages that led to the widespread defamation of this great thinker's ideas vis-à-vis science.) It was Aristotle, also, who provided the first systematic discussion of the place of science within the network of crucial human activities and institutions. In the more positive portions of this work I will, provide a discussion of science that draws a good deal upon the tradition Aristotle established. (Chapter 5.)

In our own times there are many exciting and brilliant studies about the history and nature of science, written usually by scholars who have stayed very close to science and have themselves often been noted scientists. Among the more prominent and thorough workers in the field are Israel Scheffler,[2] Stephen Toulmin,[3] Karl Popper,[4] Imre Lakatos and Alan Musgrave,[5] T. S. Kuhn,[6] Carl D. Kordig,[7] Gerald Holton,[8] Jean Rostand,[9] and many others. Despite some of the best discussions of all times within the works of these scholars, their treatment of the topic has focused mainly on the activity of scientists—as if that *alone* could tell us about the nature of the field.

Skinner, too, discusses science but he fails to dispute these men in any detail, even from the evidence of history. He states his opinions with no serious (or even casual) effort to argue his points. He does not consider any of the competing ideas about what he discusses—and since Skinner is in the field of psychology, where the topic of *how to do sound work* is still widely debated, this is all the more disturbing. Most of his references to those he considers wrong are pathetically incomplete, distorted, and suspiciously close to having been motivated with ridicule in mind, not serious challenge.

Nevertheless we must consider Skinner's ideas on science in our attempt to come to grips with his case against freedom and dignity. Not because it is a very good case *as he makes it*—but because, when made well, it is the best case he has for his conclusions against the literature of freedom and dignity. However it must be noted that Skinner does not make the case as well as it could be made, and we shall have to turn to some others in a later chapter to see what else it has going for it. (Chapter 3.)

Another point must be made to avoid misunderstanding Skinner's position. In terms of his chronological development—what he actually did in his many years of writing and experimentation—his philosophy of science may have come later than his laboratory work. He tells us here and there that he started with no theory or abstract system; he simply went to work in the laboratory. It is not clear that Skinner himself—or anyone—is the best source of information about where he himself got his ideas, which came first, and so on. Self-characterization, as well as the description of one's own mental development, is very difficult. I doubt that Skinner was without general ideas about science before he turned his attention from engineering and, earlier, literature, to psychology. His novel *Walden II* came early enough to have had to be accompanied with some broad theoretical—economic, political, et cetera—ideas during its conception.

But it makes little difference whether Skinner actually held his views on science before or after his work with rats, pigeons, and other animals—i.e., after the experimental work which he claims gave support to his views. Such work could not have given him the support without certain other assumptions, beliefs, or true understanding taken from some other sources than the laboratory. And his arguments reflect this. He does not cite the facts from the laboratory all alone but adds a good deal of language about science, its character, human affairs, and so on, that could not have been developed just from having been exposed to the experiments he has conducted. It is not important, then, that Skinner developed his ideas on science before, during, or after his experimental work—so long as it turned out that his ideas about people, society, politics, education, motivation, the causes of human conduct, and others require materials that go beyond the laboratory, ideas developed by people throughout human history and referred to by Skinner in his exposition.

B. F. Skinner's idea of science

Some of Skinner's explicit statements about science are found in his earlier works. He does not analyze and scrutinize the views he asserts. But because he knows that he needs these views to make his other ideas respectable, he does provide us with his version of a philosophy of science.

In *Science and Human Behavior* Skinner tells us that "science is unique in showing a cumulative process." (II/11) And he goes on to say:

All scientists, whether giants or not, enable those who follow them to begin a little further along. This is not necessarily true elsewhere. (II/11)

Science is first of all a set of attitudes. It is a disposition to deal with the facts rather than with what someone has said about them. . . . (II/12)

Science is a willingness to accept facts even when they are opposed to wishes . . . The opposite of wishful thinking is intellectual honesty—an extremely important possession of the successful scientist . . . Scientists are by nature no more honest than other men but . . . the practice of science puts an exceptionally high premium on honesty. . . . (II/12)

[Science] is a search for order, for uniformities, for lawful relations among the events in nature. It begins, as we all begin, by observing single episodes, but it quickly passes on to the general rule, to scientific law. . . . (II/13)

In a later stage science advances from the collection of rules or laws to larger systematic arrangements. Not only does it make statements about the world, it makes statements about statements. (II/14)

In his *Verbal Behavior* Skinner gives us additional clues to his conception of science. He calls psychology "an experimental science of behavior." (III/5) He also remarks that "Modern literary criticism [never fulfilled the early promise of a science of verbal behavior because it] seldom goes beyond the terms of the intelligent layman." (III/4). He then goes on with some additional hints:

The scientific effectiveness of . . . a vocabulary will derive from the actual contingencies of reinforcement in the scientific community . . . (III/99)

And elsewhere:

> The operational attitude . . . is a good thing in any science but especially in psychology because of the presence there of a vast vocabulary of ancient and non-scientific origin . . . behaviorism has been (at least to most behaviorists) nothing more than a thoroughgoing operational analysis of traditional mentalistic concepts. (IV/586)

And finally we get this explicit statement:

> Science . . . is an attempt to discover order, to show that certain events stand in lawful relations to other events. . . . But order is not only a possible end product; it is a working assumption which must be adopted at the very start. . . . If we are to use the methods of science in the field of human affairs, we must assume that behavior is lawful and determined. We must expect to discover that what a man does is the result of specifiable conditions and that once these conditions have been discovered, we can anticipate and to some extent determine his actions. (II/6)

In the following pages portions of the above-quoted passages are cited. The reader cannot be expected to face paraphrases and the evaluation based on them when our task is to criticize not just what Skinner believes but his way of defending his beliefs.

Because so much emphasis is laid on the scientific character of his ideas, this segment of Skinner's argument against freedom and dignity is decisive. Our task is comparable to an examination of the expertise that lies behind crucial testimony at a criminal trial. Early in his most famous book Skinner disclaims responsibility for *proving* his case. "The proof is to be found in the basic analysis. . . . " and all that is required is that the principles used in interpreting the instances of behavior cited in the book, which Skinner admits are *not* enough to prove the case, "have a plausibility. . . . " Skinner never proves his case against freedom and dignity—not here, nor anywhere else in the several books and many articles he has written. Now we want to see if his claim to be working from a scientific framework is true.

We need to consider, first, Skinner's idea of what science is. To start with, he considers it "unique in showing a cumulative process." Is this true —and what of it if so?

We must first ask what "cumulative" means here. The idea is that from the beginning of man's study of nature whatever was learned became available for members of the next generations to build upon, expand, improve, on and on, to this very point in history. Thus what we know about, say, the composition and character of our solar system is the sum total of what mankind has produced on that topic, what people have learned and deduced from studying that part of reality thus far. The store of knowledge then simply grows and grows. Facts, principles, relationships, laws, and systems are accumulated in direct proportion to the elapse of time in human history.

There is reason to think that, although somewhat simplistic, this idea is basically correct, science does indeed undergo this kind of progression. Its naïvete comes from failing to take note of serious lapses in the development of human understanding in certain realms of study—nay, in most of them. Sometimes the expectedly (and, in retrospect, apparently) smooth, upward moving (cumulative) swerve in what we understand about reality takes a considerable dip. Regression occurs. Certain theories gain currency which mislead an entire community of scientists, misdirect research for decades and retard what can fairly be called a tendency toward progress in the end. Be it in physics, where the idea of motion has been treated with both success and failure from time to time; or in chemistry where the idea of "phlogiston" led to a standstill in some special areas of study; in psychology where phrenology and who knows which of the powerful fads today (will) have clearly led the science astray at least temporarily, or in economics—where different systems have been competing for centuries, whose exponents charge those with other views with setting the field backward by years—all of them experience upheavals that do not come out to a simple cumulative process. Most of these cases can only be analyzed in terms of what might have been, what this or that scientist or group of scientists might have done differently, what someone might have done when faced with the choice between this or that idea or theory to develop, or to continue to research. One thing is evident: no clear-cut, cumulative development can be traced anywhere without omitting some more or less significant detours, without seriously assuming that the very idea of a detour in science is impossible. As it turns out, by denying the reality of freedom of will—by holding that people cannot ever exercise a genuine choice —Skinner restricts the number of conceptions of science and scientific progression he can begin to take seriously. Any view of science that takes human choice seriously is automatically excluded.

It should be fully appreciated that Skinner's rejection of free will prevents him from looking at science in a way that would allow it to be understood as the activity of human beings who can choose, who are free, and who may do badly or well at whatever they are doing. Which may point up at this stage that not all the facts about human affairs can be learned by taking Skinner's approach—with its necessary limitations in perspective.

There is indeed much in science that should caution us from taking it to be the paradigm of reliable human activities. For example, some physicists in our own day have indicted the greater part of theoretical physics as overflowing with utter confusion, being in total disarray, and by this retarding the field beyond all necessity. The idea has also been put forth that artificial demand for scientific research—which occurs when through political or some other motivation money not available in a free market is pumped into a field—generates false starts and developments by sheer force of what happens when people see the chance to take gratis money. Some commentators (e.g., Mortimer Taube) have provided a full-blown analysis of current scientific developments based on the idea that mere possibilities, with no substantive support that any progress will be made, are used to justify making time and money available for extensive research projects.

This is not to flatly disagree with Skinner. Nonetheless, if the idea of science is understood as involving the idea of cumulativeness as an essential element, we must acknowledge certain obstacles that stand in the way of this characterization. There is at least some evidence that science is not the unquestionably reliable human activity Skinner believes it to be— "the thing we do best." Sometimes scientists do worse than those in other fields. The idea of the mad scientist is not just a fictional one—the Germans and the Soviets were known at one time to have forced scientific research (based on purely ideological and political motives) with results that had nothing to do with truth and knowledge. (Both of these cultures have gone through periods of trying to bring about political and ideological desires by fraudulent work in scientific research.)

But Skinner has a point and we must admit it. When dealing with the hard sciences—physics, chemistry and its various branches, as well as biology and other fields not much influenced by the fears and wishes of people—there are certainly many visible results; so the cleanup work stemming from sloppiness, dishonesty, or just plain error can begin soon after a detour into falsehood and confusion has occurred. In this sense the only science is effective science. In retrospect we see only the well-edited version of the history of science, with the bulk of bad news left out—simply because in science bad news is no news. When major foul-ups are reported it is usually to show how they have actually spurred advances on the part of those who tried to resist them.

In the end the precise character of this effectiveness in science is difficult to discern, and we need not spend much time on it. We must note that scientists who have produced very useful and practically applicable scientific conclusions have, at times, gone way beyond what they were justified to conclude. That, too, tends to distort the cumulative picture. We have to conclude the same about Skinner, with some question about the value of his actually scientific work. (Most of those who are sympathetic to Skinner as scientist charge him with the sin of unjustified extrapolation. We will see that there is more to what he does than this rather common error in science.) What a more modest approach might have affirmed only of a limited area of reality, a bit of haste and impatience on the part of scientists led them to generalize beyond good reason. But in most cases, including Newton's, later care and work led to the eradication of the harmful consequences. And yet the damage was done; some of what received wide circulation within the community as well as outside had to be overturned, revised, and modified.

But even barring this interpretation, which can be made to square with Skinner's idea, we must look at another suggestion before leaving this point. The cumulative idea suggests a better and better understanding of nature. By what standard? Is it accurate to rebuke the Greeks for not having come up with Einsteinian physics? If not, can we say they were wrong? And if we accept the cumulative picture, is "wrong" not the correct way to characterize what the Greeks believed about motion, for example, or the causes for falling bodies? If it is, then we are in trouble. For alongside the building process there has occurred a lot of destruction—many notions of the Greeks and the scientists of the 17th century are no longer with us. In a way if we adhere to this Skinnerian idea that the Greeks did not have an effective science, we must say the same of Newton. And we may have to predict it of Einstein—for surely it is a bit premature to say that he, unlike the rest, had *the* right idea about the physical universe. In that case science is not really progress; it is the procession of successive stages of ignorance. And the only way to escape this dilemma is to admit that *within the context of their situation,* the Greeks were right to characterize motion as they did. Assuming that that was the best they could do. And indeed within the context of the available tools of discovery, including the prevalent conceptual development and machinery of exploration and experimentation, Greek science was closer to our own than Skinner and many others would admit. Aristotle understood, for example, the relativity of space and his cosmology was, within the limitations of some undeveloped concepts quite formidable, indeed, way ahead of its time.

Science and the humanities

Skinner himself admits that some of the Greeks toyed with a science of behavior comparable to his, although he dismisses their contributions as insignificant. Considering that he believes that the study of human affairs along scientific (i.e., essentially Skinnerian, mechanistic/materialist) lines has just recently begun, he cannot simply dismiss the ideas of Democritus of Abdera or, even earlier, Leucippus, both of whom propounded a strictly materialistic conception of nature. Since these views, as well as later ones, are not appreciably different from Skinner's, the latter cannot sustain his point about the modernity of his own ideas.

Of course, these are not, strictly speaking, points against Skinnerism. Being modern or ancient should have nothing to do with whether some theory is correct. But Skinner's credibility must be scrutinized when his arguments are unsubstantiated and he asks his reader to trust him. And in this matter of how modern instead of outmoded his own views are, Skinner's reports don't stand scrutiny. (The importance of his contention about how modern his ideas are is related to his cumulative view of science—after all, if people in ancient Greece already held Skinnerian views, there is something wrong about these views by the implications of the cumulative view of science.)

Let us admit that within most of the sciences progress does occur. People know more now than they did before, or at least they understand their fields more thoroughly and may even solve problems more efficiently. Predictions and control in some realms of reality where man at one time was impotent are commonplace. While it is foolish to believe that some day some conclusion of all scientific inquiries will occur—as some used to conceive of science—this alone does not invalidate the idea of frequent progress in the various branches of knowledge.

But what is Skinner's point in telling us about these things? Well, simply that we should turn all aspects of human life over to science so that everywhere comparable progress can be realized. If science is cumulative, if all human affairs could be subsumed under science, then in all areas of human life we would enjoy better and better management of problems.

As Skinner points out, philosophers are still discussing issues that Plato and Aristotle found important to discuss. And while it isn't fair to deny some progress and development in such fields as literature, drama, music, philosophy, political theory, law, or commerce, we would be stretching intelligibility in suggesting that what has occurred in these areas exhibits the kind of cumulative progress Skinner imagines science to have evidenced. So Skinner's point is that once we grant him the idea that science is cumulative, and agree that his scientific analysis of human affairs is indeed the most advanced step on this ladder of progress, we have no choice but to hand him our problems. Obviously, significant changes have taken place in politics, religion, morality—whatever one understands these to encompass. But there is every reason to believe that nothing comparable to scientific progress, a discernible growth of knowledge and understanding, has obtained.

From this Skinner concludes that we should hand the management of all these areas of human activity over to science. This is what is important here, and this is where Skinner's appeal lies as well. What he is asking for in the light of taking science to be cumulative is "a behavioral technology comparable in power and precision to physical and biological technology." (I/3) Because, as he explains, we are far "from 'understanding human issues' in the sense in which physics and biology understand their fields . . ." (I/3) Presumably, that is if we go by Skinner, only by developing such a technology, along lines followed by physics and biology, will we prevent "the catastrophe toward which the world seems to be inexorably moving." (I/3)

Skinner's comparison is totally misconceived—and his own analysis should reveal to him why this is so. He is comparing rather than contrasting. Scientific knowledge can, indeed, be passed down through history, so that we can largely disregard what earlier generations thought about a matter once we have gone beyond their advances. But the fields of art, politics, ethics, where we seem to face our major problems, deal with perennial issues. They are, more precisely, every person's and each generation's own problems. They encompass what we must face in each age, what cannot be solved for us by others who have gone before.

Skinner is asking for something impossible. That my grandfather solved the problem of getting a job after finishing college, does not mean that I would not have difficulty getting a job. Getting a job was *his* problem, as it is mine, and as *his* grandfather's was his. Just because *I* may have solved the problem of getting along with my children does not mean that they in their turn, will not have the same problem. So Skinner is involved in a drastic category mistake—confusing different sorts of problems, conflating areas that do not belong together. At least this is what the evidence would support for now. (Later we shall see just how and with what general justifications Skinner manages this.) What we should note is that Skinner does not consider that switching to the methods effective in physics or chemistry (or perhaps biology, although that itself may be a question to be answered) may not be wise. His approach is to this extent a form of reductionism.

Science vs. Skinnerism

Skinner says that science is "first of all a set of attitudes" and adds that by this we should understand "a disposition to deal with facts rather than with what someone has said about them." Here little argument is warranted. Except perhaps with the idea of "first of all." And maybe also with the specific translation of "attitude" into "a disposition." Although scientists may have the attitude to deal with facts, primarily, they do not have it necessarily in all areas of their lives. Some aren't even directly concerned with it in their profession since they would rather entertain suggestions, hypotheses, theoretical conjectures—and leave the facts to others. And here again Skinner is basically right. Science must, to be worthy of its name, focus on facts as opposed to opinions or the ideas others have about facts. Although many scientists must deal with documents, findings, judgments, which others in the field come up with, these must matter only because in the final analysis facts support them.

Whether attitudes can be translated to refer to dispositions, exclusively, we will have to consider when we get to Skinner's way of referring to human behavior. Since he rejects mentalistic terms, strictly speaking people have no attitudes in his framework. Not if "attitude" means something like a mental state, as we generally regard it. For now, dispositions will do. This means that scientists have a tendency or inclination to deal with facts, in the main, where they can.

And the next point may be well taken also. Scientists should be dedicated to dealing with facts whenever possible. So it "is a willingness to accept facts even when they are opposed to wishes. . . ." Skinner calls this "intellectual honesty." But from within Skinner's theory we will have trouble clarifying this last idea for the following reasons:

The behaviorism Skinner advocates does not allow for the possibility of human freedom, free will, or any kind of genuine free choice. He says that "The hypothesis that man is not free is essential to the application of scientific method to the study of human behavior." (II/447) We may have trouble deciding conclusively what he means by "man is not free." But it is enough for now that he rejects the idea that man can act out of "caprice," or "make spontaneous and capricious changes." This is the classical, Lucretian view of freedom held by hardly anyone in the philosophical community, at least not without very serious modifications. Skinner never confronts the view, however. He only rejects it. And perhaps science does demand this. Yet open-mindedness would seem to warrant a "wait and see" attitude instead of an outright assumption that "behavior is . . . determined." Some, like Rogers, pointed this out to Skinner at an early stage, but Skinner has not paid much heed to the objection.

Skinner considers that free will means "self-control" or "self-determination"—that some of what people do is up to them. He grants some meaningfulness to this idea but says that such behavior "eventually . . . must be accounted for with variables lying outside the individual himself." (II/228-9) Man, for Skinner, can neither "initiate action or make spontaneous or capricious changes." (VI/47)

When Skinner talks about honesty we must note that this again is troublesome for him from within his own framework. Honesty is a virtue. A person who is dishonest is considered to be free to be different, namely honest. Lying presupposes the option to tell or admit to oneself what one believes to be true. Virtues, in the only meaningful sense of the idea, cannot exist *or* fail to exist (be an "important possession of the successful scientist") unless man is free to cultivate them or to refrain from doing so.

If even part of Skinner's idea of science includes reference to a virtue, then it is questionable—no, impossible—that he can work entirely within his own position and verify his case.

Science limited

We come now to one of the more substantive and well-known views about science, one which Skinner shares with most people in one form or another. Skinner considers science to be the activity of searching for order. He says "It begins, as we all begin, by observing single episodes, but quickly passes on to the general rule, to scientific law." Thus he advances a restricted conception of what many other thinkers have, until recently, considered to be *the* correct view of science. Whatever fault there may be with this view, it should be made clear that Skinner did not originate it and should not be held responsible for its predominance in the intellectual climate. Moreover his acceptance of this idea of science appears to be motivated by a genuine desire to approach human affairs reasonably. Viewing human life along what Skinner takes to be the scientific line is, for him, the "consistent point of view." (II/9) As he sees it, "It is possible that science has come to the rescue and that order will eventually be achieved in the field of human affairs." (II/5) So we must consider this conception of science in order to make a determination of whether the Skinnerian program is viable. Without understanding why it is a mistake to view science along these lines we cannot comprehend why Skinner's arguments against human freedom and dignity are fallacious.

What is the first point of interest in this characterization? It is the idea that science "searches . . . for lawful relations among the events in nature." We might quibble at an earlier point, where Skinner thinks science searches for order but also announces that order must be one of the scientist's basic assumptions. But that would not lead to important matters. With the idea cited above we have, indeed, what is now the traditional, although increasingly questioned, view of science. So let us see if science, as we know it from the most general facts available to anyone about various sciences, lives up to Skinner's description.

The fact is that this view of science is too narrow. First, it admits only *events* as the legitimate subject matter of a science. Yet in mathematics, astronomy, physics, anthropology and others, events are clearly not the sole concern of the scientist. In these and other fields—even in psychology as practiced by non-Skinnerians—the scientist deals as intently and as often, if not more so, with *objects* or *entities*. Things, in addition to events, come under scrutiny. The belief that events alone are of significance does not rest on a candid observation of what happens within the various sciences. It emerges within the context of certain familiar *philosophical* and *metaphysical* theories about the nature of knowledge, causality in nature, and what can constitute an explanation within any field of science.

The claim that Skinner unjustifiably restricts himself to dealing with events and episodes might be challenged on grounds that he frequently mentions organisms—as when he talks about the "molar behavior of organisms." While he does refer to these—and throughout his writings allows the language of entities to occupy considerable room—it is important that we make a determination of which view of basic constituents of reality he takes as more significant. (Skinner admits to being inconsistent in his language and says this is necessary because the English language is full of prescientific notions. So when we find an inconsistency we must identify whether one or the other of the incompatible ideas represents his overall outlook more accurately.) Skinner's idea of science commits him to the event or episode view, although here and there he does talk about the organism that behaves. But he shows his preference for events by telling us outright that *his* science is one of *behavior* and defines this as "a process, rather than a thing." (II/15) And he tells us that he would "define behavior as the movement of an organism in space with respect to itself or any other useful frame of reference." (VI/8) Finally, he identifies individuals—in this particular case human beings—as "a locus in which many lines of development come together in a unique set . . . merely a stage in a process." (I/200) So the choice between Skinner's ontology—i.e., what type of being he believes ultimately makes up all of nature, including human affairs—must be clear: he thinks that processes are basic.

Again one might wonder why, if he is willing to talk about organisms,

Skinner pays so little heed to physiology. Generally, he does not think that the field can offer much knowledge about what is important in human affairs. Many physiological psychologists have complained about how disdainful behaviorists are toward them (XI/375-380)—although Skinner says that he looks forward "to the day when physiological facts will help in the scientific analysis of behavior." (VI/95) Unfortunately the physiologists think they have already reached that day, while the behaviorists deny it. Basically, behaviorists have a perspective in terms of which considerations of not just some "inner agent" like the mind but inner mechanisms like the brain get overlooked. And while Skinner is inconsistent as well as unilluminating about why this happens, we are entitled to ask for the reason and search for it in his writings.

The fact is that Skinner's entire argument relies on a view of science that admits only, or predominantly, of events. He does mention episodes, and here again one might argue that he is very close to admitting entities, since episodes are what entities carry out in action. But by choice he refuses to focus on the entities and prefers the events, so we must take this as his more basic view.

There are serious objections to Skinner's limitation on what science and his own field, psychology, can include. To begin with, science, or any other area from where we learn about the world, cannot deal with events without at once making reference to what constitutes the events being considered. An event involves the entities that comprise it. An event is something that happens and its nature presupposes entities that change, move, act, and so forth. Events alone cannot exist, since they are entities in motion. Events are what they are in virtue of what their constituent entities are, what partakes in them. The idea of science endorsed by Skinner ignores this. Nor does Skinner defend it from these charges.

What this indicates is that a simple commitment to the philosophy that nature is ultimately composed of events, not entities, cannot be asserted and used to support an entire conception of nature, mind, society, and political order; and such a philosophy is not in fact a result of scientific analysis but a basic presupposition of any given field of science. The view of science to which Skinner admits, and invokes for his implicit argument and against freedom and dignity, is itself an outgrowth of a philosophical tradition. Skinner may not have adopted it first and then constructed his experimental designs in terms of it, but once he moved out of the laboratory he had to invoke this philosophical position to give support to his nonscientific conclusions.

This admission of a philosophical commitment is important for those who disagree with Skinner. While they admit that science must be compatible with their political and moral theories, the latter needs more than what science can offer. Nor do all sciences accord with Skinner's view. Because Skinner confines science to treatment only of events, he must exclude entities—*including human beings*. The units of study within this conception of science must be events—episodes or movements. And behavior consists mainly of movement, whereas a person is an entity. While the behavior of something presupposes that there is a being that behaves, if science is necessarily restricted to a concern only with the event of behavior itself, any attention to the entity that engages in behavior, maybe even initiates it, *must* be ruled out.

Skinner's idea of science, which is not in itself the result of some expert analysis carried out by Skinner the specialist (and thus worthy of special consideration as medical opinions of doctors deserve,) must lead logically to his exclusion of the very possibility of human freedom and, therefore, the possibility of human dignity. But these opinions are not the result of a scientific analysis. They are the assumptions on which Skinner's subsequent discussions of human behavior are built. Once you accept the (nonscientific) theory of science that he advocates, the (allegedly) scientific conclusions that man is unfree and cannot achieve dignity are virtually assured. Skinner is proposing a theory of science and a theory of man, not in his capacity as a scientist but in his role as an intellectual layman who has inherited a certain view of science.

So what was said earlier needs to be reiterated: the identification of the nature of science is not itself the province of any given science; and the conclusions implied by the view of science someone proposes are not scientific conclusions. Insofar as Skinner's rejection of freedom and dignity rest on his view of science, he has no justification for claiming that this repudiation is scientifically warranted. Instead it is a view which emerges out of a philosophy and a philosophy of science.

Science and human knowledge

But we need to go a bit further to come to grips with Skinner's ideas about science. Is it true that "we all begin by observing single episodes . . . and quickly pass on to the general rule, to scientific law"? Is this what happens in a science? And is this what happens to "all" of us, from the time we begin to consider what there is, why, and what to do about it?

Single episodes are usually understood in light of the context which surrounds them. We need a perspective within which to make sense of something as a single episode of a certain kind. Suppose I see a cat jump up on an armchair in the living room. This is a single episode. But so is the movement of the cat's left paw, the rocking of the armchair, or the tearing of the material on the armchair. And if a different perspective is taken, with different purposes involved, even the contraction of the cat's leg muscles, or the movement of the air around the jumping cat could be regarded as a single episode. Whether this or that would be the single episode Skinner has in mind may depend on beginning with something other than such an episode. More plausibly we begin with some goal—even if the general one of discovering what occurs around us in the world. Then comes our awareness of episodes.

And that awareness itself requires that we first notice what the episodes consist of—e.g., a cat's leg, a cat, an armchair, or a muscle. To begin with an episode only is literally impossible. Psychologists working in the field of perception have lately given support to this. The idea used to be that babies see a conglomeration of events, a sort of messy, confused mishmash, and then begin to isolate the objects from that undifferentiated mass of episodes. But it looks like that idea is wrong. People see lamps, shadows, heads, arms, and so on, not events in which these have a role. They see these things in motion around them *when* they are in motion.

But perhaps Skinner simply means that "we all begin" when we are quite mature, self-conscious, and have acquired the skill to deal with the world on a casual, prescientific, unsystematic level—and by observing episodes or events. But here the trouble seems to be even greater. We can take any event, e.g., someone's drinking a cup of coffee. To observe someone drinking a cup of coffee involves being aware of someone as a someone (as distinguished from some thing, some machine, some group), the cup as a cup (not a bottle or hammer), and so forth. Without these there cannot be an observation of someone drinking a cup of coffee. Which is to say, we do not *begin* by observing episodes at all. What we begin with is a formulation of some goal, a purpose, e.g., to learn about what there is around us. Then we can engage in observation of things, people, cups, mom, dad, the teacher, and all of these in their very complex relationships (e.g., "I saw him go into the library and pick up the books lying on the shelf near the door" or "George observed him serving the bread to the entire family with pride on his face as they watched him doing it.")

Another point that needs to be mentioned: Skinner holds that science begins with the observation of episodes and "quickly passes on to the general rule, to scientific law." Yet, science itself does not proceed in any such direction, nor is observation by itself enough to explain how the scientist could pass on to the general rule or law. Instead it is *scientists,* human beings, who abstract from observation to *formulate* general rules and scientific laws. Anyone familiar with even the slightest approximation of carrying on scientifically can tell that passive observation produces no rules or laws or systems.

Science and language

Apparently science must, for Skinner, use language that goes beyond "the terms of the intelligent layman." He does not say why this is so. There is ample evidence that science uses technical vocabulary. But contrary cases can also be cited—economists, anthropologists, political scientists, even astronomers have managed to make clear their ideas and discoveries without using obscure language. Nor is it necessary, for purposes of making some of these sciences intelligible, that the layman's ordinary vocabulary be ruled out as expressing myths—although that vocabulary must be free of contradictory and ambiguous meaning.

There is the question, also, as to the truth of Skinner's view of the scientific effectiveness of a special or technical vocabulary. What he means is that the statements of scientists can only have significance as used in their special domain. Here Skinner is articulating an idea that is now very popular among historians and sociologists who are studying what occurs in scientific communities. For example, Thomas Kuhn holds that various branches of science are for long periods of time influenced by some basic idea, a paradigm, about what the professionals can and cannot do in their research. (But Kuhn, unlike Skinner, does not believe in science as a cumulative enterprise, nor in its smooth, uninterrupted upward movement. At least the former believes that science moves through stages of normal and revolutionary periods as a social phenomenon. (1)

The problem with this view about the importance of adjusting to a technical language, even at the exclusion of important, even fundamental concepts in a sensible, well-developed language used by people outside the field, is that the field can run amuck unchecked. That is, unless specialists keep in touch both with people in other fields and with the language of gross, unspecialized thinking about reality, they can always respond to criticism from outside that no one understands them well enough to be able to make telling points against conclusions reached in the field, methods employed, and so on. This is even more dangerous in a field such as psychology, where there are many schools with conflicting approaches, and where it is evident that the science is far from mature and free of serious confusions. Denigrating everyday language as Skinner does will emerge as a shield against criticism, not as an inherent requirement of good scientific practice. Since every science develops from people's concern with the details of what they experience and learn about outside of specialized inquiries—a point many people tend to forget but which is obviously true if one considers that early man often dealt with reality quite successfully before science emerged—it cannot end by denying the meaningfulness of all ideas not developed in its field. Even by acknowledging the need for serious reformulations of some ideas that have become imbedded in ordinary language, all of them cannot be disposed of without leading to drastic problems in the special field itself. These fields begin with ordinary ideas. They take their points of direction from them. Psychology starts when people want to know more and more about a certain evidently distinct aspect of animal and human life. The term "psyche" may initially have contained implications for people that would eventually have to be rejected or modified, but the basic idea that some such aspect of life exists can justifiably be maintained. Yet Skinner denies this by abandoning nontechnical language whole hog.

It appears, although Skinner does not explicitly state it, that the Skinnerian view of science requires that each special field possess a unique technical language. There is a serious danger of dogmatism in this, something that scientists ought to eschew. Advocating such groupism—as Skinner does by implication and others do more explicitly—an unjustified parochialism and even chauvinism becomes legitimatized, leading to an arrogant acceptance of this view by those in the field that can seriously hurt the field itself. Outsiders are excluded dogmatically as nonscientists with no consideration of their arguments or theories. This view of science may gain some plausibility from observing the workings of some of the worst of human motivations in the field of science, but by making it integral to the nature of science it becomes a supporter of what would otherwise be viewed, and quite rightly, as the less admirable traits of scientists. We cannot deny that many people in a profession—science or business or politics or barbering—want to have their well-established practices protected by some theory that they are the only *true* practitioners. And when governments step in to protect the profession from challenge—always, of course, in the "public interest"—they are simply reinforcing this wish. It is enough to report that the American Medical Association (AMA), the American Bar Association (ABA), and other organizations try to govern who is or who is not a bona fide member of the profession. Once they get the protection of laws, and in intellectual circles by the Skinnerian idea that this is how science *must* be, they no longer consider it necessary to argue for the exclusion of someone as a respected professional.

One fact that gives support to Skinner's view that the "scientific effectiveness of . . . a vocabulary will derive from the actual contingencies of reinforcement in the scientific community" is that we find scientists working in groups and with materials others have developed—i.e., ideas, discoveries, theories, principles, methods, hints, suggestions—that the membership of a community of some branch of science produces. But Skinner does not realize that a community can give support—i.e., adopt—the vocabulary of bad science as well as good science. Thus it can also reinforce the ineffectiveness of a science. But because Skinner assumes the necessarily cumulative—improving—character of science, he has to think that any support of the vocabulary of a field will be effective as science, wherever it leads.

So much for this point. Let us turn to Skinner's views on operationalism. He believes that we need an "operational analysis of mentalistic terms" which will show, or so he would have it, that such ideas as mind, agent, freedom, responsibility, and dignity are undefinable and thus designate nothing other than what the behaviorists believe exists, namely, movements of the organism (or its disposition to move, the probability of its movement). Operationalism is a theory of how to establish whether some idea or concept or term is meaningful, how to show that using some idea can help us understand and think or talk about something that does indeed exist. The term "operational" refers to the contention (of those who subscribe to this view of how to show some idea to be meaningful) that unless we can perform specific operations and measurements that correspond to some idea (and that idea alone), we have no justification for taking it to be sound or meaningful.

The main problem with this idea is that it leads to circularity. If an idea is meaningful because we can specify distinct operations that accompany its use, how do we show the meaningfulness of the ideas to which these operations refer? Some ideas have to be definable without reference to operations, otherwise we run into an infinite regress, or we find ourselves going around in circles defining operations operationally—more like in a spiral than in a circle perhaps.

Another difficulty, even more severe, about operationalism is that if we define a concept that we maintain means some existing thing or event in some context by reference to operations, how will we be able to think about that thing or event at all? If I define "table" by reference to how I measure or discover a table, then the idea "table" will not mean tables—e.g., "Please bring me a table (or that table) from the other room"—but the operations by which tables are measured and detected. But when we ask for a table—talk or think about them, refer to them in novels or poems,—it is not the operations by which they are measured or detected that we want, it is a table that we want, period.

Skinner's insistence on operationalism as the means by which to make evident the meaningfulness of ideas ties in with several other features of his outlook. For one, since he regards anything that is not directly observable—that is, not some event or episode we observe and from the observation of which we generate laws and rules—outside the domain of science (and, in the end, nature or existence itself), only those definitions can be admitted which refer to observable aspects of reality. And the (physical, observable) operations people in laboratories carry out when they measure mass, when they touch or manipulate some chemical, are all motions; they can be observed. By this stricture Skinner not only insists that such aspects of reality as mind, freedom, and dignity cannot exist, but he excludes all the theoretical arguments that might show their reality. I can point to the movement of someone's arm, so I am sure that my report on that movement can be justified by pointing, in turn, to my pointing at the movement. Although this is inadequate to show that operationalism is sufficient to account for the phenomenon of pointing, for example, it does have the virtue of simplicity—and for Skinner the advantage of being able to exclude any showing (philosophical demonstration) of the existence of something that goes beyond such simple operations.

Although operationalism is crucial to Skinner at a certain level of his discussion of his ideas (especially when he dismisses the views of others by requesting that they define their own terms operationally or go away) it is not the most crucial feature of his view of science. For although it may be concluded that Skinner has no *scientific* basis for upholding his view of science, there is possibly a philosophical or other extrascientific (prescientific?) case he could invoke. If so, we could chide him for some of his misleading polemic and yet be forced, logically, to regard his overall position possibly sound.

The conception of science that Skinner has adopted, especially where he talks of passing from the observation of single episodes to rules and laws, is a philosophical product—even if he did come up with it independently of philosophy which, by his own admission, he seems not to have done. (XI/15) Certainly many important scientists have held it also. But these ideas have not emerged from work in some special field of science but by reflecting on the character of science vis-à-vis other human activities. There is no science of science. Not unless we take the term "science" to mean something quite different in its first as opposed to its second use in that statement. Aristotle, for example, thought of philosophy as the first science, the science of being as such. But in this sense the term "science" has a very different meaning from what it means when we use it to think and talk about the special fields of physics, chemistry, biology, etc. It is only in this unusual sense of the term "science" that Skinner has offered something akin to a *scientific* analysis of human affairs. In short, Skinnerism is a philosophy, drawing on a philosophy of science. But not even that philosophy of science characterizes what Skinner himself is doing in most of his work, especially where he discusses human affairs.

What distinguishes philosophy from the sciences, or the "scientific" analysis of Skinner from the scientific analyses usually found in the special sciences? Philosophy is the field of study with the central goal of identifying the most general, fundamental facts or reality, including man's place therein. The sciences we are familiar with are concerned with special areas of reality, not its fundamental aspects. It is within philosophy that science is examined as one of many distinctive human activities. It is here that one concerns himself with what must all scientists assume before they can make sense of their own special fields. The facts identified by philosophers —when and if they do so, and even when they err in this effort—would generally be assumptions, hardly ever stated explicitly, within all other human endeavors, including science. Philosophy's scope is universal, whereas that of the special sciences is not. (All these points would be contested by philosophers, but there is no room here to defend them in full. For the time being the above is offered as a guideline to the background of the present analysis of human affairs, including of Skinner's endeavors to propose a viable doctrine.)

Philosophy and science

We need not dwell on what philosophy is, but a few remarks should be made to let the reader know what ideas govern the use of the concept "philosophy" in the present discussion. So, as implied above, philosophy studies the most basic facts of reality and man's relationship to them. Thus such questions as "What is it to be something, anything whatever?" "How can we know what there is, what would justify our ideas about some things, any things?" and "What should we do about that?" seem to occupy, in one or another form, in more or less detail, the minds of philosophers.

According to this general characterization of philosophy—which points up what sets it apart from the special branches of knowledge as well as so-called common sense—the question "What is the nature of science?" can be seen as one of the more specialized philosophical questions. Another such question would be "What is the nature of art?" It too pertains to the basics of some human activity. The philosophy of science is now a distinct concern within philosophy, although it is arguable that what its students do ought to be the province of two traditional branches of philosophy, epistemology and metaphysics. This is because in the philosophy of science the questions focus on the methodology of scientific conduct and the ideas scientists have concerning the basic constitution of reality, ideas that are often important guidelines in their own formulation of scientific problems. With these remarks we can now turn to the discussion of the background of the philosophical position that underlies B. F. Skinner's idea of science.

An important philosophical position that has been prominent for many decades—but, as most positions, it has been in contention throughout the ages—is empiricism. It is most fundamentally an answer to the question "What is the source of knowledge?" or "How must human beings go about learning about the world?" Already before the time of Socrates the basic features of empiricism had been formulated. Of course, by now there are many variations on that central theme.

In a different respect the origins of empiricism, which is actually an approach to issues that arise in just *one* branch of philosophy, namely epistemology, lie in people's ordinary, common-sense belief that we best understand something when we can feel it—by touching, seeing, tasting, hearing or otherwise experiencing it with one or more of our sense organs. From this natural but not fully considered trust in sensory evidence it is simple to jump to the belief that a clear and adequate understanding of anything at all requires reliance on what can be experienced by way of the senses. Seeing is believing, what you see is what you get, and I am from Missouri, show me—these are but loose declarations of the empiricist approach to the issue of what human knowledge is. All of this does not show that empiricism is correct or incorrect, nor does it explain why it has gained widescale adherence among those interested in understanding what human knowledge involves. Yet it does take the mystery out of empiricism's appeal—the approach is a natural one to take at least in certain contexts.

As an answer to the question "How do we best gain knowledge of reality?" empiricism provides a rather neat scientific method. In fact some argue that empiricism in epistemology easily becomes the handmaiden of the doctrine that scientific knowledge is the only kind worthy of the name "knowledge." While its purest version has never gained full adherence by those interested in these issues—the idea that sensory experience *alone* could lead to understanding is not so natural, after all—many accepted mitigated empiricist viewpoints. Among these we can list, with some risk, such diverse individuals as Francis Bacon, Thomas Hobbes, August Comte, and many of the early experimental scientists. They did not always deny a role for reason or, as some called it, "intutition" in their specifications of how human beings can acquire knowledge. But their approaches left little room for reflective thinking for purposes of obtaining scientifically reliable knowledge.

Empiricism played a crucial role in the philosophical theories of more recent thinkers also. Among others Karl Marx considered himself an empiricist of sorts—he actually claimed that dialetical materialism is a worldview that emerges after one investigates nature empirically. (Seeing himself as an empirical scientist allowed Marx to escape the charge that he himself was, like the rest of us, subject to seeing the world constrained by class consciousness—a mental bias created by one's economic conditions.) Aside from Marx—who is admittedly a special case—such famous thinkers as John Stuart Mill, Ernst Mach, Bertrand Russell, the early Ludwig Wittgenstein (who later altered his view considerably,) A. J. Ayer, and most mid twentieth century social scientists consider themselves empiricists of one or another variety.

Interestingly, the most vigorous defense of empiricism, 20th-century variety, came from a group of natural scientists who comprised what has come to be known as the Vienna Circle. This group of thinkers exerted considerable influence at the beginning of our century by insisting that all meaningful statements must be verifiable by way of sensory observation. They argued that philosophy itself had to conform to this edict lest it be incapable of making itself intelligible. Accordingly ethics, politics, aesthetics did not achieve the status of intelligibility, nor did metaphysics. It is fair to state that B. F. Skinner's conception of science owes a lot to their ideas.

Empiricism should be understood by anyone who wants to make sense of 20th-century culture, especially its scientific and academic aspects. One can appreciate a number of trends, from recent theology, to the appeal of the counter-culture attitude, the idea of human nature dominant in the social sciences, the intellectual status of the idea of morality—all the way to the phenomena of think tanks, the Gallup Poll, and Watergate—by an appreciation of the development of the empirical approach to the idea of truth. Although in philosophical circles proper empiricism is no longer so prominent as it used to be in the first half of the 20th century, the culture is undeniably permeated with the many consequences of an almost dogmatic acceptance of empiricism by many intellectuals.

Empiricism and rationalism

A characterization of empiricism is most useful when it is contrasted with rationalism—a view of the source of human knowledge against which empiricism is generally proposed as an alternative. Rationalism and empiricism have for many years been identified as the main rivals in mankind's attempts to understand the nature and source of human knowledge.

Both, in turn, have their more or less well-developed philosophies of the proper scientific method. For our purpose it is valuable to understand the appeal of both of these approaches, for through this we can better appreciate why Skinner was attracted to the empirical approach—at least as far as he gave lip service to some theory of knowledge.

Rationalism is an account of how man must gain knowledge of reality; it emphasizes the method of a priori analysis. This analysis consists of engaging oneself in so-called dialetical reasoning. Ideas are proposed, tested against opinions, counter-examples, and so forth, until some are found to be self-evident, irrefutable, unchallengable, certain, or otherwise suited for constituting the foundation of knowledge. Also close to a rationalist approach we find the process known as *deductive reasoning*—taking the self-evident truths and working out their implications. The entire program is often characterized as reaching understanding of the world by *unaided reason,* unaided, presumably, by any appeal to sensory evidence. The approach seems to promise the kind of certain knowledge we seem to have when we are dealing with mathematics or analytic geometry, where we are generally believed to start from nothing but self-evident ideas, axioms, and reach valuable knowledge at considerable levels of complexity.

The most famous rationalist was the philosopher René Descartes. By what is known as the "method of doubt," a kind of dialectical reasoning process, Descartes arrived at the allegedly self-evident principle of "I think, therefore I am." Once he arrived at this claim, he used it—probably quite questionably, despite his intentions—to derive a great many other truths. Thus he derived God's existence, the existence of physical objects, and many other things from just this one basic claim. Among the things he derived we could find a great deal of what all of us had believed to be true anyway. But Descartes wanted to provide a solid foundation for things not generally agreed upon. And he, like all other thinkers, found himself criticized severely for going about concluding what he did in the way he did.

For our purposes it is important to know that Descartes' alleged basic truth was not that he existed as a biological, living, corporeal entity, but that he existed as a thinking, nonmaterial being. So for him if there is anything that we can accept for certain, it is that we exist as thinking beings— even while we remain uncertain about whether our bodies exist. In fact, even when we have earned the right, by way of complicated arguments, to conclude that our bodies do exist, there remained, for Descartes, a very serious distinction between mental or conscious being and physical or material being. So much so, that *we* could only know *our own* consciousness or minds for certain, while about others we could only infer that they had a mind—since all we could know of others directly (once God enabled us to know physical objects) is that they had bodies.

Because of its emphasis, the rationalist approach led to conclusions that gave ample room for mental entities. Since Descartes found his own mind to be the only existing being he could know for absolutely certain, the rationalist approach appeared to allow plenty of room for consciousness, feelings, dreams, wishes, attitudes, spirit, soul, mind, and so forth. Intentions, purposes, wants, and all the things Skinner thinks to be entirely unjustifiable entities or processes had an easy enough place within most rationalist theories of knowledge. Any doctrine that would take the existence of the mind as the primary fact of reality would naturally enable one to discuss the realm of the mind with considerable comfort, without much hesitation. Some rationalist philosophies, including certain versions of a later form of rationalism called idealism, went so far as to deny that anything other than the mind exists in the universe. If, after all, the firmest knowledge we have is knowledge of a nonmaterial thing, and if all else we learn is in some manner deduced from the existence of this nonmaterial, mental thing, then it is not very difficult to pack everything that exists into the mental realm. (But oddly enough, some antirationalist, empiricist views lead to just such a conclusion as well, when pushed hard enough.)

After Descartes, the reign of rationalism began its gradual descent (just as with Plato it gained the limelight). It is basically the adoption of the deductive method, on the model of mathematics, that characterizes the tradition best (within our scope). In ordinary discourse this viewpoint is given expression when people refer to "pure reason," "purely formal," "in theory, not necessarily in practice," "it's a good idea but will it work," "logically true, consistent—but that is not what the world is like," and so on.

In spite of the ultimate demise of strict rationalism, it was in connection with what Descartes concluded about man and the universe that the way was paved for the development and character of a viewpoint that gained prominence thereafter, and is still all-pervasive in our culture. Descartes divided the world into two distinct and separable (often separate) kinds of being: *spirit* (or mind or thinking being) and *matter* (or sensible or spatially extended or physical being). Our problems with the relationship between the mind and body, consciousness and behavior, and thinking and feeling, were thus crystallized. (That these are problems is evidenced by their frequent characterization as dichotomies.) For Descartes bluntly identified man's body as a machine, and placed into it, in the words of English philosopher Gilbert Ryle, a "ghost"—the soul/mind, an unextended, nonphysical being which could be free from all the constraints and laws of nature. He argued that animals have no souls and are, therefore, machines through and through. This view seemed to Descartes to make the best sense in the light of his belief in God and man's relationship to him. But it also promptly separated part of man from all of nature.

The consequences of this view are clearly reflected in contemporary science. Skinner himself acknowledges it. But he does not trace it to Descartes. He mentions that Thorndike "showed that the behavior of a cat in escaping from a puzzle box might seem to show reasoning as Romanes had argued but could be explained instead as the result of simpler processes." (VIII/81) Indeed if all animals are machines and conform to the principles of mechanics, and yet show signs of complex consciousness, comparable to man's, is there ground to exclude man from a study guided by the principles of mechanics? Rationalistic views, in which mind is absolutely indispensible but also scientifically untouchable, lead, in the end, to the reduction of human consciousness to the movements of the body (machine), to "behaviors."

Rationalism gave way to a different approach to understanding reality with the rise of empiricism. The most renowned empiricist of modern times was David Hume. Before him John Locke had already put considerable emphasis on the role of the senses in human knowledge. (Aristotle did the same, but his reputation—to both the dismay of his followers and the misfortune of us all—was tainted by the misconceived theoretical association he had with medieval theology.) Locke was not, however, the extreme empiricist Hume turned out to be. There was room in Locke's philosophy, even if not with clear consistency, for objective knowledge of what things are, of reality, and of moral and political principles, none of which found a place in the philosophy of David Hume.

In Hume's philosophy man cannot know what there is in the world, he can never justify his beliefs concerning the nature of something. His knowledge has to stop at his senses. Reality can only be known by way of the sense-impressions we have of it. Such sensory impressions and their copies (our ideas) experienced by the mind are thus the limit to our knowledge of things. These make up our belief system of reality. This system of copies of sense-impressions is all we can know, even though Hume never claimed that nothing more exists in reality outside of them.

Essentially the Humean position was that the ground of knowledge has to be something as firmly in our grasp as is the feeling of the cold on our hands, the taste of sour on our tongues, hardness, pain. So the means to knowledge must be the human senses. The basic units of what man can be aware of turned out to be what Hume called impressions of senses. From these we come to have certain copies (as ideas) of these impressions, more or less complex, but all with the requirement that they be grounded in originally experienced sense-impressions. What in Skinner appears as the emphasis on observation has its origin in Hume's sensory experiences. And the place (observable) behavior has in Skinner's range of admissible items of existence may be compared with Hume's impressions—with appropriate, often significant, modifications. But the lineage is plain enough.

Hume's strict empiricism was only the beginning. It had to be revised over and over again, so by the time we arrive at modern logical empiricism and operationalism, we have a highly refined, although not necessarily more successful, account of human knowledge. With Hume the result of strictness was skepticism. When speaking philosophically—i.e., from a strictly logical, reasoned point of view—Hume literally thought that no

75

knowledge of reality is possible. But he also held that this is only an academic point, a caution against dogmatism; in ordinary life we should be mitigated skeptics, trust our natural instincts, our habits of mind, our beliefs. These will guide us well, despite the philosopher's discouraging conclusions about knowledge proper. (How he came to *know* this Hume never made quite clear.)

Later empiricists did not fully accept Hume; but they were deeply influenced by perhaps the most important of his ideas—his understanding of scientific causation, his view of the nature of cause.

Empiricism, causes, and science

Causes are thought by most of us to exist in nature. There are, we would ordinarily think, many things in reality, many types of things, relationships, qualities, objects, whatnot. Among these, causes take their rightful place, or so a lot of us would contend. Thus the dent in my car was caused by the truck that ran into it—and the cause was indeed a real thing, something that occurred in reality. This is just what most of us believe.

For Hume the story about causes turns out very differently: If all knowledge must rest on sensory experience, then all of our ideas must be traced back to a sensory impression (or group of impressions) for them to be valid, meaningful. He then inquired about the idea of causation. Upon which (group of) impressions is this idea based? He answered that the idea is based on the experiences we have—the feeling of expectation, the anticipation that we *experience*, that we find in ourselves, is the origin of the idea of causation.

For is it not clear that no impression of something distinctive other than the truck and the dented car exists as we experience the smash-up mentioned above? There is no impression of some third element called "cause" there. Although strictly speaking Hume has no right to talk about trucks and cars, we may forget this for a moment. Let us assume that trucks and cars exist—simply because we have distinct impressions we have come to call by the names "truck" and "car." And these impressions originate from outside our bodies. So we are entitled, with some help, to conclude that the truck and the dented car exist in reality—the impressions we have so designated have an external referent.

But with cause all we find is the experience of anticipation. This is not to say that causation does not exist—but it is to give an entirely different interpretation of the idea, one which makes no reference to something in the world. Simply because we did not get some sensory input of something that we can name "cause," we cannot legitimately believe—although our instincts will lead us to do so anyway—that there exist causes in the world. Causes exist only as anticipations within us, habits of thought that we acquire through experiencing certain impressions of things (trucks) in (constant) conjunction with other impressions of things (dented cars).

This characterization of causation has puzzled most philosophers ever since Hume advanced it. While we might well understand that someone in Hume's days, surrounded as he was with theologians who laid claim to all sorts of certain knowledge, causation, and whatnot from a purely a priori approach, would challenge our facile belief in knowledge of causation, it is quite incredible to take Hume's conclusion literally. In fact, he himself admitted this much in a classic passage:

> I dine, I play a game of back-gammon, I converse, and am merry with my friends; and when after three or four hours' amusements, I wou'd return to those speculations, they appear so cold, and strain'ed, and ridiculous, that I cannot find in my heart to enter them any farther. (XII/242)

Hume, like Skinner, operated on two different, incompatible levels of discourse. The "speculations" he spoke of are like Skinner's scientific analysis. The rest are like Skinner's use of "casual language," descriptions, approaches, activities, and so forth, in terms of a prescientific way of thought. Skinner, however, unlike Hume, wants us to adjust ourselves to the speculations and to reject the prescientific way of thought. He is not satisfied to allow his games, conversations, or amusements to go on in conflict with what his technical analysis dictates. This despite the fact that nowhere is Skinner quite able to express himself in terms of his own technical vocabulary. This and many other reasons will emerge to show that his hopes for such adjustment are in vain.

What matters here is that Hume's views on causality left an incredibly powerful imprint upon subsequent philosophic and scientific thinking. Resting meaningfulness upon contact with the world by way of sensory impressions seemed to him the right way to eliminate confusion. In this, too, he is a precursor of Skinner—except there are other alternatives open for the latter. While Hume's strict empiricism was soon abandoned, his basic analysis was not. Hardly anyone is a strict empiricist today, although in philosophical circles the ideas that are generally attributed to Hume had prominence until the end of the first half of the 20th century. What are known as the logical positivists and logical atomists drew a good deal from Hume's philosophy. And in the various sciences that have recently become well populated—sociology, political science, economics, and, of course, psychology—the methodological rules generated from these neo-Humean strains of philosophy are still very prominent. Whenever one hears references to this or that study showing that this or that is the truth in some areas of investigation of concern to people, and when one hears about how some conclusion is *empirically* valid or has good *empirical* evidence behind it, it is this mixture of Hume and some of his later followers that is making its impact, good or bad, on our age. Not that there have not been challenges put to these developments from many points of view. (Most of the challenges tend, however, to advance ideas that turn out to be almost as problematic as strict empiricism itself—e.g., Existentialism in psychology, phenomenology in sociology, Marxism in sociology, economics.)

Skinner's philosophy of science

Skinner remains, in spirit at least, a follower of Hume. I say this not because he shows full awareness of Hume's defense of empiricism nor because in all respects he shows adherence to Hume. In fact, Skinner could also be aligned with Francis Bacon and Auguste Comte, as mentioned before. But the position Skinner takes on what human knowledge is, how we must gain our understanding of the world and what it is to be scientifically proper (which is the only way we can know reality) is best defended by Hume and his philosophical disciples through the last few centuries.

Skinner tells us that *the* scientific approach consists of "observing single episodes . . . [which] . . . quickly passes on to the general rules, to scientific laws. . . ." He explicitly disallows "constructing a Hypothesis" and tells us that he "never deduced Theorems or submitted them to Experimental check. . . ." (IV/88) Whether by intention or accident, this same picture is what emerges in Hume when he says that the mind receives sense impressions from which it gets into the habit of constructing general ideas. This "passing on to general rules" could almost have been lifted from Hume, even if in some other areas Skinner and Hume are far apart. Hume also believed, however, that where event A and event B are observed or experienced to be conjoined in time, we begin to believe that they will be conjoined in the future, leading us to general rules and laws. But Hume contended that the exact nature of the A's and B's and their constituents *cannot* be known—we can only have firm beliefs about what they are.

Skinner's philosophy of science is a not very systematic rendition of a Humean epistemology carried into the field of systematic learning. To use Hume's example to illustrate how we come to believe in causal connections, we have the motions (of the sense-impressions) of billiard balls A and B, one preceding the other in time. Since we cannot really know of the independent entities, only these motions are available to deal with, recorded by our senses, registered in the form of sensory impressions or, in Skinner's way of viewing the situation, observed. This alone can constitute objectivity, the central ingredient of science—reliable knowledge. (Skinner refers to "the objective study of behavior" and "objective alternatives to thought" in contrast to mentalism, introspection, and the like. And he puts it quite bluntly that "a scientific analysis of behavior has yielded a sort of empirical epistemology. The subject matter of a science of behavior includes the behavior of scientists and other knowers" [VIII/84].) Skinner's commitment to observation as the exclusive source of rules and laws in science is the explicit philosophy of science advanced by Francis Bacon and David Hume—though only the latter provided it with forceful philosophical argumentation.

In Hume only events can constitute items of observation, just as for Skinner it is episodes and events that we observe and science studies. Hume's billiard balls were convenient fictions—the casual language of

Skinner—since all that we really can record is the motions of (collections of) sense-impressions; these prompt us to relate them in accordance with the frequency of their various conjunctions in space and time; and if we make it our task to expose ourselves to the details of such conjunctions in special areas of concern to man, we can arrive at scientific rules and laws. These, in line with a Humean approach, have the peculiarity of being the only possible beliefs we could have of the world—and yet they can never reach the status of knowledge because they are beliefs about the behavior of sense-impressions, not of objects.

This picture, with some minor modifications, is what we get from Skinner. The modification is supplied where Skinner explains that "I short-circuit Kant by going back to the British Empiricists. But I don't find myself very happy with either formulation. . . ." and points out that this unhappiness stems from the fact that "Everyone seems to feel that somewhere in the brain there should be a copy of nature. . . . But I insist that there is no copy there at all; that as soon as the organism begins to respond to the environment, it is responding and not duplicating, and that in seeing a triangle, for instance, there need be nothing in the organism which is triangular in any sense whatsoever, either physiologically, perceptually, or behaviorally." (VI/16)

This is not an important modification however since Skinner cannot make it clear. He may insist on the reality of whatever is seen or perceived or responded to, but he is not willing to deal with such things as a scientist; he insists on staying with events, episodes, or behavior ("the movement of an organism in space with respect to itself or any other useful frame of reference" [VI/8]). He never justifies his refusal to admit objects as scientifically significant. He is not concerned with these issues at all in his works. He simply accepts the idea of science inherited from the naive empiricist tradition, refuses to deal with the problems which are posed by it, and draws most of his central conclusions about man and his life and future from this inheritance.

So we have Skinner's approach. It is a relatively simple one. Empiricism is accepted without much worry about its intelligibility. Its criterion of truth is accepted even more casually—claims are true if what is said can be observed. Its logical difficulties with objects is simply ignored and their existence is asserted, though treated as scientifically irrelevant. Its idea of the nature of scientific knowledge—i.e., the demonstration of rules and laws —is taken on more or less in its entirety, and episodes, events, and (most relevantly) behaviors are made the subject matter of scientific study. Most importantly, to be a scientist is to be concerned with "order . . . uniformities . . . lawful relations among the events in nature." (II/13) Finally, all of this is taken to its logical extreme; yet without the slightest foundation in any actual scientific research, investigation, "constructing a Hypothesis . . . Experimental check. . . ," (IV/88) Skinner derives his idea of man as a bundle of behavior, an organism moving about, that has no mind, no capacity for initiating action, no freedom, and certainly no dignity. If man is not divine—and if he is a part of nature then that is impossible—he must be a machine. That is the road from Descartes, superrationalist from the 16th century, to Skinner, superempiricist and radical behaviorist of the 20th. Absolutely no contribution of the science of psychology was required to accomplish the transition.

Science, pseudoscience, and Skinnerism

Skinner's idea of science alone, not his activities as a scientist (his research, his theories) have led him to conclude that man has neither freedom nor dignity. His idea of science is questionable. The philosophy on which it rests—as part of an answer to the more general epistemological question of what human knowledge is—entails the vision of man which he advocates. Yet Skinner never confronts that philosophy, never considers objections to it, or defends it against the formidable criticism that it has received through the centuries since its documented origins in pre-Socratic times. Basically what Skinner does is simply reiterate a philosophy of nature which has been with us at least since Democritus. And his only contribution is the development of a new vocabulary by which to describe the implications of this ancient philosophical position.

None of this proves that Skinner is indeed wrong. A philosophy that is ancient is not therefore false. But Skinner never establishes his position. He asserts only that this is what he has done, that these matters "have been worked out under more precise conditions." (I/20) He tells us that "The instances of behavior cited in what follows are not offered as 'proof' of the interpretation. The proof is to be found in the basic analysis." (I/21) And he tells us that his book (BFD) "could have been written for a technical reader without expressions of that sort [which] may seem inconsistent . . . [e.g.] 'keep a point in mind,'" but neither do his other books make any effort at confining themselves to permissible, technical, and according to Skinner, consistent language.

So what are we to say of Skinner's claim that "In what follows, the issues are discussed 'from a scientific point of view'"? What must we do with the announcement that "A scientific analysis shifts both the responsibility and the achievement to the environment"? Are these claims proven by Skinner? Does he establish them for us? Does he defend himself against criticism of what he takes to be meant by a "scientific point of view" and "a scientific analysis"?

Our reply must be that Skinner leaves us entirely to our own independent resources for purposes of ascertaining whether what he says about these matters is true. And a bit of research will reveal to any careful person that his point of view is more philosophical than scientific, especially when he avoids dealing with other than such narrow issues as how to condition the behavior of certain animals. The most Skinner does is to present an out-

80

line of a philosophy of science, and then use this unscrutinized, undefended idea about what science has to be in order to support his claim that such ideas as human freedom and dignity have no scientific validity. Since for Skinner science is the source from which truth can be expected, once these ideas are excluded, by implication and by Skinner's declaration, they amount to nothing more than myths.

Skinner's idea of science is indefensible, aside from his failure to defend it. Even though some share it, of course. Even some of the empiricists admit that far more than the observation of events is needed to come up with sound conclusions in any field. Experimentation, developing hypotheses that have to be tested, are closer to what science must involve, and Skinner gives all this short shrift. Finding out about the nature of the atom and what can be done with atoms and their constituent particles is not possible via Skinner's method. There is question about how much science there is in Skinner's most primitive experiments—some consider them activities science needs but, by themselves, they can only constitute single events with no scientific significance until integrated with other elements of a field. But when Skinner goes beyond these he has left all semblance of what must be done to be scientific about some subject matter.

Science vs. freedom and dignity

But none of this *proves Skinner wrong*. Clearly, if someone in New York City asserts that the Eiffel Tower collapsed in Paris he *could* be saying what is true, even though he has absolutely no evidence for his claim. We have to consider whether Skinner is in this position. We have to consider whether his (intentional or implicitly assembled) deductions from his philosophy of nature and man are right, even though he has little proof to offer in their support. We must investigate whether his implicit philosophy of reductive materialism—the idea that everything is one kind of thing, that is, physical motion or events—is correct. We must understand that the Skinnerian announcement of faithfulness to science and dependence on scientific method for the development of conclusions about human freedom and dignity is highly specious and unsubstantiated.

Skinner nothwithstanding, it is hoped that we can avoid falling within that segment of the literature of freedom which "may inspire a sufficiently fanatical opposition to controlling practices to generate a neurotic if not psychotic response." (I/157) No doubt, the literature in behalf of any point of view that makes a difference as to how societies will be designed, governed, and so on, or simply how people will deal with each other, *may* inspire fanatical opposition. But it need not do so.

Nor is there an occasion for another practice Skinner ascribes to "the traditional libertarian": "a bitterness with which he [the libertarian] discusses the possibility of a science and technology of behavior and their use in the intentional design of a culture." Some harsh terms may emerge—

after all, Skinner does not spare these either in BFD when he blames the libertarian for many harmful practices in the culture, including the encouragement of too many people to "do as they please."

But when a theoretician asks us to abandon values and ideals which to many of us have at least appeared to be very significant, we can demand good, solid backing for his arguments. Freedom and dignity are important, even if mistakenly so. They have had a lot to do with people's lives—at least as ideas, words to rally around. Even Skinner admits this much. Anyone who chooses to debunk them, to eliminate them from the human arena, has a responsibility to meet certain standards of argumentation, of precision with terms and, yes, of intellectual honesty. That Skinner fulfills none of these in carrying out the project that promises to accomplish this enormous and significant task must be noted. Perhaps others who choose to get involved with the issues will avoid the same omissions and negligence.

3

Simple and Complex Reductionism

SKINNER'S CONCLUSIONS CONCERNING human nature and human behavior reach far beyond what his own scientific analysis permits us to conclude. As a result we are forced to consider what other source he might invoke to give support to his extremely important and consequential conclusions. And they are important and consequential if one only realizes that he aims to derive from them an entirely passive view of human action and a political theory in terms of which Skinnerian behavior technologists would be empowered to govern society by their particular methods. Skinner wants to construct society on the model of an experimental laboratory space. This he admits outright—no need to make doubtful inferences here. So before we dismiss his supposedly scientific grounds for making these drastic suggestions—for proposing that only by accepting these will we be able to cope with the terrible troubles the world faces—it behooves us to consider what extrascientific support he may be drawing upon.

Clearly, Skinner himself denies that he is being philosophical in his discussion of human behavior. He denies that he is involved in some kind of metaphysical investigation of such issues as free will and determinism. Not only does he deny that he is philosophizing, but he often shows explicit disdain for the philosophical approach. It must be evident that he wishes to assimilate all the humane studies into behavioral analysis—what else might explain his bold embarkation upon economics, political science, ethics, and the philosophy of science? We need not accept this lumping together of many clearly distinguishable fields of study; we can look for Skinner's philosophy and metaphysics, even if he denies that they exist. This is because his arbitrary assimilation rejects the need for distinctions even in the face of clear differences.

83

Let us consider for a moment, just to provide our analysis with some reputable support from Skinner's own community, what two self-proclaimed Skinnerians (Boakes and Halliday) say about Skinner's work:

> ... The uneasiness that [Skinner's] extentions evoke appears to be based on more than a lingering resistance to the idea of continuity between animals and man. ...

This resistance, the authors say, appear to have the following grounds:

> ... Whereas Skinner's initial work on animal behavior concentrated on [defining units of subject matter] and stressed the need for empirical solutions, his explanations of human behavior are framed in terms of units defined on intuitive grounds. ...

Furthermore,

> ... the extrapolations are made by rather limited aspects of the behavior of rats and pigeons ... [and] ... preference for situations that allow refined methods of experimental control has influenced the kind of problem that Skinnerians have tackled. Thus, for example, almost every experiment is performed upon adult animals and the extrapolations to learning in human childhood are not based on comparative developmental evidence. If one is interested in the way that language is acquired and wishes to compare this with the behavior of birds, then the acquisition of bird song seems as good a place to start as the control of pecking in pigeons.

The authors then add:

> ... A very important problem in human behavior arises when consequences are not immediate and there is no apparent chain of intermediate responses and secondary reinforcement to bridge the gap. (XI/371-72)

These conclusions, advanced by authors who say that they "have taken [an] essentially Skinnerian" approach which "includes all the really crucial features of Skinner's position," support the conclusions drawn earlier. Let us now see if Skinner's speculative support might not, after all, be adequate. Admitting that strictly speaking he is not doing any sort of scientific analysis in his discussions of human affairs, Skinner may simply reply that a certain *philosophical* framework or point of view he uses does provide him with correct answers to questions about the whys of human behavior.

Actually this is fantasy. Skinner flatly denies that he is "debating [e.g.] the issue of free will ... when [he] questions the supposed residual of freedom of autonomous man. ..." Nor is his book *Beyond Freedom and Dignity* a work of "mataphysics." Instead it is "an exercise in interpretation" based "on the existence, or at least the imminence, of a science of behavior." (XII/257, 261, *passim*) So Skinner tells us, "It is dangerous and foolish to deny the existence of a science of behavior in order to avoid its implications."

But whether there are implications of any science of behavior for what we need to know about human affairs is nowhere discussed by Skinner. He simply asserts it. And one is hard put to remain calm when such blatant pretentions are nowhere backed up even by attempts at logical argumentation. Even to this Skinner has an answer. Thus in his discussion of operationalism (as a view of how to define terms) he concludes that "If it turns out that our final view of verbal behavior invalidates our scientific structure from the point of view of logic and truth-value, then so much the worse for logic, which will also have been embraced by our analysis." (X/594) It is clear then that nothing could possibly count as an objection to Skinner as far as he himself is concerned.

Skinner's philosophical commitments

Still, let us assume that Skinner has admitted offering an interpretation of human behavior based on a philosophical or metaphysical outlook; this is certainly what he has done *in fact*. What is it, and can it stand up under scrutiny?

Before answering, we need to note that all we get in the way of clarification and help from Skinner himself are sample interpretations. To characterize the view which underlies his comments on human behavior requires considering some examples from his discussions. But, so as not to give the impression that Skinner's inadequate treatment of the point of view from which he is working is the only one, other renditions of it must be examined.

Skinner's metaphysics and philosophy is a loose, rather disorderly version of reductive materialism. What this version states is that reality is composed of *one kind of entity,* namely matter, and it is the motion of this matter that we know when we know anything at all. Accordingly, unless we can show that our statements refer to such matter-in-motion, we really have not accomplished our purpose. Reductive materialism in general amounts to the requirement that everything that exists be composed of nothing other than matter.

There are more complicated versions of this viewpoint, needless to say. Some philosophers are reductivists but not materialists, others are materialists but not reductivists. Still others are mitigated reductivists and wish to reduce certain terms in the language to other, more meaningful ones— e.g., "national purpose" would have to be reduced to "the purposes of the majority of those who have legal authority to support certain goals everyone in the country is compelled to pay for." For the time being we shall go by the first, loose, and open characterization.

Why should Skinner be considered a reductive materialist? He never admits to being one and offers only a few clues by way of self-identification. He says that he accepts as real only that which can be *observed*. He does align himself with the British empiricists in the competing tradition of philosophy. He does regard all prescientific ideas and positions inferior to scientific ones, which means (to him) ideas that emerge from an experimental analysis. And the latter he says, involves the observation of episodes and events. Clearly, then, he accepts only episodes and events, and only ones that can be observed, as meaningful candidates for what actually exists in the world.

Skinner vacillates between simple empiricism, where only sensory evidence can give us knowledge, and materialism, where we must accept that the sensory evidence is produced by material *objects*. He tells us that he has no use for "perceptual entities . . . since . . . there is nothing to which you can relate" them, and notes that "the triangle you see is out there." (XI/16) By this he denies that only sensations exist—something that many philosophers associated with David Hume and the strict empiricist tradition have believed. But in his adherence to operationalism, with observations as the only clue to and basis for knowledge, Skinner goes back to those who rest all knowledge on sensations. The existence of objects could not be affirmed if all we had were sensations. The sensation produced through my fingertip or my ear is simply that—a sensation. And if this is all we can know of the world, everything turns out to exist merely in our minds, not "out there," as Skinner would contend. Bertrand Russell is the last of the many philosophers who posed this problem, originally encountered by David Hume.

Episodes and events, not actual objects, constitute the stuff of the Skinnerian universe. With this Skinner explicitly joins hands with Alfred North Whitehead (VI/15), whose philosophy affirmed the existence of a basic unit in the universe not as a thing or an entity but as a *process*. Ordinarily we would think that any process must involve *something* in *procession, something* that proceeds. But for Whitehead the process itself is the basic stuff of existence. Skinner, in his way, borrows this outlook; for to him behaviors (events), not objects and people that behave, constitute the basic material of analysis. Skinner is always talking of "bits of behavior." It is clear then that he is a *kind* of reductionist and a *kind* of materialist: everything *must* be an observable physical process.

Reductionism in Skinnerism

There are some central concepts by which Skinner achieves reductionism. These are the ones he uses to refer to the variety of events, items, things, and processes that we ordinarily refer to with what he calls prescientific terms. Choice, intention, purpose, decision, and the like are all such "prescientific" notions. Skinner takes it that in the end they mean nothing, since they do not refer to any material process we can observe and measure. So he substitutes other terms to indicate *something like* what these ideas can be used to talk about; but in the process he considerably restricts what is being referred to and we will have to see whether he does not omit or conceal what might be very important. For example, when someone chooses to do something, is he merely exhibiting bodily movements in some environmental context? This is what Skinner argues. He wants to prove that although we might *wish* to mean more than a bodily movement, nothing more in fact *can* be meant and we would do better to give up terms such as "choice"—terms that supposedly deceive.

Skinner does not advocate *linguistic* reduction alone. Linguistic reduction amounts to a mere *substitution of terms* for the sake of convenience or precision. In Skinner's case this would mean that for his own limited purposes the term "choice" does not serve him well, so another term has to be adopted. Thus in a laboratory experiment Skinner finds it more effective to talk about behaviors instead of choices, without actually denying the existence of choice.

But this is not the case. Skinner believes that choices do not *exist*, that people do not make them, that decisions, intentions, purposes, and the like are ideas that have no meaning inside or outside of the experimental space or laboratory. (In the sense in which we all believe that unicorns and Martians are fictitious and mythical entities.) So Skinner is not just a linguistic behaviorist. He actually believes that the universe is composed of only one kind of stuff, namely matter in motion—material processes. (Philosophers such as Ernst Mach and Alfred North Whitehead have advanced more elaborate versions of this view.)

Behavior

Specific manifestation of this position should be considered in connection with several important Skinnerian terms. First, the most fundamental concept: behavior. "Behavior . . . is a process, rather than a thing." (II/15) The definition is filled is elsewhere when Skinner says "I would define behavior as the movement of an organism in space with respect to itself or any other useful frame of reference." (VI/8) We recall Skinner's insistence that science studies relationships between events as well as that psychology must study behavior. All that he develops in the way of technical concepts rests on these basic points. When we add his belief that a scientific analysis *must* assume that man is not free but environmentally determined, we can generate virtually everything else that Skinner proposes.

What, for example, are the items Skinner considers bits of behavior? Everything from finger movements, muscle spasms, blinking of eyelids and twitches, to toothaches, pains and itches, gestures, characteristics, habits, traits—all the way to thinking, memory, conversation, designing, composition, poetry, contemplation, in fact, everything must be considered either as an actual bit, or grouping of bits, of occurring behavior. Attitudes, virtues, vices, emotions, beliefs, hunches, suspicions, or whatever we might think would constitute a fact would be, to Skinner, some bit(s) of behavior. Provided, he would add, that there is something to observe, to point at, to

87

define operationally, to work with in a technology—to manipulate and control. Otherwise we are talking about mysterious and thus nonexistent entities or processes.

Skinner admits that some prescientific talk does make *inadequate* reference to behavior. He accepts that we all have something in mind when we talk of consciousness, feelings, attitudes, choices, and the like. But we never really know what we are talking about—we are confused and believe that these have features which in fact they do not; that a choice is something beyond a series of happenings in which the human organism partakes; aside from meaning certain bits of behavior by such terms we mistakenly believe we mean more by them. "Attitude" must refer to some type of behavior, nonetheless we tend to think there is more there, or something significantly different from matter in motion. But for Skinner this means claiming a distinction without any evidence for some actual difference. (But the evidence would have to be material evidence, observable and operationally definable.)

Skinner does not consider that when people refer to trees, dogs, cows, mosquitos, the moon, tonsils, and so on, they rarely know precisely what they are talking about—few have the technical knowhow needed. Yet we have no reason to believe that we are assuming the existence of mysterious, mythical entities just because we have no technical knowledge. Botanists or astronomers would know a lot more about many things we talk of day in and day out. Yet there is no reason that we should change our language because we use some words with less than the degree of precision possible.

Incidentally, in general Skinner does not bother to explain why it is that we all have such mistaken ideas about man and his life. He does not even explain this *as mistaken*, since a being that is fully determined makes no "mistakes"—in the animal kingdom hardly any creatures make mistakes. The bird does not neglect to fly when that is called for, a fish always "knows what to do," a lion makes no error when he roars and, interestingly enough, animals in general do not "miseducate" their offspring. Yet, according to Skinner, man has developed just as other animals have, but with a largely mistaken language. Most of the things we say are plain wrong, but we are nonetheless no more free to goof than are other kinds of animals or plants. That is Skinner's thesis.

Reduction at large

Can all features of human life, from muscle twitches to the conception of a plot for a novel, be successfully reduced to bits of behavior? Not just Skinner but hundreds of social scientists as well as physical scientists believe in some form of reductionism. And their mode of operation is very similar to Skinner's. In the final analysis the conclusion to which this position leads is embraced by people in many fields, including physics, chemistry, biology, physiology, psychology, and sociology. There is nothing novel about it—from every epoch we learn of people who thought along these lines. The central point of this view is well expressed by Gerald Feinberg, one of America's most renowned theoretical physicists and philosophers:

> In the widest sense, physics is the study of all the phenomena that occur in nature, and its problem is to understand them. (XXVII/5)

It should be mentioned that other physicists of almost equal prominence have called such expressions nonsense. Underlying the reductionist creed we find, however, not evidence but faith. K. Lashley, a biologist, provides us with a candid picture:

> Our common meeting ground is the *faith* to which we all subscribe. . . . I believe, that the phenomena of behavior and mind are ultimately describable in the concepts of the mathematical and physical sciences. (XXVII/12)

The following passage clearly indicates the type of reductive translation Skinner advocates.

> Consider a young man whose world has suddenly changed. He has graduated from college and is going to work, let us say, or has been inducted into the armed services. Most of the behavior he has acquired up to this point proves useless in his new environment. The behavior he actually exhibits can be described, and the description translated, as follows: he lacks assurance or feels insecure or is unsure of himself (his behavior is weak and inappropriate); he is dissatisfied or discouraged (he is seldom reinforced, and as a result his behavior undergoes extinction); he is frustrated (extinction is accompanied by emotional responses); he feels uneasy or anxious (his behavior frequently has unavoidable aversive consequences which have emotional effects) . . . (I/139)

There is much more, but this suffices to illustrate Skinner's idea. He admits that his "paraphrases are too brief to be precise" but adds that "they alone suggest the possibility of an alternative account, which alone suggests effective action." (I/139) The action he has in mind is, of course, making "progress toward a world in which people may be automatically good." This can only be achieved if we accept his advice that "it is the contingencies which must be changed if, e.g., the boy's behavior is to change." (It should be noted that "contingencies" mean for Skinner pretty much the same as "factors" or "circumstances" or "the make-up of the environment.")

The passage indicates Skinner's viewpoint in several ways. His own characterization of what occurs when a young man's life changes: It is his world that has suddenly changed—yet, of course, he is inducted into the armed services by very special features of this world, namely other people. He "has acquired" behavior—he did not *learn* how to behave, develop habits, or evolve ways of acting in various circumstances. He "exhibits" behavior—he does not engage in it or act in various ways.

This is another illustration of Skinner's insistence that whatever people do, feel, think, or even remember must be reduced to "behaviors."

Reduction to describables

The above-quoted passage from BFD also illustrates reductionism in another way. Skinner writes of "describing" the behavior that is exhibited and proceeds to cite "lack of assurance," "feelings of insecurity," "being unsure of oneself," "dissatisfaction," "discouragement," and "frustration," while his parenthesized phrases suggest alternative translations of such descriptions. But it is questionable whether his caricature of an ordinary account of the boy's behavior can be considered a *description* at all. This idea could be used very broadly to include such features as traits, characteristics, moods, emotions, and attitudes as "descriptive phrases." Thus to say of someone "he is a wonderful friend," or "he was depressed all last week" may be construed as descriptions in the broad sense.

But "describe" is closely related to "picture" or "portray." Thus it is usually taken in a stricter sense to mean: provide the observable aspects, features, attributes of something or some situation. So where Skinner would lump together characterization, evaluation, assessment, and classification all under the term "describe," that term would be better used to differentiate other things we say that would more appropriately be termed appraisals, interpretations, delineations, or whatnot. Skinner insists on grouping all this under "description" in an effort, it seems, to restrict everything to observable matters.

This tactic has a firm foundation in the history of philosophy and theories of meaning. Descriptivism is one of the competing doctrines for an explanation of what makes ideas or terms in a language meaningful (*full* of meaning!). According to this view only words that can be used to describe what there is, but not words that can be used to do anything beyond that, can be used to speak meaningfully. And "to describe what there is" means to specify the observable, sensible attributes of things, events, and people. In this respect behaviorism and descriptivism are very close, the latter containing the theory of meaning that corresponds to the former's theory of being. That is to say, behaviorism holds that nothing but behavior exists in the world, while descriptivism specifies that none but descriptive terms can have meaning. Incidentally, Skinner's theory of definitions—operationalism—ties in very neatly with the above, since operationalism says that we must accept only those terms which can be defined by reference to the operations we undertake (i.e., can pinpoint or observe) as we concern ourselves with the thing being defined. (Thus a hammer is something we grab, strike with, put into the tool kit, all of these being observable operations performed on or with hammers.)

Reinforcement

Throughout all of Skinner's works, technical or popular, the concept of reinforcement carries enormous significance. He defines it as follows:

> When a bit of behavior is followed by a certain kind of consequence, it is more likely to occur again, and a consequence having this effect is called a reinforcer. . . . (I/25)

Now Skinner did not invent the term "reinforcement" as a means to scientific precision. The term is in use constantly in everyday, "prescientific" discourse. The walls of a building may be reinforced, and the braces some people need to wear reinforce their injured hip or leg. One might get reinforcement or support from a friend when undergoing personal struggles. And some military units certainly needed, could have used, and maybe received reinforcements in the wars that have been fought throughout the world. The idea is also related to *en*forcement. When a person cannot get his way, enforce his wishes, goals or purposes, he may need reinforcement; this goes with military units and other matters as well. The legs that cannot be used to "enforce" someone's will to walk require reinforcement from crutches. It is always something that already possesses some strength, support, force or whatnot—and is therefore normally expected to do a job on its own—that may require reinforcement. Nor is whatever provides reinforcement able to carry the weight on its own. Reinforcement serves as support or supplement, not as initial effort.

Skinner's special use of the term is not very different. But he wants to have an arsenal of concepts, which serve to identify and reveal distinctions and express nuances, reduced to one. From the boy's predicament in the above quoted passage, it is apparent how effective Skinner believes the term is for purposes of expressing what is going on. For Skinner a reinforcer is *anything* that promotes the development of some pattern of action, some habit, practice, skill, trait, on and on into career, profession, and even life-style. In fact, everything that can be truly and correctly said about human conscious life (which *must*, however, be said about behavior only) must be a consequence of reinforcement.

There is only one area of human behavior—one instance of it—where Skinner admits he cannot explain it by his own scheme. This is the original bit of behavior that is strengthened by different types of reinforcement. In lower animals Skinner can account for this by referring to such factors as hunger, drives, or other states of "need-deprivation." In the case of complex human behavior he departs from experimental evidence and blandly asserts that it is the environment that "prods or lashes" and even "selects." "Its role is similar to that in natural selection, though on a very different time scale." (I/16)

But asserting this simply won't do. Skinner has no argument to support this contention, no theory of human evolution, no scientific basis on

91

which to deny people the capacity for choice but to assign some ambiguous thing called "the environment" a significant role in human affairs.

The trouble arises when Skinner identifies original behavior as a response. He admits that this concept "is borrowed from the field of reflex action and implies an act which, so to speak, answers a prior event—the stimulus." (II/64) But he never adjusts his theory accordingly; he leaves the impression that he has actually established that all behavior amounts to nothing more than the response of the organism. Nevertheless he cannot account for the origin of the (first) behavior that is yet to be reinforced.

With animals it makes sense to view their behavior patterns as responsive. This is the most reasonable conclusion, since what we know of their brains' sensory-perceptual mechanisms does not warrant the conclusion that anything other than environmental or physiological stimuli contributes. (There are some questionable cases even here, but so-called intelligent behavior by animals usually emerges in laboratories. Here researchers induce behavior we do not detect under normal circumstances or in the wild.)

In the case of human beings, the assumption of complete and exclusive environmental stimulation does not account for the plain facts evident to anyone who looks and thinks. Not even the complex environmental determinism, proposed in the theory of operant conditioning, escapes this inadequacy.

Operant behavior

Skinner proposes his theory of operant behavior to explain what we generally consider to be purposive activity. "Operant behavior . . . used to be dealt with by the concept of purpose." It is "behavior which operates on the environment and produces reinforcing effects." (XI/19) The idea here is that operant behavior occurs when a person does something *in order to achieve* a goal, so that when he succeeds, his behavior is reinforced (or supported or rewarded) by his success. In plain terms, a person engages in operant behavior when he acts with a purpose and succeeds. The result is "reinforcing" because, after all, he aimed for it to begin with. It serves to give support to that sort of behavior in the future in similar circumstances. For example, if I want some ice cream and yell about it a lot, and get the ice cream, then the next time I want ice cream I will yell earlier and louder. Thus Skinner explains the yelling by reference to the resulting ice cream.

But all this does is explain future yelling. Skinner himself admits that the original yelling is not what is predictable. "We can only predict that similar responses will occur in the future." (II/65) He is not concerned (although by his views he should be) with the original behavior. Thus he avoids having to face the crucial question: Where does the first "operation" upon the environment emerge, what causes it? In the case of rats and pigeons he suggests that unreinforced behavior is prompted by need-deprivation—a state of hunger, thirst, or some similar biological condition. And that seems to be a reasonable belief, especially after one has made sure that the control animals in the experiment have not eaten for relatively long periods of time. (Animal trainers know this very well.) So while Skinner does not explain the first instance of operant behavior by reference to the environment, he does explain it by reference to certain simple biological conditions—at least when simple biological entities are at issue.

Not that it is unreasonable to think that *some* things people do can be explained in part by reference to hunger or thirst, i.e., simple biological needs. (Yet many human beings have resisted hunger when other values were at stake.) While some things people do may be explained, in part, by reference to factors in their environment, and other things by reference to biological needs, Skinner has fallen far short of providing an explanatory schema that would account for such complex activities as scientific research, baseball, engineering, dance, art, philosophy, or bird watching. In these the idea that some event in the environment caused someone's (complex) behavior must be shown true whenever it is suggested, because it is quite clear that this is not what happens. Here there is no clear evidence of physiological or environmental causes for such actions in normal cases. Skinner's schema fails to make sense of *human* behavior as such.

All right, so environmental determinism does not even explain rat or pigeon behavior (since hunger is not a fact of the environment). But there at least Skinner can refer to physiological determinants. With complex human activities, mostly those dependent on *mental* effort, neither of these forms of determinism—environmental or physiological—is defended by Skinner. He does not even *try* to trace out such cases as functions of a person's environment or physiology; all that he does amounts to unsupported assertion and question begging description to the effect that such activities *must* be environmentally caused.

If it were not for his grand claims about making the environment responsible for all that people do, Skinner would not be in so much trouble. As a behavioral technologist he could simply be interested in what means we might use to achieve the ends we seek. Thus if we want to dance, read faster, ride a bicycle, he can show us what "schedules of reinforcement" will suit us best for that purpose. (Although it is questionable that this schema is *always* useful.)

But he wishes to go *beyond* this. And of course if he did not, he would not be of much interest: parents, teachers, employers, and others concerned with encouraging learning know that certain kinds of encouragement work well, others badly. Skinner wants to show that everything we do, even our selection of goals, aims, and purposes, is caused by the environment. But since he cannot explain the *first phase* of operant behavior, he fails at this task significantly. Especially when it comes to complex human actions.

Reductionism and its consequences

Skinner wants to go beyond providing good advice to those who have already chosen their goals. He wants to deny that any behavior is initiated by man. Although he says that "we may say that voluntary behavior is operant and involuntary behavior reflex," he wants to reject the idea that any behavior is, in the final analysis, voluntary. Yet his inability to account for the first phase of operant behavior—the selection of the reinforcer (goal!)—leaves room for choice.

What Skinner fails to acknowledge is the distinction between initiated and responsive behavior. In spite of his own admission that the term "response" is simply borrowed (not systematically introduced to make the appropriate distinctions), and that "well-establish usage" is his only justification for employing it, he refuses to face the difficulties all this poses for his supposedly scientific analysis. Both initiated (unreinforced) and elicited (stimulated) behavior are responses in Skinner's book. In all cases he flatly ascribes causality to the environment—even while admitting that making all these kinds of behavior contingent upon the environment must be done "without identifying, or being able to identify a prior stimulus." (II/64)

All this is required by Skinner so long as he adheres to his shaky view of science. But we are slowly beginning to realize that no scientific analysis or experimental data give support to this line of reasoning and set of assertions which he advances. Instead, it is his commitment to the philosophy of reductive materialism that leads Skinner to consider human affairs on the level of the affairs of pigeons and rats.

What emerges is that in the case of what he calls operant behavior—everything that people do purposively, intentionally, deliberately, and the like—Skinner reduces human activities to responses, never mind that no stimulus has been found. Problem-solving, artistic creativity—he once called poetic creation "having a poem," on the model of "having a baby"—or anything akin to baking cakes, forging checks, publishing magazines, sweeping floors, plugging in telephone lines, managing baseball teams, choreographing dances, or any other activity from the most exactingly creative to the simplest type of behavior—all of this is operant behavior and thus can be subjected to operant conditioning. The only support for these conclusions is controlled experiments with animals and with some people in jails, mental hospitals, and in other curious circumstances. Less curious ones, such as managing a factory or a department store, are sometimes cited as cases of operant conditioning (via schedules of reinforcement). But none of these is taken up in detail and no alternative analysis of such activities is offered. It is said that when Skinner's class at Harvard started to pack up their books and things before it was time to go, he devised a schedule to the effect that he would continue to lecture past the closing time more often. Gradually the students stopped packing up on time. Skinner trained them to stay around until he was finished.

Well, this may be one way to avert such troubles in class. Since I have described it loosely I will not try to further scrutinize the case. But whatever the details, it seems to me that asking students to wait until one has finished speaking (and when necessary to politely remind one that the time is significantly up) does quite well—even better. The same goes for examples in management. The manager of a singer, or of other employees of a firm, or of a football team, and the like (trainers, coaches,) could use some reinforcement such as a pat on the back, encouragement, better pay, and so forth. Most often it is more helpful and useful when it has not been scheduled—deliberately designed for purposes of getting results—but offered spontaneously, with sincere judgment and feeling, not with ulterior goals.

So Skinner is systematizing certain forms of human relationships; he is trying to give a full rationale to something we have known for some time: that people will more likely than not do something in return for gains of their own. Supply and demand. But his focus is narrow in that he wants that form to explain all human relationships. Thus justice, love, morality, friendship and all other human relationships, as well as relationships between people and things, life conditions, and emotions, are all described in terms of one kind of relationship and some mathematic varieties of that one kind. But the fit is uncomfortable, logically as well as in practice. (Can one seriously imagine analyzing two lovers' emotional, physical, and even moral relationship in terms of control and schedules of reinforcement? Come to think of it, quite a lot of people ask just that. But usually not as a universal claim about how persons relate to their own worlds and each other.)

What emerges from our inspection of the related ideas of reinforcement and operant behavior is this: the principle of reduction is employed to make sense of human affairs, but this amounts to an unjustified imposition costing the enormous expense of obliterating significant, essential, irreducible differences that we find in those affairs in general, and in virtually any person's life in particular. (To say that these are *irreducible* means that no rational justification for reducing them to simple behaviors of the organism has been offered in the face of very good grounds for viewing them as distinct. No Platonic, absolutist proof is needed. There is no science in support of Skinner. Science seeks to discover, not to impose. The imposition is, plainly, a philosophical one undefended by Skinner.

As he announces with unusual candor:

In the present analysis we cannot distinguish between involuntary and voluntary behavior by raising the issue of who is in control . . . since we assume that no behavior is free. . . . (II/111)

Why is it that we "cannot" distinguish on the basis of who is in control? Because we "assume that no behavior is free." But "cannot" means, in this context, to "have no grounds for and are unjustified in doing so." For

Skinner admits elsewhere that people have in fact introduced such distinctions, albeit without justification—or so he wants us to believe. So the "cannot" is a theoretically alleged inability, not a natural (behavioral) impossibility.

Control via reductionism

But an assumption is just that, something we choose to take for granted. *Should* we take it for granted? Instead of offering grounds for why we should, why that is the rational approach to dealing with human affairs, Skinner simply assumes we must. And this assumption is clearly grounded on philosophical, metaphysical convictions left unargued.

What Skinner tries to do is to translate the idea of control so it can fit his assumption that man cannot be free. (If man *can* be but often *is* not free, Skinner's analysis can apply only in limited, highly conjectural situations.) In BFD Skinner tries very hard to classify a number of different types (mental, physical) and kinds (intentional, deliberate, emotional) of factors in human life under the undifferentiating idea of control:

> A scientific analysis of behavior dispossesses autonomous man and turns the control he has been said to exert over to the environment. The individual . . . is henceforth to be controlled by the world around him, and in large part by other men. . . . (I/96)

In what sense does the environment, including other men, exert control over the individual?

> . . . The surfaces a person walks on, the walls which shelter him, the clothing he wears, many of the foods he eats, the tools he uses, the vehicles he moves about in, most of the things he listens to and looks at, are human products. The social environment is obviously man-made—it generates the language a person speaks, the customs he follows, and the behavior he exhibits with respect to the ethical, religious, governmental, economic, educational, and psychotherapeutic institutions which control him. . . . (I/96)

The idea of control embraces for Skinner all the factors we may identify, in "prescientific" terms, by the use of such concepts as influence, make, produce, induce, advise, affect, incite, impel, teach, convince, persuade, warn, organize, create, devise, invent, constitute the conditions of, force, and require. Whatever has some relationship to a person's life—immediate, intermediate, contingent, necessary, voluntary, inherited, accepted, heard—must, for Skinner, constitute a factor that *controls* it. Anything encountered in the most direct and unavoidable or slight and optional fashion constitutes control.

Thus in our prescientific way we might believe that when we deal with others by choice and free association, instead of force and coercion, we are clearly not controlling them. They have options from which they can select, and dealing with us in these ways is an alternative they could choose.

Skinner disagrees. He denies that there is a distinction between control and being left to one's own resources and efforts. And his denial is supposed to accomplish the task he refuses to undertake—to justify the reduction and the consequent obliteration of distinctions that he opposes. When coupled with his belief that "The task of a scientific analysis is to explain how the behavior of a person as a physical system is related to the conditions under which the human species evolved and the conditions under which the individual lives" (I/12), this shows his total commitment to reductive materialism.

Materialism

There are many other instances of reductive analysis in Skinner's works, but the above has shown how he employs it in the fundamental concepts of his theory and the consequences of this approach. Now we must explain Skinner's materialism, his belief in the priority of material processes (matter in motion) as the constituents of reality. Three stages are involved in the process.

First, Skinner tries to disown the "push-pull version of causality of nineteenth-century science," frequently advocated by materialists (e.g., Hobbes). Instead, he says, "The causes referred to are, technically speaking, the independent variables of which behavior as a dependent variable is a function." (I/207) This means that instead of causes and effects, Skinner prefers variables or factors, some of which determine the behavior of others, as when used in laboratory experiments, their "conceptual home." Factors in the environment are independent in contrast to behavior which is shaped by (dependent upon) them. (Yet despite his relegation of cause and effect to "causal discourse," Skinner does not exclude the idea of cause even from his technical texts!)

The variables in question, however, must all be observable in the narrow sense of this term, meaning capable of being evident to the *senses* and requiring nothing else whatever—a point emphasized by Skinner's disavowal of hypotheses, experimental tests, and so on: his analysis requires sole reliance on the observation of episodes or events. Obviously, if he were interested in *variables* as such, he could not rule out nonobservable factors. Specification of variables for purposes of explanation of some occurrence *does not presuppose what the nature of those variables must be.* But Skinner presupposes their nature because he is more interested in variables as manipulables than as explanations—they must be events in a *physical* system. Without that assumption he could not rule out as a variable the capacity for initiating some action. This would have to be considered as an explanation of human behavior. Skinner *prejudges* that behavior *depends* on causes other than man.

Second is Skinner's explicitly philosophical suggestion that mind can be fully reduced to behavior (i.e., physical events). This is important because when he complains that the prescientific view of man cannot provide adequate explanations of human behavior, he intends "adequate explanations" to mean the identification of causal factors—more specifically, certain kinds of causes—of human behavior.

This again is a Skinnerian *philosophical* thesis, not the result of any scientific analysis or discovery. Scientists are interested in what causes something to occur; they are working on finding the actual or possible causes of various events. It is not they who identify what can *count* as a cause—e.g., could ghosts, mental events, wishes, prayers, or ritualistic incantations cause things to happen? This is of concern to some scientists, but they do not generally make an issue of it within their professional (scientific) roles.

What *can be a cause* is something philosophers have made many attempts to identify. It is usually philosophers who have asked the question (in this and other connections): "What constitutes knowledge?" or "What may count as knowledge?" This is actually the central question of epistemology, the theory of knowledge. Usually those who address themselves to this question have a lot to say about whether various kinds of suggested things could be known about the world. In our case, could we know that mind can be the cause of material changes? If man cannot know anything but what is strictly observable by his perceptual organs or sensory mechanism, can he possess anything like a mind (as distinguished from the brain)? If not, then clearly mindlike things or events can not be known as causes of anything and *must* elude scientists.

Skinner indicates his idea of causation in the following extracts.

> . . . Careless references to purpose are still to be found in both physics and biology, but good practice has no place for them; yet almost everyone attributes human behavior to intentions, purposes, aims, and goals. (I/6)

Clearly, for Skinner such items as purposes, aims, and goals cannot constitute causes of behavior. What could?

> . . . If we ask someone, "Why did you go to the theater?" and he says, "Because I felt like going," we are apt to take his reply as a kind of explanation. It would be much more to the point to know what has happened when he has gone to the theater in the past, what he heard or read about the play . . . (I/10)

It is evident that to Skinner what *happened* can count as a variable or cause; hearing, reading, observing, and other past events can be used to explain human behavior. In fact, these alone seem to be satisfactory to him as scientifically proper units by which what people do can be explained— by which people are, as it were, *pushed* around in the world.

The problem with explaining what people do by reference to how one feels or felt, something we do on occasion, just as Skinner notes, seems to be that "Whether we regard ourselves as explaining feelings or the behavior said to be caused by feelings, we give very little attention to antecedent circumstances." (I/11) So for Skinner, (antecedent) *circumstances* are another factor in the causes of human behavior. What is the nature or character of a circumstance? One of Skinner's examples suggests an answer: he says that "The contingencies of survival responsible for man's genetic endowment would produce tendencies to *act* aggressively, not feelings of aggression." (I/12) These antecedent circumstances, namely the contingencies of survival, lie in the environment, and they would then *produce* such acts.

These factors with such incredible productive powers of their own—so that everything in human history, from the first tools to a novel by Dosto- evsky, has been caused by them—would include social and nonsocial types. Behaviors make up the first class—human behaviors, that is—while natural, observable events make up the second. Candidates such as opinions, attitudes, feelings, intentions, motives, or purposes of both (others and oneself) are ruled out by Skinner; to him only events can be variables. Objects, strictly speaking, cannot. This by Skinner's explicit, though oft- forgotten, commitment to behaviors (events) as the units of scientific analysis. His talk of circumstances or contingencies supports this point. All these come down to being basic units he calls episodes.

To clear this up further, let us note that episodes are sets of actions, a sequence of events involving actions (e.g., on stage, in movies). But this suffices for Skinner only if he equivocates between actions and events. In general, he cannot do this by his own analysis since acts, at least where human affairs are concerned, involve intentions and purposes. This is because there is a counterpart to the concept "act," namely the actor—a person capable of initiating behavior, carrying out some action, under- taking to do something. And for Skinner people are not free to do or make things, to act, or to produce. They can only *respond;* i.e., what occurs involving people can be nothing more than happenings brought on by (antecedent) happenings. As the long quote from Skinner, where he trans- lates prescientific parlance into his "scientific" vocabulary, indicates, people "exhibit behavior." (Even in this Skinner is granting too much to man; exhibitions are what *people* put on, sometimes, maybe, of their own free will, as it were.)

Thus we can see that for Skinner "episode" must mean "event." He supports this when he announces that science identifies relationships between *events.* (II/13) In short, the only factors in the world that can count as causes (make up causal relationships) are events. This confirms Skinner's basic position that science studies matter in motion.

All the objections that are applicable to Hume, including the strictly skeptical ones that Hume himself derived from his own views, apply to Skinner's philosophical underpinnings. Most important, Skinner prejudges and insists on what *must* be the causes of human behavior, thereby aban- doning the scientist's required stance of relying on discoveries, not assumptions derived from prescience or philosophy.

When Skinner rejects "autonomous man," "inner man," feelings, mind, consciousness, and all the other candidates for possible explanatory factors (causes) of human behavior, he is not *concluding* anything. He is simply voicing the a priori requirements of his philosophical predisposition.

Third (but of less significance), Skinner makes much of the advanced stage his own approach achieves for a study of human behavior. In *Beyond Freedom and Dignity* he never tires of pointing out that for the ancient Greeks man had been "divine" because he was believed to have intentions and purposes, to originate and create, as well as to initiate actions. (I/12) Actually, among the Greeks, as in our midst, there were plenty of people who adopted a view identical to Skinner's.

Windelband makes the point that "Galileo . . . went back to the idea of the older Greek pre-Socratic thinkers, who applied the causal relation only to states—that meant now to the motions of substances—not the Being of the substances themselves. Causes are motions, and effects are motions. . . ." (XIV/410) On the other hand, as Professor Randell points out, Aristotle advanced many ideas that are once again considered respectable—for instance, the relativity of space (a la Einstein).

Skinner's errors in the history of ideas show up even more when he talks about the status of individual human beings in the evolutionary flow. "The individual is at best a locus in which many lines of development come together in a unique set. . . . the individual . . . remains merely a stage in a process." (I/200) Windelband notes that it was Heraclitus, one of those "prescientific" Greek thinkers, who tried to establish an "order of events . . . as the only constant amid the mutation of things"; but he adds, for Heraclitus

> change and counter-change run side by side, and the semblance of a permanent thing makes its appearance where for a time there is as much counter-change upon the one way as there is change upon the other. . . . (XIV/49)

The permanent thing is comparable to the individual in Skinner's "process metaphysics." Windelband notes also that "the fantastic forms in which Heraclitus put these views envelop the essential thought of a sequence of change taking place in conformity to law." (XIV/50) The similarity here to Skinner's notion that science formulates the general laws of event relations is obvious. If we focus on this flashback on the history of philosophy, it is clear that Skinner has no way of justifying his own work as *advancement* in the history of thought. Skinner's "science" and philosophy are certainly not anything radical that has just now had the fortune to develop. This may not be important; but it is significant to know that his *claims* to the contrary are false. The suspicion that he pleads the case too vehemently at least suggests that validity and truth are not the primary strengths of his conclusions.

Skinnerian reductive materialism

There is, of course, nothing wrong with advocating ancient views. Man has managed to produce almost any variety of the basic views or ideas he holds in any epoch of his known history. This is why it is difficult to explain the lack of cumulative development in the humane sciences along Skinnerian lines (people stayed at a standstill about human behavior but kept getting smarter about physics and biology—supposedly by reason of their history of reinforcement, whatever that explains). This is why "developments" in art and philosophy are not the same as, or equivalent to, developments in physics and biology. Man produces the answers to the questions he re-asks over and over again; he seems to require *of himself* both the asking and the answering.

To recapitulate: Skinner is a reductionist and a materialist, adhering to both the detriment of science and an understanding of human affairs. This is not yet to say that his philosophical inclinations are absolutely wrongheaded—we need to consider additional renditions even to make the milder claim that these are not justified and, thus, unacceptable. Nor are his suggestions concerning avenues to the understanding of what human beings do entirely wrong. Taken consistently, not by his non-scientific theories, Skinner as scientist does not actually close off the possibility of human freedom, despite his commitment to environmental determinism: some operant behavior, so far as his *experimental findings* are concerned, could be initiated. But his stated position runs counter to those findings and is unjustified; thus his claims about man and his life are ill-conceived.

Before taking up other philosophical versions of reductionism let us consider something Skinner emphasizes a great deal. He says physiology is not so potent a field for the study of human behavior as is behavioral analysis. But he does not justify this as we might expect.

The reduction of the mental to the physiological is a common strategy in psychology. One major objection to Skinner's disavowal of physiology is that there is no reason to believe that controlling behavior can be better accomplished by manipulating variables in the environment than by fiddling with the brain. Physiologists have ample evidence for some kind of behavioral control via psychosurgery, brain implantations, and so on. This is not to say all of them advocate its use or take it as a cure-all; only some. (The brain is surely a serious *candidate* for locating certain conscious capacities.)

Much could be written about the claims of psychosurgery also. There is probably more evidence showing abuse of people with that technique than with Skinnerian proposals. In many ways that requires more overt control of the individual.

Unfortunately most forms of determinism flourish today. Most of them promise instant improvement of mankind. They rarely address individuals. This implicit political feature of determinisms deserves further scrutiny. Skinner offers just one variety—perhaps more forthrightly at that—which should certainly provide an object lesson.

Advanced reductionism

It must be recognized that Skinner does a disservice to some of the views he is espousing. These views could be defended better than he makes it appear with his simple refusal to offer a defense. In a way, Skinner has demonstrated that he is not up to challenging freedom and dignity—simply because a decent challenge requires greater preparation and rigor. Although he is in the mainstream of contemporary social science, this itself is something that only appears to render his a minor task.

Most of those involved with the social sciences may already hold the same fundamental beliefs as Skinner. But these people usually confine themselves to the areas they know about; there is ample confusion even there to discourage embarking on grandiose tasks of extrapolation and reform of all disciplines. Skinner is more ambitious. But that also requires more work. He needs arguments to back up his assertions; or at least he ought to give an indication of which arguments—whose, published where— he wants to make use of, so we can go and find out.

Perhaps Polanyi is right when he exclaims that "Any mechanical explanation of human affairs, however absurd, is accepted today unquestioningly." (XVI/26) But Skinner has promised to defend such explanations as the only adequate ones, not just to present one for some particular event of interest. We can understand that someone who has been working within Skinner's model might want to explain the Watergate affair in terms of the contingencies and histories or reinforcement encountered by all the figures involved. But Skinner is supposed to be *defending* that kind of explanation, not simply offering it for one or two cases. He is a theoretician, not a practitioner. He is B. F. Skinner, the father of contemporary radical behaviorism, not a researcher in some laboratory who is merely employing the methods of the master.

There are hypotheses to the effect that Skinner may have embarked upon a grand experiment with *Beyond Freedom and Dignity*. Reading it has been thought to be the sort of reinforcement that is modeled on the Skinner-box experiment. You read it and want more of it—and that will make the travel beyond freedom and dignity a consequence of a well-designed, culture-wide schedule of reinforcement.

But we are not yet at a stage where we can take this seriously. Somehow too many pieces do not fit. And Skinner was supposed to make them fit, so that we could then submit to expert control. Instead he provided something that does not offer the arguments needed to constitute a successful schedule. (Unless he never made provisions for any critical minds when he designed his experiment. In that case, as Noam Chomsky has asked, why bother to try to reinforce those who need no reinforcement?)

In order to leave reductionism in the shape that it deserves to be left, namely with a better representation on the philosophical scene, let us critically examine it in some of its different formats. There are reductionists and materialists who actually *argue* their cases. And they deserve a hearing, even if only in outline.

The appeal of reduction in science

First, a suggestion as to why reductionism has such an enormous intellectual appeal. For too many centuries in recorded intellectual history a powerful philosophical bent toward the dualist/separatist theory of mind and body existed. Starting even before Plato, but given full exposition by him, and then powerfully and influentially reinforced by Descartes, people concerned with these questions tried to explain what seems to be an obvious distinction that man has in nature. The gist of the dualist explanation of this distinction has been that man is in some way separated from nature. And the mind or soul has been the prime candidate for the element in man that could be outside the natural realm. This view gained a good deal from the long and diverse history of many people's insistence that man is partly divine. Then, since God has been identified as separate (or at least fundamentally distinguishable) from nature by the greater portion of the literature of theology, man's *partial* divinity encouraged similar considerations. But with few exceptions, such as Spinoza (who then was charged with atheism), this is a fair representation of what theology has contended.

It thus seems that for experimental science we have to make a decisive choice. Man is either divine and unsuited for study by scientific standards, or man is natural. The latter alternative has been taken by most to mean that man is, therefore, to be regarded exactly like all other more familiar aspects of nature. The first systematically developed and significant natural sciences to gain prominence dealt with the motion of relatively large physical entities, their relationships to each other, and the general principles governing their behavior. The way in which the various aspects of these fields are studied seemed to be an appealing model for the study and treatment of all natural phenomena.

The related ideas in philosophy and in the philosophy of scientific methodology have acquired the widely applied characterization of materialism and mechanism. Materialism is a theory about the *kind* of thing that constitutes the basic, fundamental substance of the universe, of whatever exists in reality. Although there has never been any clear identification of just what kind of entity this basic substance is—for various reasons related to the constant change in the conception of the most likely candidate—it is usually referred to most broadly as matter or physical substance. Some basic object, an atom or, later, something smaller than an atom, has generally been considered as the candidate for this basic substance. Or, alternatively, some basic process, state, or event has been suggested to constitute the basic unit of which all of nature is constructed.

Mechanism is one system of principles by which, allegedly, some of what occurs in nature must be explained and understood. When generalized, this view explicitly rejects the explanation of anything by reference to final causes—i.e., something *toward* which motion of entities proceeds—and affirms the idea of efficient causes—reference to *antecedent* events or entities—as the *sole* source of explanation. Accordingly, any consideration of some realm of reality that aims at truth, i.e., a correct understanding of what is going on and why, *must* employ some variety of mechanism in order to succeed.

Few of the innovators associated with either of these traditions can be identified as advocating them for dealing with everything that may be considered to exist. Some admit that there are aspects of nature that do not conform to these philosophies and methods of examination, others hold that there are at least some supernatural phenomena and beings that must be considered in an entirely different vein. This admission has usually been coupled with the advocacy of a doctrine that does not require that all of the things of interest and importance to mankind need be approached consistently. Thus, for example, some things must be studied scientifically, with the application of rational, rigorous, and precise standards, while others must be attended to by some means on the order of intuition, revelation, or mystical awareness. Known as fideism, this view upholds the inapplicability of human reason (broadly understood to include both scientific and philosophical inquiry) to certain matters such as religion, ethics, and other areas well known to be controversial and enjoying diverse opinions throughout the history of man.

Still, problem-solving in general has been associated with science and technology. Skinner is clearly committed to this view. And there has been considerable effort within the intellectual community, especially by some philosophers who have a background in science, to assimilate all efforts to solve problems to the sphere of science as mechanics. It is this attempt at assimilation that produces various philosophies of science, of which reductionism and physicalism (today's version of materialism) are examples. Although the two cannot be distinguished in most instances, the treatments of the topic vary a good deal, so hardly any generalization suffices to characterize the situation.

Reductionism in psychology and philosophy

Throughout its history psychology has experienced the impact of most of the ideas within the philosophy of science. Skinnerian behaviorism is clearly an outgrowth of the optimism with mechanism and materialism as unambiguous systems and avenues to truth. But perhaps because man's mind has been considered the main subject for scientific study that could not simply be reduced to physical substance, mechanism in psychology came before out-and-out materialism. (Exceptions occur only because some, like Hobbes, who were philosophers, theorized a great deal about the mind. And Hobbes was a philosophical materialist who denied free will and advocated associationism and mechanistic accounts of everything that exists. (I)

The early psychologists, not yet materialists, tried to make their field an experimental science with the aid of introspection—at the same time invoking the principles of mechanics. Thoughts, images, feelings, memory, and the varieties of mental phenomena (quite distinctly mental, still) were treated according to the methods and principles fruitfully applied to material bodies (planets, atoms, elements) in the physical sciences. But this did not last long. The insistence on publicly observable, measurable, controllable units of study overcame much of the resistance to materialism. Introspection did not jell with the dominant empirical trends in science, even if the introspectionists were the first to try to divorce psychology from philosophy and make of it an independent experimental science.

This is the point at which behaviorism, with its initial denial of the significance of consciousness, and later its denial of the existence of mind, entered and promised psychology a respected place within the growing number of "legitimate" (empirical) sciences. Behaviorists generally consider themselves the only true scientists within psychology, even though their model of science is no longer considered valid even by physicists and most scientifically oriented philosophers.

Nonetheless, there are many philosophers and philosophically minded scientists (or pseudoscientists) who deny that mind exists. The more prominent of these deserve at least an overview. Their positions support Skinner's philosophy—as well as the point made earlier in this work that Skinner's attack on freedom and dignity is not justified by science per se but has a philosophical origin that Skinnerians and other social scientists often accept without scrutiny.

In the era of the Greeks and even in the 17th century, materialism was argued mainly as a metaphysical theory. The idea was that existence is composed of nothing but "atoms and the void." Today, however, the arguments tend to be linguistic, even when they have metaphysical and ontological implications. The issue is no longer what there *is*, what really exists and what is illusion, but what it is meaningful to *say*, how do we talk most felicitously. (Metaphysics has not been in vogue since Hume and Kant concluded that man could never really know nature as such, things as they really are.) There are exceptions; but the majority of contemporary philosophers eschew metaphysics even when they consider such ancient and clearly metaphysical problems as whether there exists a kind of entity, an aspect of reality, properly distinguished by the concept of mind.

Many philosophers today espouse the doctrine that when we use the concept "mind" to mean some aspect of the entity variously known as man, human being, or person, the meaning is exactly the same as when we refer to man's brain. This is the mind/body or mind/brain identity theory. There are numerous versions of it. Basically, those closest to Skinner hold that whatever mental (or conscious) properties may be identified in our consideration of human beings, all of them are the same properties that we identify when we discuss or study certain parts or processes of man's physical organism. In short, the mental and the physical, properly isolated, are the same thing. Frequently the point argued is illustrated by the example of the relationship between the Morning and the Evening stars. Both are really the same, but once we thought they were two different stars. A bit differently, loosely ("casually") we talk about temperature, but we now *know* we are talking about kinetic energy. The two are the same. This is the story then given with mind and brain, all protest notwithstanding. And along these lines, some people admit that it may be useful to retain the two different terms, "mind" and "brain," just as it makes sense to retain two names for one thing or person, given different purposes. But in reality there is (we *mean*) only one thing, the physical brain.

Pain: mental and/or physical?

One of the best-known starting points for the identity theorists is a discussion of pain (or some other sensation, which is taken as representative of mental events). Thus they often begin by trying to show that having pain, and the fact of certain bodily (neurophysiological) events occurring in one's organism, are simply one and the same fact.

In arguing for this view many of these philosophers invoke the very same appeals found in Skinner. In the main they believe that talking about the mind is prescientific and will prove to be unnecessary once science has provided a complete enough description of the processes of the human brain. Thus simplicity is one reason to prefer abandoning reference to the mind. Another is that features of the mind are not observable or publicly verifiable. These Skinnerian objections have been proposed by philosophers from Hume to Rudolf Carnap and the contemporary W. V. O. Quine of Harvard. For Quine the events of the mind are just "states of human bodies" and are found cumbersomely placed "behind" physical behavior. All "mind-talk" is, therefore, simply redundant. (XVIII/264)

The above-mentioned philosophers and their less famous partners—Herbert Feigl, J.J.C. Smart, U.T. Place, D.M. Armstrong, Hilary Putnam, *et al.*—find their views accepted as absolute truth in the circles of some psychologists. I.E. Farber tells us

. . . It is notable . . . that the term "choice" usually refers to nothing more than the descriptive fact that an organism behaves in one way rather than another.

. . . Since the evidence of the decision is the behavior itself, attributing the behavior under these circumstances to choice is exactly as useful as attributing it to demons. (XIX/172, 73)

K. Lashley's remark that "the phenomena of behavior and mind are ultimately describable in the concepts of the mathematical and physical sciences" (XXVIII/12) merely echos Carnap's remark that "psychology is a branch of physics," made back in 1932. (XXXIII/197)

All this should not lead one to suppose that Skinner's treatment of the topic is anywhere as detailed and careful as the treatment offered by the philosophers cited above. Most of these thinkers offer elaborate arguments for their theories. It is worthwhile to focus on some of the main points they raise in behalf of their view that *consciousness is nothing more than brain processes,* that is, the mind/body (mind/brain) identity theory.

The bulk of these theorists rest their claim that mind is identical to brain on the contention that having a pain (for example) is identical to the occurrence of certain events in the body. A recent proponent of the theory tells us that

> The characteristics whose identity I attempt to make more intelligible are particular characteristics. . . . They are such as, for example, the present throbbing quality of this particular toothache of mine and the particular fluttering or pulsating quality of a certain excitation pattern now occurring in my brain . . . (XVII/13)

It seems quite plausible that having a pain is nothing but the occurrence of some neurophysiological event in one's body. If there is any mental event that seems reducible to nothing more than a physical occurrence in one's body, a pain seems to be the closest to such a case. (Otherwise it would not be such a good clue to tell a doctor where it hurts or what region of our body aches in an effort to locate what ails us bodily!)

Looking at this point closer however there is something definitely missing if we characterize pains as nothing but bodily events. Such a characterization omits any reference to our awareness of pains as pains. Although this realization does not serve to refute the claim that pains are dependent on bodily events, it does point up the fact that having a pain is not *just* a bodily event. Having a pain involves being aware of a certain bodily event by way of "introspection," to experience an aspect of what is going on in our bodies. And since this awareness does not rely on the senses we use to identify the physical universe, it is *prejudicial* to deny that nothing but a physical aspect of pain exists in nature. If nothing but a physical aspect of pain exists, how would it be possible to be aware of pain in ways other than we are aware of, say, the heat of boiling water, the color of the trees, and other physical aspects of things around us? It makes sense to take it, even with something as closely linked to our bodies as our pains, that there is something nonphysical about them—granted this may not be *separable* from what constitutes the physical features of the pain.

Most of the arguments that deny that mind exists as a distinctive aspect of reality rest on the belief that all that is known and knowable about the world has to be perceived by the senses. Here the tradition behind the identity theory again goes back to David Hume—something these theories have in common with Skinnerism, not surprisingly. As Epstein characterizes the issue,

> . . . the interpretation of the mental as an inner something, an immaterial entity or property that exists "behind" (or "over and above") the physical is an empiricist distortion of the terms "mind" and "mental." The conception of the mental as immaterial stuff, "subtle matter" or hidden and occult property, is the legacy of the empiricist tradition which tried to make sense of the mental by attributing to it a special kind of immaterial existence. As a matter of fact, the intellectualistic or rationalistic tradition never adopted this point of view since it wasn't restricted by the narrow criteria of philosophical acceptability that hampered the empiricists. (XXXVIII/120)

A final point should be noted in connection with the most recent defenses of the notion that consciousness is nothing but brain processes—the general view that there is no mind, except as some historical illusion, an accident that somehow developed in the minds(!) of people. (For virtually all identity theorists are at the same time reductionists, entity or process materialists, who claim that physics is the only science and physical matter or processes the only things that exist.) This point has to do with a recent attempt to make the identity theory a scientific claim, not a philosophical one. (Earlier we noted that Skinner would like to believe that reducing mind to brain is a thesis of science. In opposition we have argued that Skinner's is a well-known, ancient, and recurring philosophical position for which he does not argue. If this last attempt is successful, we would have to retrace our steps and argue the case against Skinner on strictly scientific terms.)

Some philosophers claim that saying that mind is just body is no different from claiming that the Morning Star and the Evening Star are the same object/process or that termperature is nothing but kinetic energy. Both are real but both are the same. Morning Star and Evening Star are names for the same thing, and "temperature" and "kinetic energy" are different concepts which (at least within statistical mechanics) mean the same thing. The idea is that "mind" and "brain" stand in the same relationship.

Going back to the toothache example, we are told the following:

> [the] toothache example . . . provides for just one excitation pattern, p, in my brain that is triggered off and sustained by impulses coming from my broken tooth and is correlated with my feelings of pain, and it enables us to say that my direct *awareness* of my pain is nothing distinct from my *having* this pain, and that my having this pain is identical with the occurrence of the excitation pattern, p. . . . (XVII/20)

Ziedins now adds the important point for our purposes. This is that "What is assumed is that there are certain correlations between introspectable characteristics of physical events; but that is an empirical assumption." (XVII/20)

The problem here is, and has been noted by many critics of this line of thought, that by proposing to test the assumption *empirically*—this means, by reference to a process of investigation that relies *exclusively* on evidence that may be detected by extrospective, sensory observation—the theory begs the most important question. For if there are mental events that are distinguishable (although not necessarily separable) from bodily events, their distinctive characteristic involves precisely that they are not open to extrospective, *sensory* detection. It is bodies that can be so sensed, and minds that cannot.

Whatever a mind is, one way in which it manifests a distinctiveness from the body is by not being detectable in just the way bodies are. Just how a mind might be evidenced is a different issue, but the test proposed by Ziedens would appear to beg an answer. It is within the assumption of *empirical* testability that this prejudice lies. So the idea that this approach *might* secure for the identity theorist what he is after is incorrect—it *must* secure it for him. By restricting the matter to an *empirical* test, the theorist cannot even begin to consider that there could be something other than an empirical aspect to the being of man, that a human being might possess attributes that are neither illusionary nor reducible to bodily characteristics.

The reason for this lengthy excursion is that the most recent discussions of the mind/brain identity thesis have concentrated not so much on whether the identity exists, but on how one might establish whether it exists. Earlier, most philosophers argued for mind/brain or mind/body identity from a preestablished metaphysical thesis about the nature of the basic constituents in the universe. Once they concluded that these are material, mind/brain identity followed logically. This is the approach taken by Skinner in the final analysis. It is his commitment to the view that basically there exists only matter in motion that leads him to deny the objective reality of mind (or consciousness or awareness or thinking). And the above use of "objective" does not imply materialism. All it means is that the existence of something can be established by rational argument, without prejudging that this refers to observed items.

But this is not the popular approach today. Metaphysics is in ill repute. Many philosophers, especially those who have achieved academic prominence, try to argue independently of metaphysical commitments. Ziedins tells us explicitly that "There is not supposed to be any special metaphysical link between the mental and the physical which would constitute their identity. . . ." (XVII/21) So the arguments are usually centered around what is referred to as the "logic of the concepts" involved in the consideration of mind and body. Just what this means is not necessarily clear, although we may assume that it has to do with the most intelligible, coherent way of *discussing* these matters. The "logic of a concept" is supposed to reveal what the sensible, natural, admissible way of using it in common discourse amounts to.

Mind/Mirror

There is another way of handling the mind/body identity that is more metaphysical but less popular today (although it is tacitly accepted by most in the intellectual community, East and West). Marx's materialism popularized the idea that knowledge consisted of the mind *reflecting* the facts of reality. (Thus, for example, the environment of a given class—its modes of production, its economic conditions—produces the *consciousness* of the members of the class.)

According to this theory, what one knows, e.g., that Los Angeles is one hundred miles away from Santa Barbara on the California coast, or the names of all the U.S. Presidents, or the tenets of materialism, is "put into" the mind by reality itself. And the mind (brain) records the facts somewhat like a camera.

A basic problem arises here in connection with ideas that refer to something beyond what is being experienced by the senses. The thought of next week's party, Junior's graduation two years from today, or the development of the future society itself—all these cannot be reflected in the mind, if by reflection we mean anything akin to what happens when we see ourselves in a mirror. On the level of simple perception this theory carries considerable appeal. But when ideas—schemes, plans, designs, conjectures, theories—are brought into focus, there seems to be no way to make sense of anything like reflection going on. (This passive view of knowledge could not be upheld consistently even by Marx, although part of his entire system of dialectical materialism suffers with its rejection: once the mind is allowed a creative role, there is no reason to believe that people with similar economic circumstances *must* believe what is produced in their own consciousnesses by these circumstances.)

So the problem is obviously quite severe when we consider what it is to have an idea of something general, an abstraction, in the first place. This problem is difficult to handle from any perspective—dualist, dual-aspectivalist, or materialist. But the materialist/reductionist school has the worst of the difficulties. This is because the *idea* of "chair," or "justice," or "philosophy," does not exist "out there" to be produced in a way that we can imagine the perception of *a chair* being caused by the existing chair before us. The concept of chair is not in itself a chair—there is no chair in our heads when we think about chairs. Nor is there a photograph in our heads. There could not be one, not just for the obvious reason but because the thought of a chair need not be of any particular, but could be of some yet unspecified chair. Only the basic, crucial *aspects* of a chair are held in mind when we think about, e.g., a chair we will have to buy when we move into a new apartment.

The notion of the existence of ideas becomes entirely unintelligible if we deny some element of mental productivity, some original creativity that has not simply occurred in response to matter by identical matter. If we consider the mind to be nothing but a passive (collection of) material substance, with no properties that are lacking in stones, or even plants, then we cannot account for the existence of ideas.

Skinner anticipates these objections by eliminating the problem of having to characterize ideas and their origins. All such items are for him reducible to matter in motion, behavior bits, or the probable occurrence of the same. He fails, or course, to explain what makes it possible for such "behaviors" as waiting for a train or planning a vacation to either occur or to be on the verge of occurring. *What* is it about human beings that results in the complex behavior we have plenty of evidence for, if all that we are is globs of flesh that move around in response to our environment?

Reductionism rejected

Outside the mirror/mind theory there are others as well that try to reduce mind to matter. But the mind/brain identity theory discussed above is the most prominent alternative in current contention and its difficulties are enormous. The outline offered above, both of the doctrine and of some objections to it, should suffice for the present purpose—which is to indicate that these theories exist and that debate about the matter is very much alive. Nor is there any reason to suppose that it will ever die away. As long as people continue to want to make sense of their world, themselves, and the relationship between the two, the various kinds of answers we have come across will vie for acceptance. That in itself seems to be borne out by man's capacity to move along the paths of being dead wrong and quite right—or anywhere in between. This again testifies to the uniqueness of the human animal.

Our point has been to indicate the character of reductive materialism, both as accepted by Skinner and as espoused by some others. The thesis is not a scientific one; that much is clear, although Skinner speaks as if the conclusions which flow from it were established by scientists in the process of carrying out investigations in accordance with strict scientific procedures. But to Skinner a scientific analysis means a reductive materialist analysis, with some variations of his own thrown in here and there. He does not give attention to the point raised by Stephen Toulmin that

> If we ask about the validity, necessity, rigour, or impossibility of arguments or conclusions, we must ask these questions within the limits of a given field, and avoid, as it were, condemning an ape for not being a man or a pig for not being a porcupine. (XXI/256)

To assume that it is possible to prove that there cannot be any manifestation of reality other than what physics has been investigating is certainly neither scientific nor philosophically justified. Why should there be only matter? Faced with persuasive evidence of significant dissimilarities, why should we deny all forms of existence other than the physical?

To all reasonable appearances there are important differences among the things that exist around us. Surely stones are different from plants and animals. And surely man has shown characteristics that have not been found, to any appreciable degree, in the rest of the animal kingdom. The simple fact that man worries about his nature, where to place himself in reality (or outside of it, at least partially) is undeniably unique. So it is surely up to the opposition to provide the proof that none of this is true, that universal equality reigns among all things, all evidence of observation and experience to the contrary notwithstanding. Theirs is the affirmative case: man is nothing but matter; man is mindless, thoughtless, passive, unfree, a purely physical entity on a par with the rocks and the rats (or pigeons). These are propositions to be proven. And it seems that the attempts to that effect are at best meager and at worst dismal.

It must be noted that there are many attempts beyond those mentioned here which have the purpose of showing that no such entity as the mind exists in the world and, of course, that human beings have no minds, only bodies (brain parts) in motion. We have called many different theories of the identity theory and, more specifically, varieties of reductive materialism. When philosophical discussions become very specialized, one cannot ignore such differences, for each is in its way a new attempt to justify the Skinnerian conclusion. This conclusion is that man has only a body, and that what we call "mind" is really nothing but the body or brain with a few illusions attached. The position is as old as man's mind, but support for it changes in every epoch.

The few theories in contention include the three versions of eliminative materialism. They are, first: "mind" is a meaningless *term* because it is unverifiable by evidence, and anything said by using it is false; second: "mind" is a category of a *type of thing* which exists and may be meaningful but has no use in an attempt to identify or refer to something, only in indicating certain dispositions of the body or brain; third: "mind" is a term which makes sense in a (wrong) theory of human nature, as "the will of the people" *makes sense* only in the (wrong) theory that the people can have a will, but with a right theory the concept is not needed. In the end none of these work. Traces of them all, especially the first, are found in Skinner—he relies on all of them but only by hinting at them haphazardly.

Another contender in this debate is a form of reductionism that argues backward and claims that there is only mind; it is the body and the brain that are in some way fictitious. (Christian Science argues this view as do some very strict forms of idealism and solipsism). In all these cases some kind of entity or process or some type of linguistic expression is considered the basic unit of being or meaning, at the expense of the multitudinous kinds and types of real things, features, or aspects that constitute existence. This won't do either.

112

At this juncture, before the alternative position is given, we may embrace the conclusion about reductionism that Isidor Chein offers so succinctly:

> I take it for granted that no mental or behavioral event can violate any physical, chemical, biological, or sociological laws, and I take such laws to have an objective status independent of our knowledge or misknowledge of them; but I also take it for granted that there is an order of law, psychological, that also applies to mental or behavioral events, and that other orders of law must be consistent with it, and I assume that an adequate accounting of mental and behavioral events will have more occasion to refer to psychological law than to any other order of law. In admitting only one inclusive and consistent over-all order of law I am, however, a monist. (XV/180)

And Chein's indictment, leveled at the bulk of contemporary experimental psychologists, is very much to the point in the present discussion:

> I am charging that psychologists maintain the image of Man as a passive corporeal entity governed by a thermodynamic principle because of their philosophical precommitments and in flagrant disregard of contradictory information. (XV/9)

Despite the fact that for Skinner it may seem that to be scientific means to make the science of human conscious life conform to the principles of some older and productive field of inquiry, it is clear that his approach is in disregard of contradictory information. If he confined this to the field of his specialty we might consider him as one of those holding up a certain tradition within psychology proper. There is evidence that he has been productive within that field, after all.

The mistake is that Skinner has allowed his name to give weight to very questionable politics, ethics, and philosophy. He has denounced freedom, dignity, human rights, democracy, and other human achievements that have brought happiness and security to millions of people everywhere. Being wrong in his attack, and out of his specialty to boot, cannot easily be chalked up as simple misfortune. No more than we could dismiss scientists who advocate questionable nuclear policy, troublesome political candidacy, or any other enterprise about which they know no more than their less prestigious and yet possibly wiser neighbors.

4

The Values, Goals, and Wishes of B. F. Skinner

WHAT ARE VALUES? What are the values defended by Skinner? Perhaps these two questions are not obviously related. But once the answer to the first is set out the connection will become clear.

Values are whatever people choose to pursue, preserve, protect, promote, or advocate. Some values are significant, others of little importance. One might have no explicit knowledge of his own values. Another person may profess to some values but in fact hold others more dear—and this usually shows in his private actions. People can also be self-deceived about their values—as when they characterize themselves as patriots, with utmost sincerity, but give absolutely no thought to the question of what exactly is the true interest of their country.

The occasions for communicating one's values arise infrequently and for unusual reasons, but when speaking about general human problems one should take a stand. A book that seriously reflects one's moral/political commitments should certainly deal with values.

Yet it is also true that dealing with values is not smooth sailing for everyone. If a person advocates that values really cannot be conceived of along ordinary lines, he is referring both to what we all do and to what he is about to do. Thus Skinner, when he speaks of values in his works, must accept that his conception of them will be used to analyze his own thinking. Perhaps Skinner, like some others, does not really mean what he says. Perhaps when he identifies them he is quite aware that he knows nothing about values but merely believes that what he wishes to write about requires that they be given coverage.

We certainly do find balderdash here and there, even in works by most

114

respected and eminent figures. So this possibility must be kept in mind, especially when the message can be accepted only with difficulty. Maybe the person is kidding—or even deceiving us about what he thinks. (Anyone who writes about a topic which necessarily refers to himself also may mislead us not only about the topic but about himself: someone who misunderstands what it is to be a parent may still write a good deal on the topic. But his misunderstanding will very likely extend to a poor conception of himself as a parent, also.)

We are committed to taking Skinner at face value. That he waived technical vocabulary in order to be understood by those not familiar with it, should indicate that he wants what he says and what he means to be taken as one and the same. That it might all be a grand concoction, a clever or not so clever attempt at mind manipulation, is something one cannot consider by simply reading Skinner's or anyone else's books. Even where the temptation is great, it would be wise to accept matters as they stand at first. Surely a person can be dead wrong—but in all sincerity. It happens all the time. Nor is sincerity the only relevant virtue—"I meant only good," said after a disaster simply won't conceal the damage or the culpability.

Clues to Skinner's goals

At this point we ask what Skinner's own values are: what is he seeking, what is he promoting, what is he advocating, what does he want in this world, that there is none or too little of now? Further, we ask, what hints does Skinner give that will help us to discover the answer? This is what it means to take his own statements at face value; it is Skinner's own characterization of values which must reveal what he wants known of them. That is the safest course, without too much idle speculation about ulterior motives.

Consider what Skinner means by "good," "ought to," and "should." This is crucial because when these terms are used to characterize basic conduct—what people as human beings do or fail to do—we are talking about ethics. "Courage is good," "A person should be honest," "One ought to help one's neighbor," and beliefs of this kind are ethical notions. They generally serve the function of guiding human conduct under virtually any circumstances. (Only when some more important value is at stake may one of the principles be disregarded, perhaps.) But Skinner believes that "ought to" or "should" means "is approved by the group of which [one] is a member" and "approval of [one's] fellow men is positively reinforcing to one." (II/429) In an ethical context especially the claim that someone ought to do something means, to Skinner, that one will do what is approved by those in the group of which one is a member.

This analysis of what "ought to" means does not occur in *Beyond Freedom and Dignity* but in *Science and Human Behavior*. In the latter Skinner does not specify that he will use "casual discourse" in order to accommodate the prescientific thinking of his reader. So we are justified in believing that he is arguing for his scientific analysis of such terms as "ought to" and "should." This is important because those who object to criticism of Skinner and behaviorism in general often dismiss it on grounds that the critic fails to see the constraints imposed by the (English) language.

But this inexpressibility cannot be carried to all corners of Skinner's work: he would have to claim knowledge of a language that is entirely ineffable, private, and spoken only by himself—so that no one else could speak it. (At times Skinner does appear to be saying that if we would only yield to his conception of science, our entire world-view would have to change, in *all* respects. Yet the idea that we have been dead wrong all along is absurd. If Skinner were the only one who knew the truth, he would have had to start with at least something like what we ignorant ones have to deal with. If so, then we can be assured that at least some of what we believe is right—it can at least start us off in the right direction.)

At any rate, what Skinner says about statements containing "ought to" and "should" is partly correct. His translations do capture what *some people* intend to mean by those terms. Or more accurately, what some people would *like* to mean by those terms. The idea that ethics is the field that identifies what "society or the group approves of" has been around for centuries. Many eminent people have argued that "morally good" or "ethically right" means "to be approved of by one's fellow men." If Skinner is taken literally when he tells us that such statements *may be* converted into what he gives us, he is certainly right.

But we have already seen the trouble with taking Skinner literally. "May be" is so open that if we accept it at its face value, we have to dismiss Skinner as an idle, groundless speculator. But do we then have a "scientific analysis"? If we consider what Skinner expects us to do, we can be sure that he'd rather have us forget about the literal meaning of "may be" but remember his insistence that his is a scientific analysis. As such, "may be" must be taken as strongly suggestive of "should." So when Skinner says that "ought to" or "should . . . may be converted into" what he chooses, the true meaning must be that these must be so converted, if they are to make any sense at all.

In short, according to Skinner the only meaningful, scientifically respectable sense of "ought to" and the like amount to his own interpretation. But put under scrutiny this would have to be considered a mistake. Such blatant social relativism has something very fundamentally wrong about it, i.e., when people endorse something they can often be criticized for their approval. Two groups could thus disagree as to what is to be sanctioned, what doesn't matter, and what is objectionable. So if there is to be a meaningful sense of "ought to," approval could not be it. There would emerge contradictory applications of "ought to," which would have to be accepted on Skinner's analysis.

Alternatively perhaps Skinner wants us to pay attention to the bulk of the population or membership of a group. So the approval of the majority is what establishes the truth of what ought to be done. "Ought to" then means "what is approved of by the majority of the group."

To this we must object that it is precisely the point of some of our values, if we take them seriously, to override mere majority approval. Skinner may consider this unbelievable, but in the observations of great novelists, dramatists, and even in normal, day to day characterizations of human life, the terms "ought to" or "should" often capture a meaning that goes squarely against Skinner's own translation. Actual and fictitious individuals of great moral virtues—courage, honor, integrity, loyalty, justice—have exhibited them in circumstances where they received the approval of no one. If it is possible to understand the meaning of "ought to" in, for example, "One ought to judge and treat people according to their moral qualities," then we must also recognize that one ought to do so even in the face of overwhelming denunciation, prejudice, bigotry, and disapproval. Any virtue worth its name deserves more than acquiescence in the face of popular acclaim.

Perhaps Skinner believes that such loyalty to values is a brand of the fanaticism he attributes to some who have fallen under the influence of the literature of freedom and dignity. Indeed many look with dismay upon those who choose to be loyal to values in the face of wide-scale attack. Naïve, idealistic, unsophisticated, and stubborn are only some of the terms dragged in to account for such a trait. But there is no reason to believe that those characterizations are sound. Most of them carry normative overtones, and thus require independent justification as better ideals to adhere to than those professed and fought for by the condemned. Calling someone naïve or stubborn simply because he shows loyalty to values is veiled disapproval of the values in question, no matter what the rhetoric.

Skinner's pseudopsychological notion that advocates and defenders of human liberty and dignity show signs of "emotional instability" merely gives expression to his condemnation of freedom and dignity, nothing more. His own vehement opposition to its literature is no more a sign of emotional instability and repressed childhood fears of taking responsibility for one's own life than are love of liberty and dignity signs of a neurotic need for independence and moral excellence. Such disparagement on either side simply subverts some of the useful functions of these psychological concepts.

There is a conjectural interpretation of Skinner's reference to the approval of one's group that has a ring of truth about it. Perhaps he means that mankind at large determines what is good and bad—what ought to be done. Here, by "mankind at large," he may mean something very esoteric, namely the idea of "man," or "human nature." In this sense what ought to be done in a specific situation may refer to the standard of conduct he should appeal to. And this standard of what is right or wrong, good or bad, might be a comprehensive understanding of the idea of man. Human

117

nature would then provide the guidance to human behavior. This is just what some philosophers have argued throughout human history. Man *qua* man is the standard of right conduct acording to Aristotle and quite a few other thinkers. In that sense the group one is a member of has something to do with what one ought to do.

But this is too farfetched an interpretation of Skinner. Certainly he has no thought of the nature or essence of man as the guiding standard of human conduct. He rests his case on approval. And to approve of something is not the function of an idea of ideal but of other people. So we must conclude that, for Skinner, what one should value is that which others approve of. This also makes good sense in terms of Skinner's theory of meaning.

The Skinnerian meaning of words

Skinner believes that words have meaning only if they can be defined operationally. That is, unless one can show what activities or procedures enter into the actual use of some term it does not mean anything. Operationalism and empiricism are very closely related. Empiricism is the theory of knowledge that goes hand in hand with reductive materialism, Skinner's own metaphysical point of view. In operationalism a word is meaningful only if one can show or point to (experience with one's senses) the rules for using the term. Thus "ball" means "experiencing roundness or bouncing" in an object. (Actually these are not so much aspects of the thing meant as of the *experience* with that thing. That is, operationalism concentrates on the subjective or personal actions of the user of language, e.g., measurement, when the terms being defined are employed. These operations serve as the standard of meaningfulness and correct application. But an infinite regress soon stifles the success of the theory.

In line with the above, the concept of value or good is meaningful to Skinner only as something that is "empirically observable," "operationally definable." This is why he specifies the meaning of "ought to" in terms of something as concrete and immediately experienceable as public approval. In stricter language this would come down to something like "People around someone shouting 'hurray'," or "Paper being given to someone with words such as 'Yes, do it,' 'It is all right that you do such things,' " or the like. Approval is generally thought to be recordable, visible or audible, and measurable in terms of physical units. In view of that, it is taken to be the closest thing to signifying what the terms "value," "good," "right," "ought to," and soon must mean within a reductivist schema. After all, as long as we stick to approval, we are dealing with a manipulable, observable factor.

So we have here a theory of value which holds that what is good, right, worthy, and ought to be pursued must be what is approved of by one's peers. That's the essence of the theory. In order to discover what *Skinner* takes to be valuable, what *his* values are, in the broadest sense of that term, we must apply this theory to what he tells us about his own desires—or at least his hints to that effect.

Theory of value in practice—survival of a culture?

In identifying Skinner's values one has the impression that he is trying to hide them. He very rarely comes out and says point blank that he approves of the survival of the culture. Instead we get the following:

> . . . Our culture has produced the science and technology it needs to save itself. It has the wealth needed for effective action. It has, to a considerable extent, a concern for its own future. But if it continues to take freedom or dignity, rather than its own survival, as its principal value, then it is possible that some other culture will make a greater contribution to the future . . . (I/173)

> . . . A culture is like the experimental space used in the study of behavior. It is a set of contingencies of reinforcement, a concept which has only recently begun to be understood. The technology of behavior which emerges is ethically neutral, but when applied to the design of a culture, the survival of the culture functions as a value. (I/174)

> . . . We are concerned here, however, not merely with practices, but with the design of a whole culture, and the survival of a culture then emerges as a special kind of value . . . If his culture has induced [someone] to take an interest in its survival, however, he may study the contribution which people make to their culture as a result of their early history, and he may design a better method in order to increase that contribution . . . (I/143)

In none of these places does Skinner tell us explicitly that the survival of the culture is an important or supreme value. In each case there is a qualifier: it is of prime value *if* we are concerned with designing cultures. He does declare that "We are concerned here . . . with the design of a whole culture." But it is not clear whether he means that *he* is concerned with it as a matter of wishing to let us know its importance, or whether he is simply doing this in a "Well, let us suppose we are concerned with the survival of the culture" fashion. Once again his use of "may" does not permit a clear interpretation.

However, while Skinner leaves some room for different interpretations, his work would make no sense unless he believed very firmly in the propriety of designing cultures. Perhaps he wrote *Beyond Freedom and Dignity* as a money-maker only, a sort of cook book for those interested in political theory and activism although he himself prefers fasting to eating. He certainly affects a tone of indifference in various places, and there are passages where he makes it appear that he cares very little about what kind of culture should be designed. Thus, for example, he tells us that

> If the designer is an individualist, he will design a world in which he will be under minimal aversive control and will accept his own goods as the ultimate

value. If he has been exposed to an appropriate social environment, he will design for the good of others, possible with a loss of personal goods. If he is concerned primarily with survival value, he will design a culture with an eye to whether it will work . . . (I/144)

In the first place, Skinner just said that in designing a culture, its survival functions as the value for the technology of behavior. But here he says that in the case of the individualist designer it is "his own goods" that function as such. Yet nowhere has he demonstrated that the individualist cannot make use of the technology of behavior. As a matter of fact a number of commentators have argued that Skinner's schema accommodates individualism quite well—provided it is not centralized into a massive bureacracy. Alexander Comfort, a philosophical anarchist, believes that "In essence, Skinner with his technology of behavior is answering the libertarian or anarchist dilemma—how to educate men to be social without the use of a coercive apparatus generative of abuse and of acting out." (VII/207)

Still, despite his unwillingness to come out squarely for the survival of the culture, Skinner does advocate action that will lead to its survival. He believes that certain recognizable problems can be solved by the technology of behavior. He describes the tools we already have, "needed for effective action." And he foretells that it is our choice of freedom and dignity (rather than the culture's survival) as the "principal value" that could make it possible for some other culture to "make a greater contribution to the future."

These declarations are never distinctly pro culture and its survival. We certainly use the concept "culture" to refer to habits, practices, widely ingrained attitudes, or policies, and it is questionable whether all these should survive. This may explain why Skinner is so vague about what he means by "the survival of a culture." Since he does not bring up those aspects which might require extinction, and mentions only the wealth and science the culture now has by which to solve such problems as pollution, his basic substantive values are never apparent. At least this is so according to what he ways.

What does Skinner advocate that can give us a hint about his substantive values? As he says, "We have the physical, biological, and behavioral technologies needed 'to save ourselves'; the problem is how to get people to use them . . . What are the principal specifications of a culture that will survive because it induces its members to work for its survival?" (I/150) The clue is right there: members of the culture must be induced to work for its survival. This, of course, is not consistent with the values of freedom and dignity, or individualism.

Cultural survival à la behavioral technologists

It must be obvious to anyone that Skinner is advocating the survival of the culture through management of people and at the expense of freedom and dignity. Specific measures aside, this is the central substantive point. Freedom and dignity must be abandoned as principal values. Why? Because freedom and dignity conflict with the means by which the survival of the culture may be secured. How? They are the opposite of what is most required for the survival of the culture. What is that? Getting people to use science and technology to make the culture survive; inducing them to act with that goal in mind; forcing them to devote their lives to these values as opposed to ones they might select if they were free.

How people will be induced to act appropriately is not difficult to discern. Skinner gives very clear clues:

> The application of a science of behavior to the design of a culture is an ambitious proposal, often thought to be utopian in the pejorative sense, and some reasons for skepticism deserve comment. It is often asserted . . . that there are fundamental differences between the real world and the laboratory in which behavior is analyzed. . . . These are real differences, but they may not remain so as a science of behavior advances, and they are often not to be taken seriously even now. (I/151)

What is crucial is not any of the differences, but that Skinner considers the comparison a meaningful one in the first place. In a passage cited earlier he says that "operant conditioning shapes behavior as a sculptor shapes a lump of clay." (II/91) In fact it is not operant conditioning that shapes behavior; the conditioner himself does, if anything. Skinner apeaks of displacing responsibility to the environment, but he is plain enough about where the environment itself will be shaped: at the hands of operant conditioners. Skinner or his designers would arrange the contingencies of reinforcement so that the other members of society will work for the culture's survival. And one of the contingencies involves reducing anxieties about viewing culture on the model of a cage.

We have already seen that there are grave difficulties with this arrangement. Apparently Skinner (himself) and other behavioral experts do not stand in the same relationship to the rest of the members of society, in any objective sense, as a researcher stands to his rats. The latter involves two very different kinds of entities. The idea is similar to suggesting that perhaps we should have human zoos on the model of animal zoos. It is not a resistance to science that induces people to question the sense in this proposal. It is quite the opposite—their awareness of the enormous confusion underlying the suggestion. The same kind of awareness led to the abolition of slavery, even in those cases where the slave was declared to be "perfectly happy." The relationship is scientifically intolerable because some scientists (who at one time were not) have now declared that the issue of whether someone will or will not be a scientist (or singer or actor or animal feeder) is not something that each potential scientist has the right to decide. Instead *some* scientists will assume the capacity to decide for others whether they ought to be scientists (or whatever).

The problem of reflexivity arises again where two things are treated differently in view of accidental differences but in the face of essential similarities. Sir Karl Popper, H.B. Acton, Michael Polanyi, and others have long since shown that the planned society is destructive of science. This is because it leads to confusion and misidentification of what is what, as well as to closing off the paths to the growth of knowledge and mispredictions concerning what is likely to occur as a result of the influence of planning, misplanning, and other aspects of the confusion between cultures and experimental laboratory space.

But what is at issue now is not the internal errors of what Skinner advocates. We are concerned here with his goals. He tells us vaguely that the survival of the culture ought to be our goal, that science and technology ought to be employed to accomplish this. But we have not learned from this what his own values are, what it is that he wants. He may be "ethically neutral" in one sense, i.e., he will not commit himself explicitly to any specific kind of culture. (Hardly any of the famous utopians specified what their great society was to consist of.) There is for Skinner no reason to defend the one admittedly vague value he does endorse: ". . . we do not need an explanation [of] what we might call a pure concern for the survival of a culture . . ." He tells us only that "to the question: 'Why should I be concerned about the survival of a particular kind of economic system?' the only honest answer . . . seems to be this: 'There is no good reason why you should be concerned, but if your culture has not convinced you that there is, so much the worse for your culture.' " (I/131)

It appears that although one reason freedom and dignity should be rejected is that they stand in the way of an explanation of human affairs, now Skinner himself contends that in some cases no explanation is necessary. What is even more important is that he discards explanations just when the most significant aspect of his positive, affirmative thesis is introduced—i.e., where the central value is announced. Concern with the survival of a culture need not be explained, justified, or understood. As he tells us, "The simple fact is that a culture which *for any reason* induces its members to work for its survival, or for the survival of some of its practices, is more likely to survive." (I/130) And apparently that is good, no matter what those practices are (e.g., genocide or class extermination). "Survival is the only value according to which a culture is eventually to be judged, and any practice that furthers survival has survival value by definition." (I/130)

This is all well and good, but why is survival "the only value according to which a culture is eventually to be judged?" Skinner does not answer this question. And it seems that he need not answer it, at first. This is because on the one hand he makes it appear that the valuation of the culture's survival is automatic. He compares this "concern for the survival of a culture" to "the origin of a genetic mutation." (I/129) Then, since the latter is not generally considered to be a matter of choice, it would be silly to debate whether the mutation should or should not occur or have oc-curred. Thus, by analogy, talking about concern for a culture is, at least for the present, like talking about planetary motion or the growth of finger-nails—either it will be or it won't.

But Skinner spends chapters in the effort to convince us that the sur-vival of the culture is worthy of concern. So he cannot mean that we will be concerned anyway, automatically. Why bother trying to induce people to work for it? But if this is not automatic—but rather something that we must produce, make happen—we are entitled to an answer to the central question: "Why should we work for the survival of the culture instead of personal happiness, artistic excellence, or the will of God?" Skinner can-not simply dismiss this question as not needing an explanation. (He *can,* but at the cost of remaining unintelligible in a crucial—no, *the central—* aspect of his entire thesis.) Not if he wants us to take up where he left off and go to work on behalf of the survival of the culture. That value is his primary reason for attacking freedom and dignity. Science, as we have seen, has very little to do with Skinner's attacks on these concepts. The metaphysics of reductive materialism and the ethics of culturalism provide the framework for his entire thesis. The two reinforce each other and a very interesting picture emerges.

Skinnerianism vs. the conventional wisdom

A main feature of the philosophy of science which grows out of reductive materialism consists of prediction and manipulation. Observable, material variables can lead us to predict what will happen; arrangement of such variables enables control of what will happen. For someone who wants to produce certain results, the reductive materialism concept of man and science seems to come in very handy. The goal is the survival of the culture (whatever its details does not really matter); the means is the arrange-ment of variables in ways that will produce that survival. And only those who are qualified to do this know just what will be involved—what will be the details of producing the results. The conclusion is that only experts in behavioral technology should contribute to the design of cultures, since only they are knowledgeable about the science and technology needed.

One problem with arguing against Skinner's suggestions is that a good many of them are being practiced today. Skinner himself admits that certain ways in which government now operates are comparable to what he has in mind. For instance, when the government declared certain occupations to be in the national interest and therefore those preparing for them would be eligible for draft deferments, it was practicing rein-forcement. Skinner actually defines law as "a statement of a contingency of reinforcement maintained by a governmental agency." (II/339) Ac-cordingly, the way the society is run today, by those who take on the roles of administrators in their particular ways (however we might eventually evaluate them), involves several of the principles or methods of getting people to work for the survival of the culture. True, Skinner renounces all "aversive control." But an adequate response to his ideas must recognize that many of his suggestions are in effect today. If Skinner can be countered, if his views are in error and his conclusions false, some credence may be lent to the contention that some of what is going on in our society has no viable foundation either in science or any other discipline of human learning.

Obviously the manipulation of people is not impossible. While some things are going on above board, it is possible to manipulate people to do what they never chose to do, nor would have agreed to do, had they been aware of it. Everyone knows that government officials do not obtain our *consent* for every scheme in which many of us play an explicit role. Sometimes the average citizen is more of a guinea pig than are volunteers in hospitals and prisons. What with all the public domains to which government workers have access (not to mention all the information they have in their files about people), experimentation is relatively simple. Perhaps not all the control Skinner wants is available—our culture is admittedly not yet very much "like the experimental space in the analysis of behavior." (I/195) This means that the distinction between the two is retained as well as recognized, despite widespread obliteration of it within the minds of certain people.

In arguing against Skinner the problem is that his ideas, in one or another of their versions (determinism, manipulation of people, the importance of the group, society, or culture) are quite popular already. That means that serious opposition to them is bound to go against a number of established views. Chomsky himself recognizes these two factors that make resistance to Skinner's ideas difficult: the prestige of science and the tendencies toward centralized authoritarian control. (XXIV/19) This is important to remember because although in some respects Skinner may seem outrageous, his is indeed a very conventional idea: let us use the government to further the survival of the culture by employing whatever scientific or technological means are available, with the best expertise around. This notion has been advanced since the 16th century optimism in science; Jeremy Bentham and Auguste Comte, for example, argued for the application of science to social ills largely on the basis of its enormous success evidenced in Newtonian physics.

Not just Skinner but many other behavioral technologists advocate and receive almost unquestioned backing for technological solutions to all problems. The financial support given today by the Federal government to experimentation in psychosurgery, the fact that Skinner's own project was financed by the Department of Health, Education and Welfare (HEW) and the National Institute of Mental Health (NIMH), and similar facts should bring this point home forcefully enough. This is not the place to launch into a sustained attack on the meddling which governments (i.e., their officials, with the support of Skinnerians, *et al.*) engage in when it comes to people's personal and professional lives. Indeed Skinner's unpopularity in some circles may well be due to the fact that few people want to put the matter as explicitly as he does. In this respect he is a far more courageous person than those supporters of government regulation, manipulation, and intervention who continue to pay lip service to freedom and dignity.

At any rate, with these points in mind we can investigate why it is that Skinner believes the survival of the culture to be our primary value. Although he says here and there that concern for this value will be forthcoming anyway, he also announces that people must be induced to have it. And *Beyond Freedom and Dignity* gives evidence that he is committed to the latter position rather than the former. A conspiracy theory might suggest that he was paid off by the government to give scientific respectability to the already widespread but largely unconfessed practice of human engineering. But that is not a hypothesis that we can take seriously in the present context. In spite of this he declares that no explanation of this value is needed. However it would be valuable to have an explanation for Skinner's own preference for the survival of the culture.

Survival of the culture and Skinner's values

In a way Skinner's declaration that this survival is of primary value is entirely consistent with his analysis of such terms as "ought to" or "should." According to this when we say someone ought to do something, we mean that the consequences of doing it will be approved of by others, members of the group, peers, or the culture. (Skinner never specifies the size of the group he has in mind.) So the culture's survival is something that one should be concerned about, i.e., something (some, all, wise?) people approve of. The question of what *kind* of culture is approved of does not come up. The main point is that if people *want* it to survive, that means it ought to, and we ought to act accordingly.

There cannot, for Skinner, be any further question as to whether people's wants are right or wrong, good or bad. The merits of a particular culture cannot be identified—it depends entirely on the subjective factor of whether people want it. Since "people" is vague here, one has to assume some form of majoritarianism. Nothing else makes sense to Skinner when we talk about what people want or approve of. There are, of course, some who have no feelings about these matters, who neither approve nor disapprove. These include most children and quite a few adults. So "people" would indicate "those of the concerned individuals who enjoy at least a plurality of consensus about whether they want the culture to survive." This leaves plenty of room for taking as established the value of the survival of virtually any kind of culture. (If we include the requirement of knowledge of one's culture, we narrow down the criteria even more and there will remain only a handful of people, mostly those of the so-called establishment, to be polled on the question.)

Again, all through this there is still no revelation of just what kind of culture Skinner supports. But we are getting closer to discovery. Thus far dignity and freedom have no place in the culture (barring some inconsistencies in his own discussion of what kind of cultures could be supported by a technology of behavior). On the other hand, he adds, "When it has become clear that a culture may survive or perish, some of its members may begin to act to promote its survival." (I/127) Ignoring now our standard problem with his use of "may," what is he after? Is it simply that those who want to can take action to promote survival? Again, this is not consistent with Skinner's deterministic picture of human behavior. According to that picture, people cannot begin to work for anything—they either will or they won't. But there is some justification for ignoring this here, for Skinner is no longer preaching the science of determinism; he is now trying to make out a case for why anyone *should* worry about such remote, quite possibly unintelligible, notions as the survival of the culture.

At this point perhaps his use of "may" should be taken seriously. He could mean that when some people consider the culture in danger of collapse, they *may*—i.e., are permitted or entitled to, at least have the support of Skinner's *good judgment* to—act to prevent it. This meaning is quite open to Skinner and, without trying to be sinister, his book certainly suggests that certain expert behavioral technologists should take upon themselves the task of promoting the survival of the culture. And it is a meaning consistent with his translation of "ought to." "Some members of the culture may begin to promote its survival" then amounts to saying that "some are permitted to do it." And "the survival of the culture is a primary value" amounts to "the survival of the culture ought to be promoted." All of this means to Skinner that "promoting the survival of the culture will be reinforcing to some of its members" and "the survival of the culture is approved of by other members of the group (i.e., the membership of the culture)."

And surely Skinner is right about the second. If we go by what many people say—via interviews, talk shows, Gallup and other polls, magazine articles, church podiums, classrooms, and political platforms—the survival of the culture is widely approved. Here and there variations, changes, and improvements are desired, but in general few people want to oppose as noble a goal as the survival of the culture. Since the culture is, by Skinner's definition, "the customs, the customary *behaviors* of a people" (I/121) it is almost a foregone conclusion that people want it to survive.

And Skinner seems to be right about the first point also. Some people no doubt like to work directly for the survival of a culture. This category of human activity can be so enormous that anyone working with diligence on practically anything that is likely to survive him will qualify as working for the survival of the culture. Moreover those who like their jobs can be characterized as being reinforced to work in behalf of this goal.

126

Skinner's confession

Yet all this is a bit too simple. What is the crucial, distinguishing aspect of the Skinnerian schema? What is it that renders his politics unique? We have not yet gotten to the bottom of Skinner's system. The main thesis he offers is that we should approve of the *kind* of action toward the survival of the culture that *he* is advocating—namely the design of the culture by expert behavioral technologists.

This is how he defends his preference, ultimately: He is among those who may (meaning: should) begin to act to promote the survival of the culture. This promotion means to Skinner the expert control of people in all respects of their lives. Since he (and perhaps some other specially skilled and knowledgeable people) approves of this, it is what he ought to do. Starting off neutrally, as an observer of empirical episodes (in this case his own approval), he discovers that he (his behavior) supports the expert control of other's lives (starting with pigeons, rats, and other experimental animals). Then, in line with his own (mistaken) view of science, he moves from this observation to the announcement of the law or rule that the lives of people ought to be controlled by his kind of experts so as to ensure the survival of the culture.

It is easily seen that this does not even square with Skinner's own approach. He does not say that from observing one episode alone we are entitled to pass on to laws and rules. Yet he moves from the observation of himself approving the control of others (for purposes of the survival of the culture) to the far more sweeping judgment that everyone ought to value the expert control of people for that purpose. Not even the crudest form of empiricism, at its very worst as a philosophy of scientific methodology, allows for that kind of logical howler. Bacon advised that the mere gathering of data will generate laws of science. But one's sample must be larger than one event, i.e., his own approving (behavior) of some means to an end.

One might object that this is a misreading of what Skinner is saying. After all, he could refer to *many others* who approve of the survival of the culture. So he does in fact have a large enough sample from which to draw his conclusions. Moreover, we have noted earlier that many people in this culture approve of a good deal of control from the government, so that too must be taken as part of the scientific evidence concerning what people approve of.

The crucial issue is not however that people approve of the survival of the culture. Had Skinner informed us of nothing more, that would not have been very enlightening. In the vague, value-free, ethically neutral sense in which the term "survival of the culture" appears in Skinner's books, everyone can agree that the culture one is a part of ought to survive (provided certain important changes are made). What is *crucial* is his advocacy of leaving the design and control of these matters to *behavioral technologists*. It is the people who hypothesize the possible collapse of the culture (based on their "scientific" investigations and understanding of human behavior) who should begin to act now. Not other people, not those who are reading his books or hearing him lecture on television or radio. We are supposed to accept that the behavioral technologists are to take the first step, to begin the *expert* moves to promote the survival of the culture.

Skinner has endeavored to give a scientific justification for the claim that *he and his colleagues ought to run the culture* and everyone's life within it so that the culture will survive. It is this, not simply the survival of the culture or even governmental control, that is Skinner's primary goal and value; it is his expertise that he wants to induce us to accept and promote. His would be an uninteresting outlook if it only suggested that all of us in our different ways ought to go to work to improve our society, that we should *all* help to support the survival of our culture.

That would be simple conventional ethics. Most high school commencement exercises serve this kind of marmalade. "Go out and serve your society" is standard diet for conventional moralists. (Then, when the kids have spent ten years working for the welfare of society or the culture, they run to the psychologists and learn of their need to develop greater respect for themselves, pay attention to their own feelings, speak their own minds, and not succumb to the will of the culture. But all this is well known.)

What Skinner is out to do is much more ambitious and presumptuous. He is after the doctrine of the divine right of behavioral engineers to do as they design and prefer, whatever it is, and with whoever must be involved ("induced"). Is the interpretation too absurd? Maybe Skinner would flatly reject the inference. But it does flow from his own interpretation of the nature of values, of what we mean by "ought to" and "should." For "It is not true that statements containing 'should' or 'ought' have no place in scientific discourse." (II/429) And these end up to be what we can identify as his own *observed* desires. What ought to be done by all is what Skinner wants from all. And the justification for it is that he wants it or approves of it. "You ought to promote the survival of the culture by means of expert behavioral technology" means "this is reinforcing to you and (or because) others will approve." But the others in this case are a *very* small group of people who understand what is being said—so small that it includes no one other than Skinner and those who fully agree with his behavioral technology and its suggested role in our world. And the ones to whom it *is* reinforcing are the members of the same group.

So when we take it that Skinner is simply trying to convince us that he and his ilk ought to begin to act so as to promote the survival of the culture, we are entirely correct. Skinner himself would admit this. His books are designed to convince us that expert behavioral technologists ought to run the country, culture, or world—whatever is available. But he might object to the characterization of his argument given here as starting from such a solipsistic basis. Nevertheless, this is actually all he leaves room for, the only remotely scientific treatment that can be given to his proposal—we ought to accept that they ought to do this because they approve of it being done by themselves.

The value and threat of Skinnerism

For many of us the Skinner phenomenon has become a kind of expected oddity in our culture. Some people get panicky when they hear of yet another advocate of totalitarian measures, clothed this time in a different garb called the science of behavior. The idea that some people should be ruled by other people, that the expertise some acquire in understanding an aspect of nature entitles them to force others, if even ever so gently, to live by their wisdom—is not new. Usually the advocacy of such notions is coated with sugar and morality, sometimes with science. One really cannot consider Skinner very formidable in his political message. Whatever impact he has had in the field of psychology, there is little danger that his techniques will be adopted by agents of any government on any general, broadly based scale. Most people have more to do living their own lives with reasonable success than to invest energy in Skinner's proposals.

Nonetheless it is important to realize to what extent Skinner is successful in his pursuit of leadership. (He may disavow any personal interest in being seated as some federal czar of behavioral technology. But the idea that such a controller should be appointed is quite consistent with his own thesis. [VI/54]) We do live in times where troubles seem to be piling up at a dizzying rate. The nightly news can be frightening and most of the creeds so familiar to us are out of favor. Intelligent people do not have a solid organizational dogma to rely on. Science is still very potent, despite the attempts of the counterculture to take us back to nature. Although there is some doubt that our age is any more crisis-ridden than other ages have been, there are many people who believe that drastic measures are called for, often just as evidence that something is being done, never mind whether it provides a remedy.

It is the time for shortcuts that turn out to be dead ends. Transcendental meditation, vegetarianism, scientology, sensitivity training, and hundreds more each claim the final solution to all of the problems of mankind. If one only had a lusty primal scream, all would turn out well! If only this and if only that. In this case, if only Skinner and his colleagues could take over the government, arrange enough schedules of reinforcement, discontinue aversive control, and abolish punishment, the world would turn out much better.

As with most fads, some people definitely make valuable use of the various techniques and formulas provided. No doubt sitting in a deep trance for a while each day can make a difference to some people, just as giving up meat can be of help to others. Some people and many animals have learned to behave quite well by way of the science of behavior. The field has made valuable contributions to the treatment of some alcoholics,

129

retardates and unruly children, to the development of classroom materials, and so on. But the blow-up principle is very tempting, so that many people who have seen results in one area are perfectly willing to encourage the implementation in others. Even if human freedom and dignity are at stake.

On judging Skinner and his work

There are some practical and by all means valuable uses for Skinner's technology. To be objective about him requires that one admit this openly. But being objective and being neutral about Skinnerism are not the same thing at all. This itself requires some treatment: can one be objective and yet take a position when considering matters such as Skinner's point of view? Well, first of all, if one could not it's doubtful that anyone could be objective about anything he has an interest in.

If it is accurate that people are the sort of beings for whom making decisions is an essential aspect of living, then neutrality in crucial issues is rarely possible for any of us. It must also be kept in mind that a good case for objectivity is possible without requiring that it involve neutrality. For example, as Skinner himself expresses it a bit obliquely, a scientist *commits* himself to a policy of being objective. And even if he is not always, that policy would make little sense if it spelled self-defeat at the outset—if having that commitment rendered it impossible for him to be objective because it violates the neutral stance.

Objectivity is a way of dealing with a subject, neutrality is how one stands in relationship to its various tenets and conclusions. And it is quite understandable that being neutral about something would lead one to care little about whether he is objective in dealing with it.

At any rate, having said this, it will make more sense now to consider the way some people *regard* Skinner and his views. Some have said, for instance, that Skinnerism is dangerous. It may be true that some of Skinner's claims can lead to actions that are harmful. But in one respect *any* viewpoint can be transformed into a destructive weapon. Moralism, i.e., going about blurting out praises and condemnations when these are ill framed and irresponsibly substantiated, can lead to all kinds of conflict and damage in human relations, even in one's own personal life. (Overly self-critical approaches are well known to contribute to a distorted view of oneself and one's capacity to deal with the world.)

One thing that any conscientious examination of Skinnerism does not warrant is fear of *all* the behavioristically explained and justified *techniques* used in, e.g., education, psychiatry, psychology, or therapy. Often what goes by the name "behavioral technology" is no more than sound advice about how someone might deal with his problems, even with the problems for which advice or help has been sought. Take for example Skinner's idea of schedules of reinforcement. While anyone desirous of a healthy physique, getting rid of some well-entrenched habit, or developing some valued skill will most likely find some of what Skinner offers useful, he may indeed already be making use of the technique without having associated it with behavior technology. (Note, for example, the non-Skinnerian use of the term "conditioning" in sports.) Obviously, we frequently devise systematic ways by which to learn or change some things, including things that are very personal in our lives. People handle many problems rationally, systematically, thoughtfully, and the cash value of this is often something like a Skinnerian program by which to acquire or rid oneself of modes of behavior.

Thus far there is nothing wrong with Skinner and what he suggests except the misleading language and theoretical framework within which it is presented. As argued earlier, almost anything people offer for serious consideration—ideas advanced as helpful, useful, effective, and reliable—seems to be upgraded by some scientific-sounding jargon and rhetoric. And the behaviorists have indeed conducted respectable studies to show that their methods produce results that some people will find helpful and may desire and value. Mostly this is done in connection with a clear understanding that the results, short- or long-range, are wanted by those for whom the method is employed.

What is not to be confused with a partial defense of Skinnerism (and behaviorism) is full regard for it as a world-view by which to make sense of human affairs en toto, and aspects of them such as moral conduct, political systems, economics, friendship, creativity, love, and so on. Not that even in these some of what the behaviorists offer cannot be made to pay off. But as a psychologist friend once remarked: some people benefit from being hit by a falling brick—but that is no reason to make a federal policy of it.

And here there is a clue. When you or a trusted aide in problem-solving endeavor to make discriminating use of behavioral technology, that can be fine and dandy. But in his world-view and political recommendations Skinner goes beyond anything so sensible. He denies the distinction between our choosing to employ his findings in this or that realm of our lives and the applicability of these methods independent of choice, as well as by those who would use them in disregard of people's wishes. For Skinner advocates that his techniques be *imposed* on us by expert behavioral technologists. Using the model of animal training and psychiatric wards, and only limited cases therein, he blows up what he has found there into a grand picture. He thereby succeeds in obliterating the very insight he might have provided: that *in some circumstances* his *methods* are helpful. Psychiatric wards and the premature state of human infancy—other of his models—are not what a human community is or ought to be about. We can admit that lots of things seem crazy in the "normal" world. But we must also admit that a lot of things are the outcome of irresponsibility, not simply craziness.

By obliterating this distinction Skinner's view becomes dangerous. It lends a phony rationale—a rationalization—to practices that destroy human life, almost literally. Thomas S. Szasz, a professor of psychiatry and a writer, has provided an impressive account of how the cloak of mental-illness labeling has permitted incarceration of people who do not "behave well," whose behavior we do not like, and who can be removed from our lives by calling on the police and a willing physician. Skinner himself shows some awareness of this but slides over the problem as he does over others connected with his own theory and the implementation of his advice.

Aside from these rather obvious consequences, which are clearly not to be laid at Skinner's feet alone (since Freudian psychology, as others, offers rationales for this kind of barbarism as well), there are the more massive and remote consequences arising from Skinner's quasi-political rumblings and mumblings. Again, his views do not have clear implications for a particular kind of society and political system. But in the end they do reach a rather definite point. This is that some people—expert behavioral technologists—should have total control over the lives of the rest of the society's membership. Such a result does not entail a specific purpose or goal or value for the control that would in fact be exercised—Skinner's vague notion that it ought to be the survival of the culture is just that—extremely vague.

The fact remains that Skinnerism requires the acceptance of and support of the survival of the culture as construed by the controllers themselves; they should be provided with the legal power (which in our society means initial democratic consent) to set up methods by which all of us would have to promote the goal selected by the experts. There is every reason to believe that Skinner's entire schema, from his scientific pretensions and naïve philosophy to his bizarre political, economic, and technological proposals serve this unspecified goal.

On resisting Skinnerian institutions

Chomsky has said only that "a theory of human malleability *might* be put to the service of totalitarian doctrine." It seems more reasonable to take it that such a view offers that sort of alternative a far better chance of philosophical respectability than would a philosophy that viewed human nature as essentially consisting of the capacity to choose rationally from the alternatives in our lives. Perhaps there is no necessary connection between deterministic philosophies and authoritarian political recommendations—David Hume was a mitigated determinist who advocated a free society, but some of the greatest intellectual supporters of planned societies believed in determinism (e.g., Plato, Hobbes, Hegel, Marx). The racial determinism of Hitler and the historical determinism of Stalin cannot be construed as mere accidents—ideas, as Richard Weaver observed so aptly, have consequences!

But whatever fears one might have of Skinner's ideas, they must be put into perspective—to prevent, so to speak, throwing out the baby, even if there are gallons of bathwater to get rid of. The sort of steps to be taken when that is understood are not easily specified. People in various circumstances find different occasions to make decisions regarding their political ideas and action. We can conclude, though, that since Skinnerism is wrong as a general viewpoint, it *ought to* be discarded as such. Thus it is appropriate to challenge those who cater to this view, even though some of what they say or do is valuable for certain purposes. But when it comes to action, then debunking, boycotting, and rejecting ideas is one thing; suppressing them by force quite another. It would be playing into Skinner's and other totalitarians' hands to take that approach.

Some people who consider Skinner's political notions an affront have of course recognized that the idea of cultural design can be stretched to include the institution of a legal system that *prohibits* just the sort of practices he advocates. After all, if design for design's sake is advocated, what objections can we have to designing a system that would disallow expert universal behavioral control by agents of the state? (This is why Skinner is not really advocating design for design's sake but design along Skinnerian behavior-shaping lines.)

Many people are inclined to react to Skinner by virtually adopting his own recommendations under a different guise, i.e., by advocating the regulation of Skinner and his disciples by censuring their views. (Others, like many liberals in Congress, simply want to keep Skinnerism and psychosurgery under political supervision—demonstrating their own inclination toward the position of expert controllers.) This is wrong and flies in the face of freedom and dignity. Unfortunately too many people approach politics in an unprincipled fashion and are willing to use measures on their enemies against which they want to protect themselves.

On the other hand boycotting Skinnerians and the institutions employing them, and refusing to provide funding for their kind of experimentation, is the appropriate approach. Unfortunately here again many complexities emerge and one might need to act in a quasi-political fashion, seeing that so much is already under political management. Thus, where one is not free to refrain from involvement—e.g., in compulsory public schools that might adopt some Skinnerian program (which might be fine but tends to promote the Skinnerian idea beyond the educational realm)—political advocacy and pressure become necessary. The kind of action to be taken will probably be different for different people. But on all levels the principle which should guide one is that no one's liberties must be abridged unless he himself acts in violation of others' freedom. The rights of Skinnerians to engage in voluntary experimentation must not be violated. But because their practices are so often fused with government-financed programs, the proper course to take may be difficult to identify.

In this connection we should note that *designing* a culture is not in itself immoral and objectionable, whereas imposing it is. Skinner opposes human rights and considers them to have "only a minor bearing on the survival of a culture." Yet these rights are precisely the basic principles of the system that libertarians advocate. They differ significantly from Skinner's ideas of organizing society, needless to say. He is the first to admit this and act against the libertarian ideals of freedom and dignity. The crucial difference is that in a free society all people, not just "experts" are responsible for the control of human lives—namely *their own*. Some experts, such as judges, policemen, and administrators would find a place in a free society—just as they do in the performance of any specialized professional activities. In many areas we assign to experts the jobs we need to have done. We engage barbers, doctors, mechanics, lawyers, butchers, teachers, and a host of other people in our desire to get skilled service and quality products in return for payments we are willing to make. This is *voluntary* exchange, which is fundamental to acting within the framework of a culture organized around the basic principles of human rights. And this is just what we have to contrast with Skinner's advocacy of expert, total control of all that we do, whether or not we ask for it.

We have already noted Skinner's attempt to avoid being implicated as a totalitarian; first by saying he does not like the use of aversive controls, and second by referring to the control of the expert controllers by those being controlled. This amounts to a poor attempt to avoid responsibility for the implications of much of what Skinner concludes and advocates. It is clear that he differentiates between voluntary relationships and control by some experts who have decided to run the culture along lines they believe important. It is equally clear that Skinner denies the reality and possibility of the former by claiming it is a mere coverup for ascribing random chance and causelessness to human affairs. He fails to see that voluntary interactions among people can be rational, well planned, organized, sensible, intelligent, even somewhat predictable—and without some behavioral expert controlling them.

Skinner fails to understand that sound behavioral technology is only a *means* by which some goals can be achieved more efficiently than otherwise. And that our purposes and goals cannot be rendered wiser, more admirable, or better suited to our needs, welfare, and values simply because experts in behavioral technology control them. Means or ways of acting are not good or bad *without* reference to goals—so a good runner may save *or* hurt himself or others by employing his expert skill, as could a surgeon, a safe cracker, a scuba diver, or a behavior technologist. There are no experts on human life and morality; there are no experts on what is the right thing for a person to do—except perhaps the person himself, provided he has considered the question in depth. In short, behavioral technologists are automatically no more *good* than any of us—so why entrust *them* with the control of our lives rather than anyone else who has some special skill? *Being* good must be a personal "skill."

There are all kinds of crackpot theories floating around and even being published that reduce man, human behavior, social organization, and so on, down to one simple formula which, if that formula were only adopted *right now,* would instantaneously lead to the salvation of mankind. From transcendental meditation to smashing dishes on concrete floors, from living by the stars to hypnosis, and from having a nice, clean, bloody revolution to gassing all members of some vaguely identifiable group of people—every week another miracle formula is advanced that purports to guarantee human happiness.

But there is wisdom in the idea of the human right to life, liberty, and the pursuit of happiness. It suggests that matters are, most fundamentally, in the hands of each of us—not some experts or philosopher king. This is why a good society will avoid imposing anyone's instant formula on the population; it *cannot* be done that way. People really must live, judge, and act so as to succeed on their own, and only by voluntary interaction is this enhanced without likely harm to anyone.

Skinner, like so many people, is impatient with this idea. He wants final, mathematically conclusive certainty. And he wants to do something about it, something effective, of course. To do so he needs control, or so he believes. But because his concept of human nature is wrong, his proposed solution to all our problems *cannot* work, even if he could somehow gain the legal power to exercise control. Ultimately, such a plan *could* only end in failure. What is likely to happen then would be something like what has come about for the "sincere racists and humane Marxists." Thus the horrors that would result from the fumbling attempts to make Skinnerism adjust itself to reality would be explained away by reference to all the "deviationism" in the ranks; by how the experts are only mock-Skinnerians, really fools and impostors who, like Stalin and Hitler, distort an otherwise scientifically valid, humane, and even artistically admirable viewpoint—which, had it been left in the hands of sincere, decent, intelligent folks, would have produced the next in the hundreds of unrealized but beautiful utopias in human history. Well, it would be nice if these excuses would never have to be offered and Skinnerism, like phrenology, descended into well-deserved obscurity before being made into a guiding formula of state-supervised advance toward universal happiness.

135

PART II

5

Science, Philosophy, and the Division of Labors

SKINNER'S EXPOSITION AND defense of the reductionist/behaviorist approach to human affairs has a central problem. This problem has to do with the belief that all human affairs must be understood in the light of analyses provided by a mechanistic/materialistic framework of inquiry. The Skinnerian view holds that there is only one way to truth—the way which is used successfully in the field of Newtonian mechanics. The "blow-up fallacy" is perhaps responsible, more than anything else, for leading Skinner to his unacceptable conclusions about human affairs.

One could ask: "Why go about considering such matters in the fashion being used here? What rationale might there be for proceeding along these as opposed to other lines of inquiry?"

What must be offered first is a brief outline of the case for a division of labors within the arena of intellectual activities. When so many believe that something called experimental science alone can produce knowledge, this sort of "defensive action" is perhaps quite understandable.

Psychology and political theory

While the study of political matters was once of central concern to a philosophy, today it is less and less so. Perhaps there is a revival of political philosophy now that many graduate students are dissatisfied with the dry philosophy taught in most of the prominent departments, but political matters are still widely assigned to the field known as political science. This field (like all the social and human sciences) suffers from terrible confusion because of its difficulties in proving that it is capable of being scientific. Since science is thought of by many to be what Skinner also says it is, political science has been under some compulsion to become more and more behaviorist oriented, reductionistic, experimental, and so on.

The connection between the study of man's psychology and his political life is, accordingly, often seen to be one of reducing political science to behavioral analysis concerning human relationships, community life, or international conduct. In the last analysis this is not really a connection but a reduction of one field into another. (Presumably each will eventually be reduced to physics or so some scholars claim.)

But one should not get the false impression that all psychologists are behaviorists. Those who are not, however, are generally concerned with the study and treatment of people's *personal* problems. Even the branch known as "social psychology" tends to stay away from the broader questions that emerge in the context of politics. Interestingly, while many psychologists oppose the Skinnerian view, and advocate human independence, self-assertion, autonomy of personality, and similar traits for self-improvement, in politics their views are closer to Skinner's than one might suppose. Mostly, however, they avoid politics so as to stay clear of the charge of pushing some ideology. To most intellectuals "ideology" is a dirty word, no matter which one is at issue. What used to be considered having a political point of view, a theory of politics, is now taken as adhering to an ideology— an arbitrary, biased, subjectivistic, visionary, unrealistic notion of human political life. This is the logical consequence of denying that values are a variety of facts pertinent to what human beings *ought to* do. This denial in turn follows from the image of man as a being fully controlled by his environment and not faced with the need to choose between alternatives that must be *evaluated.* So political theories can only be expressions of the kind of "values" Skinner admits into science: the feelings people have, their *approving behavior,* toward some form of social arrangement. The ground for such behavior has to be independent of questions of right and wrong. Such behavior simply is as it arbitrarily came to be—*via* someone's history of reinforcement.

Some schools of psychology do not embrace Skinner's view of man. They include those generally classified as humanists and Existentialists. Most adherents to these schools avoid commenting professionally on the political aspects of human life. When they *do* comment, they all too frequently support the same general type of society that Skinner advocates, namely the paternalistic welfare state. This despite their advocacy of personal traits that run counter to such political ideals. But even more problematic is the fact that these schools join hands with Skinner, in the main, concerning the status of values in human life. Most humanists and Existentialists adhere to a subjectivist theory of value: what values a person has must be incapable of objective justification, universalization, and generalization.

These schools, therefore, provide no opposition to Skinnerism where politics and ethics are concerned. The fight between them and Skinner is

140

confined to a very narrow therapeutic area, including, sometimes, the issue of whether Skinner's view of science should be accepted or should be given up in favor of excluding man from scientific study.

We must admit that despite himself Skinner is at present the only major psychologist who has made even the slightest attempt to offer us political advice based on conclusions allegedly derived from studies in his own field of psychology. Notwithstanding that these conclusions have little or no support in fact and logic, the point is that Skinner has attempted to draw an explicit connection between psychology and political theory. To this extent he must be respected. He believes he has made some important discoveries about human nature and life, and he is concerned to make these discoveries effective for purposes of the highest order: to manage the political affairs of people as well as human knowledge will permit.

Although the particular conclusions Skinner draws are unjustified, and a great deal is wrong with what he says, his conviction that man *can* be understood and that his problems *can* be solved, is not without foundation. Nature, of which man is clearly a part, is being managed with considerable signs of success. So why should man be so elusive? It is not true that this basic conviction supports Skinner's belief that the means useful toward the successful management of nature in physics, biology, or even animal psychology will fit the purpose of solving man's personal and political problems. Yet the basic conviction need not be rejected on that account.

Science without reductionism

Can we provide a means by which to approach political life that is no less realistic or natural than those found useful in other fields of study—even if the appropriate methods are not reducible to quite the same things? Although a racehorse may run faster when struck relentlessly during a race, is this what will get a person to hurry it up? Repeating words to a parakeet can get the bird to produce them but will this method teach a child to speak?

Perhaps, one may say, these are unfair examples. Look at the higher animals—chimps, porpoises, and the like. Don't baboons live in communities? Don't they communicate their needs and pleasures to each other with success? So when we find some means by which their lot is improved shouldn't that give us adequate clues about people?

Not quite. There is a logical error in jumping from conclusions about rats, pigeons, chimps, or porpoises to people. But is it not possible that these conclusions might apply? After all, these animals are "close" to man, and they do behave in some cases like man. There are even ways to get them to do things people do, to teach them feats they would never initiate on their own. So surely we cannot *rule out* stronger similarities than those suggested by the simple experiments we have been able to conduct. Especially when we are so restricted in our studies of man; we cannot put *him* under controlled circumstances as we can chimps (well, we might, but we are discouraged from doing so by "stubborn, fanatical people" concerned with freedom and dignity). So while the *experiments* themselves do not back up the conclusion that man is in no significant ways different from other animals it *might* still be true. Then why not work on that assumption?

But here a problem arises, one not observed by most people. What sort of question is "Might it not still be true?" Even if the evidence does not justify that it is, might it not still be? In a court of law the prosecution would not get far with proclaiming, "Well, the evidence that the defendant is guilty is inconclusive, but might he not be guilty anyway?" No one can be asked to yield to that kind of "argument." Yet many unsuspecting people do, even in the most highly respected fields of inquiry. The objection, e.g., to a psychologist going on with his studies of man as if he were a pigeon, is dismissed on the grounds that, well, he *might* be, so why not act as if he actually is one? What is generally forgotten is that we have every right to say that he might *not* be, so why not act as if he actually is *not* one. Especially where the idea is to abolish freedom and dignity!

Aside from the above, which to most psychologists are tiresome philosophical quibbles (but not as trivial as some would have it) there are other obstacles in the way of the reductionist stance. They should serve as our starting point for proposing a different approach to the study of man.

Consider that by merely observing people, in terms of the classifications we use to get through each day, we can identify millions of serious differences between people and other animals: from driving cars to playing football, from authoring children's stories to writing theoretical books on psychology, from building sand castles to constructing launch pads for moon rockets, from smiling to rolling in the aisles from laughter, from frowning to sobbing at a mother's graveside, on and on and on—the list is infinitely long. Is this not *evidence* that man is different? Different from chimp and porpoise, from rat and pigeon, from ant and elephant? It is!

True, the data we get from such observations is not easily expressed in some statistical correlation, some regression pattern or other form of measurement used in connection with many fields of study. But the evidence is there—anyone can discern it if he just opens his eyes and his mind. To ignore it will not make these facts of life go away. And surely the proper turn for a scientist is to make the most of the data he has before him, never mind that it does not come in the same form as evidence in other sciences.

Once such evidence is not obstructed by the blindfolds worn by so many psychologists, the picture changes from the way we left it above. It is not only logically invalid to move from rats to people on the basis of experimentation with rats; to make that kind of move flies in the face of *evidence*. Here we do not simply have trust or hope or even faith! It is blind, stubborn and irrational faith that rules the investigator if in the face of this evidence he still does not give up his commitment to reductionism. For now the question "Well, after all, might all this not apply to man as well?" is answered by "As a matter of fact, no—just take a look and see that people do not run through mazes by trial and error—they use a map or the good advice of a friend who has been there before." Of course what many of these "scientists" will do is to say "Oh, how do you know we cannot explain all that in terms of the laws that govern the behavior of rats?" And here many people nod—reluctantly, but they nod nevertheless. "How do I know they cannot? I don't know—so what right have I to make a judgment on the matter?"

But this is a fantastic hoax perpetrated by special pleading in the name of professional expertise. The ploy of *argumentation ad ignoratium* defeats many a sincere person. But it is never too late to learn about it and avoid it the next time. For it is not one's responsibility to prove that the scientist *cannot* do something; it is the scientist's responsibility to prove that he *can*. Because one does not know that he cannot, it does not follow that he in fact can, could, or will. Where it is not obvious that the psychologist can explain human behavior on the basis of his studies of lower animals—in terms of general principles he could generate about lower animal behavior— he is the one who owes the proof. The layman (or for that matter the nonreductionist psychologist) need only wait until the scientist comes up with the explanation of man in the way the latter's faith requires that man must be explained.

There is nothing wrong with ignorance—not when one does not claim knowledge and has no responsibility for having acquired it. It is far worse to imply that one knows something and then come up empty-handed, with a large dose of blind faith and arrogant commitment. Especially when this faith denies evidence that is available to anyone who is interested. The answer to "How do you know we cannot come up with what we have faith we will someday discover?" is, "I want to *see* and *hear* the *proof* that you can!" (After all, when millions of taxpayers' dollars are invested in research studies—it seems that there's been ample time to make at least a little headway toward *proving* the reducibility of human behavior to that of rats.)

It seems that we should ignore a good deal of what experimental psychologists, especially Skinnerians, have produced by way of making sense of human political life. It is precisely the element of human life that gives rise to the need for politics that these experts and "scientists" have left completely untouched. Governed, as they are, by their model of man as a passive entity that responds to stimuli (but which on its own cannot make a useful move), these individuals have no way of even beginning to understand a purposive area of human life such as politics.

Politics, correctly understood—as distinguished from despotic uses of political *tools*—has as its central feature the purpose of organizing a human community to serve the rational, moral goals of its members. (Such an organized community may make it possible to pursue irrational and immoral goals but its principles of organization can give no aid and comfort to such pursuits even while it does not prohibit them.) As such, the field is logically, theoretically inaccessible to reductionist and behaviorist analyses, since these begin by denying the reality of purposes (or by translating the concept of purpose to mean something completely different, even contradictory to it). To have a purpose is to embark upon an *active* pursuit of a *chosen* goal. Any field of study that assumes, a priori, that man is passive and completely controlled by conditions of his environment is entirely impotent to deal with human political life. (It is impotent to deal with personal life also, except where knee-jerks, twitches, chemical imbalances, routinely acquired patterns of behavior, and the like are at issue.)

Science, philosophy, and other ways to truth

The first fault in Skinner's treatment of human behavior and its ethical and political aspects is his assertion that his ideas are fully justified by scientific analysis. Whatever Skinner believes, he claims follows from *the* scientific approach to things.

What alternative view of science would it be reasonable to adopt? In a very general way, any systematic, rational, comprehensive study of some subject matter (that aims to arrive at knowledge of what is the case within its field) can be considered a science. Being systematic, rational and comprehensive, and aiming at knowledge are quite adequate to describe some inquiry as scientific. But the specific components of any given science are not detailed by knowing this much (or little) about it.

Most people consider it typical of science to involve experimentation, research, and observation. Most people expect that the data scientists employ be objective. But many (at least since the advent of positivism) conflate the meaning of "objective" and (publicly) "observable." Skinner is one. Yet there is no reason to suppose that mathematics, for instance, is not objective because it has nothing to do with observation—numbers are not observed. Unless, of course, one expands the meaning of "observe" to include "intellectually attend to." But then we are back to the very general view whereby even philosophy must be considered a science. Aristotle, certainly one of the earliest empirical scientists in Western history (especially in connection with his work in biology and medicine), did consider philosophy's branch of metaphysics the science of all special sciences, as the most comprehensive of the systematic fields of study. As he put it, "wisdom is a science of certain causes and principles . . . it is this science which must investigate the first principles and causes, and the good or final cause is one of the causes." (XXIII/14-15)

When Skinner identifies his discussion of ethics and politics as science, he is in the tradition of Aristotle (although he would be adverse to this interpretation). The connection between the two ends here. Skinner clearly does not mean by science this kind of comprehensive study. Rather he

144

means the kind of activity that involves moving from single episodes to rules and laws, based *exclusively* on observations. He does not examine the meaning of "observation" in his discussion. His empiricism restricts his idea of science to the study of that which is detectable by way of sense experience, without any theories to aid in the employment of man's senses. And such a notion as "the good or final cause" is definitely ruled out.

Perhaps it is better if we do not go all the way back to Aristotle in our search for the best characterization of science. Not that there is anything ipso facto suspect in that. In fact, Aristotle is closer to the modern view of science, including modern physics, than are the Baconians and the positivists. Still, for purposes of clarification it will be useful to distinguish between philosophy and science, even if in one sense there is no difference between the two activities.

There are many branches of philosophy (e.g., epistemology, aesthetics) just as there are in science and in art. What often appears to be the difference between philosophy and science is that the former has many schools, orientations, methods, and factions while the sciences are considered by most people to be entirely homogeneous; i.e., whatever is current is accepted as the most up-to-date knowledge of what is. On the other hand, there is disagreement not only within philosophy, but also about its nature and purpose—and even about whether it has any. Anyone who has taken philosophy courses in college should be aware by now that it is neither taught nor learned in the ways one approaches the sciences. (This however is not conclusive. It could be that the teaching is wrong, not that the fields are different.) Thus Aristotle may be presented as a legitimate proponent for the right view of some problem, while in science Ptolemy and Galen are dismissed.

Many teachers of philosophy, as well as some philosophers themselves, believe that there is no such thing as philosophical *knowledge*—the most we may expect of the field is that it foster a serious doubt about all the things we take for granted in life. But this view is contested as much as all the others. And in each age there is a kind of silent, though often feverish, competition among members of the various schools of philosophy for the dominant position of "most likely to be true," "most sensible," "most meaningful," "correct." What is at issue here is this or that approach to life in general: often expressed by the ordinary man in such phrases as "The world is completely confused (or orderly)," "We cannot help what will happen," "Men can manage their affairs," or "Anything is possible." The issue is which one will be the most successful when given full intellectual backing. Even where it is denied, the attempt is to solve the perennial problem of how a human being should approach his life here on earth, what is the best understanding of existence as he encounters it *qua* man. As such, philosophy seeks a generalizable, sometimes even timeless, approach to living as a human being.

We are not concerned now with whether this search must ultimately be considered absurd, an oddity in itself. We only call attention to the fact that it goes on not only in each epoch of man's history but in each individual's life, sometimes explicitly and other times only haphazardly, impressionistically. The only commitment we make now is to the fact that two contradictory approaches to human life cannot both be right. If that could be, we could have a view that is both appropriate and inappropriate for human beings. The idea that one view only might be unanimously agreed upon may be absurd. But that two contradictory one's could be *has* to be absurd. In philosophy as in other fields, contradictions cannot exist; what is propounded cannot be both true and not true.

In philosophy we experience more disagreement than in the so-called hard (natural, physical) sciences. Philosophy is often criticized for not being more like science—for not living up to the standards of rigor, precision, accuracy, and testability assumed to be all-pervasive within the sciences. To many it seems frustrating not to glean from philosophy what is at least offered from science.

Yet, is it fair to look at all fields of knowledge and ask that they accommodate the standards and methods of just one or some of them? Even more, is it wise and prudent, is it truly scientific? Surely it is prejudicial to the inquiry to be conducted. The approach taken in the hard sciences—and it is by no means obvious that only one approach is taken there at any time—is *accepted* by many to be the paradigmatic road to knowledge. The achievements we call technological are often attributed to the hard scientific method, although here again it is by no means clear that the ascription is justified by the facts. More often the *rhetoric* points to hard science as the launching pad for such achievements, whereas the truth lies closer to a mixture of people's common sense, personal effort, and the combination of many fields of inquiry converging upon each other to produce our technological gadgets.

Science exhibits controversy

One of the crucial issues not faced by many and obscured by such people as Skinner, is that within many fields of science disagreement rages with as much if not more vehemence than in philosophy and in art. What to us, with our cursory knowledge of the special sciences, appears as calm, is often turmoil when seen closer up. In biology the explanation of the development of the basic cell; in physics the description of light; in astrophysics the evolution of the solar system; in anthropology the identification of the "missing link," and everywhere about one thing and another, usually at the fundamental level, debates prevail. And the behavior of the scientists is at times more erratic than that of philosophers when engaging in comparisons and argumentation. (The recent upheavals surrounding the theories of Immanuel Velikovsky[10] illustrate that the claim many would

146

like the layman to accept is not there to be found. But this is understandable as soon as one abandons the idealized view of science and scientists, especially behavior technologists, that Skinner advocates.) The arguments and disputes within the sciences do not usually occur at the levels at which most people encounter the various fields during their college education. It is more on the horizons that we find the turmoil. A glance at the scholarly journals within any field of study indicates that none of them is immune from the controversy which many believe afflicts only philosophy and, perhaps, the humane sciences.

In addition, while theoretical sciences are in constant upheaval and do not obviously differ from philosophy, the applied sciences compare with what might be called applied philosophy, at least on the simpler levels. Admittedly, it is not widely agreed what the application of philosophical studies amounts to. Yet we are not far off when we associate the practical results of philosophy with such expressions as "You are getting philosophical all of a sudden." In short, one's optimism, pessimism, distrust or trust of other people, acceptance or rejection of faith, belief or disbelief in the possibility of objectivity in social studies, all are the practical results of philosophy—and they do have their payoff. But not quite in the same way in which the practical utilization of the atom has its concrete manifestation. Yet even here both disastrous experiments and medical "cures" have occurred; differences in the degree of success of science can be seen in every area where it takes some effect.

This also tells us that we are not quite correct in accepting technological breakthroughs and progress to be the exclusively scientific phenomenon they are often considered. Moral, political, religious, economic, and many other factors contribute to what happens in the areas of automated gadgetry, transportation, appliances, and so on. The alleged "scientific method" is not alone responsible for creating the technology of any age. There is evidence also that philosophical ideas can both advance and retard technological evolution. It is, for example, more than likely that the vigorous philosophical propagation of a certain methodology employed in the physical sciences for all fields of inquiry has retarded the development of the social and humane sciences. This by the insistence that only by *imitating* physics can an emerging, identifiable field of study make meaningful progress—that is, achieve scientific status. Reductionism has done much damage to progress in the life sciences by requiring that *all* realms of reality be studied according to the methods appropriate for one or two.

Alternatives to reductionism

In the present epoch the philosophy of science is becoming less and less reductionistic. There are many who have offered a different approach to the understanding of science from that offered by those in the positivist epoch, from Bacon on to Rudolph Carnap and Carl Hemple. Anyone who takes it upon himself to discuss the relationship of science to human life and culture owes some treatment of these developments. For instance, the idea that a scientist can simply identify *raw data* without developing a theoretical framework in the process of approaching the data is unwarranted. What a thing *is* cannot be learned without invoking a conceptual framework for purposes of understanding reality. The furniture of the universe must be arranged and organized (understood in relation to the various pieces) *before* we can identify new items with consistency. The nature of truth is not simply "contacting" things "out there" by passively exposing ourselves to them. Knowledge is produced—which means that it is neither invented nor simply *found* out there. In the works of such philosophers as Thomas S. Kuhn, Stephen Toulmin, Israel Scheffler, A. R. Louch, and others, one can meet these kinds of issues head on, without getting the misimpression that there is nothing to worry about and that the ingredients of a scientific approach to human behavior are self-evident.

At this point we find the question of what we *must* mean by "scientific" to be still unsettled. The indications offered earlier are not conclusive. For example, is it the study of physics that should be our guide to the proper methods in any science? But before we identified physics as a field, we made certain divisions, distinctions, apportionments in the world. A certain distinct realm of reality developed into the domain of physics, and the constituents of this realm dictated the methods of its study.

In philosophy, too, it is the subject matter that must be our guide to suitable methods. Philosophy, to use an analogy, deals with the foundations of the structure that supports all realms of human knowledge and activity. As such, it cannot be assimilated into any *special* field of inquiry. The methods must be appropriate to the nature of what is being investigated. We won't get far in economics with a microscope, in physics by way of opinion polls, in chemistry by light-year measurements, or in ethics by the use of high-energy bubble chambers. In practical matters as well we need to know first what it is we *want* before devising a sensible approach to its achievement. So achieving economic prosperity by throwing away time and money makes no better sense than using a knife and fork to sew a dress.

The resemblance between philosophy and the sciences as activities in which we seek to identify *what* exists, and why, consists in the mutual requirement of clarity and precision; but the details of what makes something clear and precise are different. Philosophy includes the investigation of how we can best distinguish different kinds of things, including the various branches of science. The question "What aspect or realm of existence does the physicist study?" is not answered by the physicist as physicist—although many physicists do turn philosophical about what they do. But then they are no longer doing their special jobs. Within his own field it is the physicist who is best equipped to answer questions; about his field's relationship to other fields he is no better equipped to draw a conclusion than are others. Just because most of us occasionally express opinions about these issues (as we do about medicine, sociology, economics, and psychology even though we are not skilled in these fields) we have not become philosophers. The idea is to make sure that the best and most up-to-date methods of inquiry are being employed. Then one can support one's conclusions and defend them against opponents who are sincerely critical. Skinner's strategy is to tread on grounds he assimilates into his own by fiat, and to proclaim that he is not interested in those whose provinces these are. Not even when their criticism is sincere, serious, and aimed at solving problems.

Science vs. mysticism

Today even the humblest kind of science is under attack from the mystical elements in our society. Charles Reich and Theodore Roszak come to mind. Many such people advocate the rejection of science on grounds that it necessarily leads to a disregard of the elements in man's life that do not fall within its sphere. Well, sound scientific procedures do not have to encroach upon what does not belong within science—e.g., art, ethics, politics. The "value-free" approach that has passed as a paradigm of scientific procedure with its accompanying presumptuousness on the part of the scientific community has infuriated many people.

Actually, only a few pompous members of that community make it their task to exclude all and everything from the rational and meaningful in our lives except that which can be treated as the objects of physics. But these few manage to encourage those who would chuck science in favor of Eastern mysticism and the current fad of drug-induced intuitionism. This artificial and yet wide-scale division of mankind into two camps of pro- and antiscientism is supported by stubbornness in the membership of both camps. The Skinnerians can send some members fleeing into the obscurity of hocus-pocus, while those advocating "blowing your mind" may only encourage people who seek some semblance of reason in life to head for Skinner's behaviorist, pseudoscientific mumbo jumbo. The two approaches are equally irrational, both promising panacea via some quick formula, e.g., operant conditioning, expanded consciousness, or mystical intuition.

To be logical, reasonable, rational, productive, integrated, honest, and objective are requirements of any serious human endeavor. Which is to say that consistency, making good sense, thinking in terms of the highest standards of accuracy (being factual) are universal requirements of a fruitful approach to knowing the world and ourselves. By not accepting these requirements, we are saying, in effect, that inconsistency, meaninglessness, falsehood, and error are just as effective in learning and acting— if not more so. And while some people, even with great reputations, would have us think along these lines, it is absurd. If it is absurdity that one would endorse, however, he faces a further problem: he simply cannot express even this *meaningfully*. The abandonment of logic as a fundamental guide to the discovery and recognition of reality must lead to meaninglessness, i.e., the inability *to mean* anything by what one is saying and thinking, especially in the long run.

In order to learn about people in general, what they can do and believe and how they can feel, we need to take account of the utterings of advocates and practioners of absurdities. Most of us choose to endorse absurdity only temporarily (e.g., when we get discouraged, desperate, overwhelmed by life's obstacles and misfortunes). In such cases we should examine the emerging "world-view" to see if it may not contain (bits of) merit. Many full-blown expressions of man's life and thoughts contain germs of insight out of which not absurdity but further understanding can evolve. So they should be considered.

There is another remarkable thing about philosophy's relationship to the various sciences. The remoteness of the objects of scientific investigation makes possible, at times, their calm consideration and use, leading us to associate the possibility of truth with total detachment (which many associate with objectivity). Things about which most of us feel neither excited nor frightened, like the pigmentation of dodo birds, are often studied with greater prospect for advancement than can be expected in, e.g., psychology or economics. The scholar in such fields is in a different relationship to his objects than the scholar who deals with aspects of reality closer to man's experience. Although even this is not always the case. A psychologist studies man *as* psychologist, not as father or friend.

Knowing the knower

Philosophy strikes at the basics of our concerns—and its claims can stir things up in our personal and social lives. Marxism, Existentialism, individualism, socialism, materialism, positivism, *et al.,* all elicit outcries of welcome or hostility to their respective conclusions. To advocate a philosophical outlook often means stepping on very sensitive toes—a person's most basic convictions, what makes him the kind of individual he is, especially when his own views have been consciously accepted and integrated.

But for all that, science and philosophy are not in opposing positions, simply because there appears to be more calm at times in the former than in the latter. The intensity with which the tenets of a field impinge upon our emotions probably has more to do with their widespread impact than with our general *capacity* to treat the subject matter objectively. With adequate discipline we can study even the most personal aspects of our lives, as well as the most feared ones, with objectivity. If anywhere, there it surely becomes a crucial ingredient, since mistakes in areas we care little about should not matter so much as error, prejudice, or narrow-mindedness in areas we value and need.

150

Most people will admit that ethics and politics fall within the category of the important. Assuming that there are legitimate questions as to how human beings should act, how they ought to organize their communities, we cannot deny the importance of getting right answers. Neither can we deny the importance of finding out whether such questions are meaningful. Skinner himself must at least pay lip service to the importance of values, even though he claims that only one value matters, namely the centralized, expert control of man so as to promote the survival of the culture. All philosophical determinists and materialists, despite their dismissal of ethics and politics as "meaningless areas of inquiry," must face the question of how they *ought to* approach their own activity, even if only on the professional level. Ethics is too far-ranging to fail to touch anyone who can make decisions, anyone who is not completely deranged or paralyzed.

Are we entitled to call the subsequent analysis *scientific*? If we take the broad, Aristotelian view of science, then what we do will be related to science—to metaphysics, epistemology, ethics, and politics. And a proper science of human behavior must deal with these areas. Some of the conclusions which follow are well supported by respectable scientists from both psychology and other fields. But the method by which such a science must approach its subject cannot be prejudiced in favor of Skinnerian reductionism and deterministic behaviorism. After all, it is this which such a science needs to discover—whether human behavior is to be approached in these or different terms.

Obviously Skinner has not proved his conclusions with either his pseudoscientific methods or with other, philosophical arguments. But he has managed to intimidate many people as to what counts as scientific methodology. So our lack of reference to experiments with pigeons and rats, and our failure to offer case histories of psychotics and retardates, might be considered fatal to what we want to defend. An understanding of what has just been discussed will dispel the idea that it is this sort of procedure that qualifies a person to consider such questions as: What sort of life is good for people? What kind of a society, legal system, and political organization can make a good life more rather than less likely for those who live in a human community?

6

Man, Science,
and
Freedom of Choice

WE COME NOW to the positive thesis of the defense of human freedom and
dignity. Skinner takes a similar step when he embarks upon the denial of
the claims of the literature on these subjects.

But it might be asked, why is it not enough to simply reiterate the substance of that literature? Haven't the classical liberals, the advocates of
the free society, defended freedom and dignity with competence? Do we
not have a rich political tradition in America, one that does not call for any
more padding and clarification? In some ways of course the American
political tradition, including its classical liberal origins, is in very good
shape. No other political system has done so much for man. No other
political tradition has made possible a better system. When we consider
the matter on comparative grounds, America's political tradition wins
hands down.

Restrictions in America's political tradition

There are problems in this tradition however which provide an opening
for those who wish to attack it. Especially when we consider its economic
aspects, this tradition focused primarily on *social* theory. What kind of
society is to be preferred? What sort of society will be more productive?
What kind of legal system will do our society more good? It is these and
similar questions that motivated the investigations of most classical
liberals. Adam Smith was largely concerned with the best economic system, although his moral theories have a solid place in intellectual history.
But in the main the classical liberals concentrated on political matters and
left personal, private morality to others.

Even today the two schools of economists, Chicagoan and Austrian, who advocate the free market, argue mainly on utilitarian grounds. The free market is efficient and useful. But both Milton Friedman and Ludwig von Mises divorce their theories from any argument as to which is right for man—freedom or slavery. They both believe in and *prefer* freedom. But both see value considerations inappropriate for what they are doing. (For this lack of concern with virtue, libertarians have been criticized by Irving Kristol.) Other contemporary defenders of liberty, e.g., Professors Harold Demsetz, Sam Peltzman, Armen Alchian (all "Chicagoites"), *et al,* tend to deny that the value of freedom can be defended on rational grounds. For many defenders of human liberty the worth of a free society must be taken as self-evident.

As an exception we might mention John Locke, an earlier thinker, whose theory of natural rights was clearly concerned with values. But Locke did not attempt to integrate his ideas of human rights into any scientific analysis of human nature. His investigations focused upon man as a member of a human community. And while he was somewhat involved in considerations of personal morality, he mostly attended to the political principles suited to human nature.

It can be argued that this deemphasis on the need of ethics and values in people's private conduct left a gaping hole in how the free society had been defended. Maybe because liberty is not consonant with such duties as self-sacrifice and altruism—the most prominent ethical stances through mankind's history—those who advocated freedom stayed away from developing a moral code that could give human political liberty some justification. John Stuart Mill tried to argue for liberty on utilitarian grounds, to the effect that free men contribute more to the common good than oppressed ones. But there always seemed to be something odd about this argument and Mill himself had to reject his support of a free society at the end, very likely because that support was inconsistent with the view that people are good only if they work for the benefit of society.

This confusion at the level of ethics and moral philosophy is still difficult for those who try to defend the free society. Recently John Rawls[13] advanced a theory of justice that tries to defend the maximum liberty for every person in a just society. He tried to divorce his defense of freedom from any specific moral point of view, but some philosophers suspected him of advocating egoism. He was roundly attacked for this in the journals. Yet it is indeed difficult to imagine that one could advocate human freedom, the rights to life, liberty, and the pursuit of happiness without implying some sort of egoistic moral code. Why should the organization of a community defend human life, the liberty of people, and their pursuit of happiness if people are wrong to live for their own happiness?

After the fact of this confusion in libertarian moral theory, and despite the basic soundness of its political program, something needs to be done to show that both liberty and dignity can be defended on rational and scientifically valid grounds. Otherwise it is not surprising that opponents of liberty and human dignity are able to attack libertarianism. They can present themselves as the compassionate, concerned caretakers of mankind and demand that we give them our lives to lead, to control, for the survival of not our own lives, liberties, and happiness, but for the culture.

The basis of choice

Earlier we noted that Hume denied the existence of necessary connections in nature. He also denied the possibility of moral knowledge, and to this date the intellectual climate depends a great deal on Hume for providing such respectable grounds for moral skepticism. Hume's other skeptical conclusions have been largely abandoned. But his moral skepticism remains influential, despite the efforts of the utilitarians Mill and Bentham to dodge the force of his arguments. They too fell into disrepute at the hands of the English antinaturalist philosopher G.E. Moore.

Moore, who turned out to be very influential, especially concerning the philosophy of language and the study of the character of ethical judgments, believed that we could not define "good" although we could know it. But the kind of knowledge we could gain about it is unlike any other. Moore believed that good is an indefinable quality but still an objective one. It is a quality that cannot be perceived by the senses, therefore it is not a natural quality. Now while it may be possible to know good—what is good, what is evil—this knowledge is indeed mysterious. In the end, most philosophers abandoned any speculation about what Moore might have had in mind with his "knowledge via intuition" and remembered him only for his very effective argument against the idea that good could be anything on the order of what Mill and Bentham argued it might be. The latter claimed that good is some observable quality, such as pleasure or satisfaction, that we could measure.

But Moore argued that anytime someone says that some natural quality is what we mean by the word "good," he must face an insurmountable difficulty. For we can always question a natural quality as to whether or not it is good—e.g., "I agree that X is pleasurable but is it also good?" And as long as this remains a meaningful question in connection with the proposed natural quality for which the word "good" is supposed to stand, we must abandon the idea that "good" really stands for that quality. That is, according to Moore, because if it really stood for that quality, the question would make no sense. It would ask "Is good good?"

Having disposed of the idea that some natural (physical) quality that we could observe is meant by the idea of "morally good" or "morally valuable," Moore proposed something very obscure. It was his idea, mentioned above, that "good" stands for an indefinable, nonnatural quality that certain acts, people, policies, and institutions have that others fail to have. But this quality could not be sensed. Nor did he make clear just

154

how we might identify it—except to say that we would know it intuitively, whatever that might mean. The idea cannot be defined, according to Moore, because it refers to something simple, whereas definitions state combinations of qualities, or complex groupings.

Unfortunately Moore, like most British philosophers, was under the influence of Hume and could not consider anything but a description as a viable definition. In other words, to him the definition of "good" would amount to giving a description of some combination of sensory qualities. That is because language could be meaningful only insofar as it referred to sensible items in the world, namely those that could be described. But whatever the word "good" might mean, it is not generally taken to mean some sensible property—especially not when it comes to human conduct.

The story then can be put simply as follows. Considerations of what is good, right, wrong, evil, or the like could not be handled by means of how we were supposed to handle our other concerns. In science and elsewhere it was supposed that sensory knowledge could be enough to go on. Anything that could not gain support from such sensory knowledge simply had to be consigned either to the mysterious (mystical, theological) or to the emotional (expressions of feelings, sentiments). In either case, respectable studies had to be confined to what came to be called "value-free realms." Inside philosophy most thinkers looked upon ethics as a concern with the emotive meaning of certain utterances—values could not be known, evaluations could never be right or wrong, reason gave no support to judgments concerning what is or is not good, right, wrong, evil, or whatnot. These issues dealt with human emotions, feelings, sentiments, but never with reasons.

Outside philosophy the social sciences, with all their studies of human behavior, rejected the relevance of values to the method of their studies. Values may be studied, but the student himself must cast out all considerations of values. Basically values were taken to mean biases, lack of objectivity, distortions. The idea that one might discover the correct values, the right conclusions about what is good or right concerning human life, all this was entirely passe. Some political and social scientists said that perhaps we could never really rid ourselves of biases, but this was simply an expression of personal, or even human inadequacy. It did not seem to most of them to warrant reconsideration of the ideal of value-free objectivity. Few came away with the idea that perhaps when we study human conduct it is not only impossible but unwise to attempt to discard values. This is because the nature of the beast is such that understanding its conduct may require the acknowledgment of certain standards.

In the end, however, with wars and domestic and foreign disasters, many people in academia became disenchanted with the profession of neutrality, which is what "objective" really served to indicate. It simply did not seem adequate to say "I feel it is right," or "I feel it is wrong," or "It seems wrong to me," or "It is right as far as I am concerned" in attempts to justify one's appraisal of racial segregation, Vietnam involvement, the persecution and slaughter of Jews, the achievements of people fighting oppressors, and other forms of significant human conduct. The inquiry became, "OK, so that's how you feel, that is as far as you are concerned, but let us find out if it is right or wrong, good or bad." Thus during the late 1960s and early 1970s many intellectuals went back to the drawing board to consider if we couldn't come up with something better in the area of ethics and morality than "Anyone's values are as valid as any others, it is all a matter of personal, subjective feelings, sentiments." While philosophers never like to be characterized in terms of a simple rendition of their ideas, in the end the post-Humean, empiricist turn in how the bulk of them viewed ethics amounted to just this sort of crass agnosticism.

A few years ago many philosophers would have accepted Skinner's analysis of values—meaning the approval of one's peers. Today he has hardly any support among philosophers, and not much even within the psychological community, especially among the clinicians and therapists. Too many people *suffer* from trying to live up to the approval of their peers —a rather difficult task, indeed, that can leave a person drained of self-respect.

Still, after two centuries of moral skepticism, philosophers have been reluctant to do more than criticize that tradition. Only here and there do we find actual answers to ethical questions. There is no tradition in academic philosophy to build on. To answer such questions requires serious preparatory work.

First of all, we shall have to present, briefly, an outline of a theory of causality. This is needed so as to show that Skinner's explanation of human behavior solely in terms of physical variables—observable variables of a physical system—may be too restrictive. If other kinds of causes besides the type Skinner admits into his system exist, perhaps human conduct would best be explained and understood in terms of them. We have already seen that restricting causality to one type of causes amounts to begging the question—what logical right does one have for such restriction? Some may believe that the demands for simplicity justify it. But simplicity at the expense of reality is no virtue. We have seen that Skinner himself is incapable of accounting for human behavior by way of his scheme. He cannot cope with original behavior, so he simply ignores it. And when we protest, the most likely response a Skinnerian will give is that as long as we confine ourselves to behaviors specified in physically observable movements, we have a put up or shut up position, mainly we can control the behavior of organisms by arranging reinforcing contingencies in the environment. But this response requires that we first put everything under the control of Skinnerians—and wait until they bungle the job before we are entitled to say that the theory is worthless.

It seems much more appropriate to tackle the problems as we have done and propose an alternative approach. But before doing so, we must start with a different approach to the question of causality.

Causality

Some modern Aristotelians have proposed that since Hume the philosophical community has overlooked a view of causality that seems to be far more rational than that which Hume and the Humeans have to offer.[11] We need first to take notice of Aristotle's most basic metaphysical principle, the Law of Identity. There are some excellent contemporary defenses of this principle, or varieties of it, such as the Law of Contradiction. Basically, the principle cannot rationally be denied—to deny it and continue to make sense of what one is thinking or saying is impossible—unless one simply ignores that one has denied it.

At any rate, the Law of Identity states that a thing is what it is, while the Law of Contradiction states that something cannot both be what it is and what it is not. Both of these laws are so obviously true that to explain them seems superfluous. Yet the Law of Identity has been quite seriously denied by philosophers. Mostly it has been denied that it is a law pertaining to reality, and is generally accepted as a law of thought, a convenient way of thinking, a convention. But actually it is a fact about the universe, a fact of existence. It is not falsifiable—but still it is true. In other words, it cannot seriously be supposed to be false—as we might do with other statements that are true.[12]

Now this fact about this law has been lamented as a shortcoming. Yet if one realizes that the law pertains to everything that exists or might have existence, any actual or possible item in reality, it is easy to see that its subject matter makes it impossible to conceive of its falsehood.

At any rate, our concern is not directly with the Law of Identity, but with the law of causality, the law that identifies the nature of action or behavior —the most general statement that can be made concerning these. The Law of Identity and causality are intimately related. The great Aristotelian philosopher H.W.B. Joseph may be cited here to clarify this last statement. First he indicates the character of the Law of Contradiction, which is another way of stating the Law of Identity:

> *We cannot think* contradictory propositions, because we see that *a thing cannot have* at once and not have the same character; and the so-called necessity of thought is really the apprehension of a necessity in the being of things. . . . The Law of Contradiction then is metaphysical or ontological (XXX/13)

Later Joseph spells out the law of causality:

> To assert a causal connexion between *a* and *x* implies that *a* acts as it does because it is what it is; . . . For the causal relation which connects *a* with *x*

connects a cause of the *nature a* with an effect of the *nature x.* The connexion is between them *as a* and *x,* and therefore must hold between any *a* and any *x.* . . . (XXX/408-409)

It is obvious that the above is a radical departure from Skinner's view of causality—the idea of mechanical interactions of variables that may be observed. Skinner does not take "natures" seriously because he deals only with physically observable stuff, even if there may be something more to take note of for purposes of a clear understanding. But other psychologists have attempted to make use of Joseph's clarifications. For example, Branden provides the following rendition of Joseph's point:

> The actions possible to an entity are determined by its nature: what a thing can *do,* depends on what it *is.* It is not "chance," it is not the whim of a supernatural being, it is in the inexorable nature of the entities involved, that a seed can grow into a flower, but a stone cannot—that a bird can fly, but a building cannot—that electricity can run a motor but tears and prayers cannot—that actions *consistent* with their nature are possible to entities, but *contradictions* are not. (XXXI/58)

From this brief consideration of causality, a contrast emerges.

Whereas for Humeans and for Skinner the critical aspect of a causal connection is what is *observed*—conjunction between variables on the basis of which we may predict and control—in fact we need not limit causality to one *kind* of relationship. As Branden points out, "The law of causality is a very wide abstraction; per se, it does not specify the *kind* of causal processes that are operative in any particular entity, and it does not imply that the *same* kinds of causal processes are operative in *all* entities." (XXXI/59) Therefore, while in the case of some entities observing constant conjunction may be all we might need to identify the kind of causal connection that obtains, in the case of others that might not be enough. And surely there are many causal relationships that could not be understood without going far beyond the mere "observation" stage of investigation, all the way to the construction of elaborate theories, sometimes the careful development of theoretical entities, and so on.

There are some familiar rejoinders to this way of considering the situation. For instance, to the notion that "a stone cannot grow into a flower" some clever philosophers will respond by saying "Well, it might turn out that way, mightn't it, after all?" By this move the objective at hand is to force one to provide something like a logical contradiction before one is entitled to say "cannot." And if we are Humeans and deny that the nature of something is knowable, then this objection is fatal. But the Humean ploy is really quite empty; just because the judgment involving the stone and the flower reaches into the future, so to speak, does not mean that we cannot know it to be true. After all, the mere passing of time is no ground for assuming drastic changes in the nature of things.

At any rate, the present approach should yield a fruitful contrast to Skinner's analysis. Let's examine it.

Causality and human nature

If "actions possible to an entity are determined by its nature: what a thing can *do,* depends on what it *is*," then before we can consider the nature of human *behavior,* we need to know what human *nature* is. We need to identify man's nature.

Here, of course, we run into some standard and ancient problems in epistemology. The *natures* of things have been identified as independent but substantial ideas (by Plato), inherent parts of some entity (by Aristotle), workable generalizations (by pragmatists), arbitrary constructs or names used to refer to things (by nominalists), as well as social conventions adopted by speakers of a language (by some interpreters of Ludwig Wittgenstein). All of these characterizations of what the nature of something might be have serious difficulties. As a result many who are concerned with ethics and politics have given up relying on theories and arguments based on the *nature of man.* (For example, with reference to the idea of natural human rights, many philosophers have objected that human nature is simply indeterminable, so we simply can not tell what rights people have because of their human nature. More recently Ernest van den Haag has argued against human rights by noting that people just cannot agree on what man's nature is; as if *lack* of agreement could ever demonstrate the impossibility of reaching one.)

Nonetheless, of course, everyone relies on his notion of human nature to one or another degree. Whether explicitly of implicitly, all of the social sciences employ some idea of the nature of man. Anthropologists, sociologists, economists, and most of all psychologists all exhibit a commitment to some such idea. Man is a territoral being, an aggressive being, a language-speaking being, a tool-user, an imperfect (fallen) being, a being in need of religion, a social being, a violent being, a thinking being, and so forth—the list could be multiplied, and that is just what seems so hopeless about the project.

Still, while the prospects of identifying human nature seem at times doomed, there is also substantial agreement on certain matters. Thus, such diametrically opposed philosophers as Aristotelians and Existentialists find that the self-determining, self-becoming, self-actualizing aspect of each person's life is something that he shares with almost all other members of his species (excepting those, in the main, whom Skinner likes to refer to in support of his view of human behavior, namely retardates and psychopaths). Marx, too, believed that man is distinct from all other animals by virtue of his capacity to make long-range plans (and to produce for an expanding repertoire of needs and wants). Those who think that man is distinctive by virtue of his tool-making ability accept, as least implicitly, that human beings can produce things not found in nature, and reshape them ad infinitum, with a purpose to be served. Skinner himself argues the need for long-range planning for the survival of the culture. And this implies an ability not shared by other animals—at least not to as

159

considerable a degree as human beings. In fact most of these notions about human nature converge on something akin to Aristotle's idea of *rational man*. And most ethicists and political theorists build on something very close to this idea.

The problem is that whatever man's nature is, we need to be able to *justify* our idea of it, otherwise our theories cannot be defended against those who would question it either with sincere curiosity or with malice.

Justifying human nature

In our attempt to make sense of the world we start with the general background we acquire as children, knowledge mixed with belief, hunches, and dogmas. By the evidence of having survived reasonably successfully with what we acquired from others as we grew up, we can surmise that we do have at least a substantial stock of accurate beliefs. These are often statements or claims we would *make* but might not be able to *justify*, even though in the end they might well turn out to be justifiable.

Not too many people will bother to investigate whether what they accept during their early years is in fact true, but at least in special areas many of us become competent at understanding things. Thus our beliefs get ironed out, some are abandoned (if we are consistent), some retained, some sharpened into knowledge. If we insist on consistency, and if we make sure that what we believe squares with our experiences and the experiences of those who are worthy of our trust, gradually we achieve our purpose of getting to know about the world around us. (This knowledge is not some kind of "absolute, final, unchangeable, unrevisable or un-updatable truth" needless to say. That idea of knowledge makes no sense and the complaint that we have not got "knowledge" of that kind is un-justifiable.)

We find when we reflect on it (philosophically at times), that getting to know the world involves the organization of our experiences, the grouping of our awareness of what there is around us into different classes, abstractions, generalizations, and theories. Then we might, and at times do, consider what *had to be done* to gain mastery over some area of reality, including some fairly well-distinguished field of activity or study in more mature years. From that and other things we know, we can tell what was required: i.e., to distinguish, classify, differentiate, and integrate what we needed to know about, according to the differences and similarities we could detect by use of our perceptual organs. The more intensely we inquire into some field or the greater importance it may have for us, the more precisely we need to perform this kind of mental activity.

To justify all our judgments in this kind of undertaking would require proficiency in numerous fields including, eventually, the theory of knowledge. And there it becomes clear that some accounts of definitions are more defensible than others; some provide greater, others lesser, comprehension of just what can lead to a correct definition of the concepts we use to think and to communicate.

Such division of labor is quite understandable in a complex world. And if all goes well with the special jobs people take on, matters can move along quite smoothly in coming to grips with reality on many levels. People are free however to disregard rules of sound procedure. This, coupled with honest mistakes, can lead to grand and destructive detours. Many people make claims about matters they have not examined—one need only consider the thousands of books published each year and the many contradictory theories, claims, ideas, and whatnot they all contain. Obviously not all can be true, right, on the mark.

The same goes for definitions. And here, as everywhere, there are those who take it upon themselves to organize objections to the possibility of arriving at correct definitions, often simply to put those who argue for its possibility through the hurdles that could emerge when their guard is down. Those who charge ahead to gain knowledge and understanding can get impatient, so challenges to what they propose are often quite useful. Nor is it always wise to assume that everyone involved in the undertaking is trying to achieve the same goal. Some people strive to show that definitions are *impossible;* not that they are difficult to produce, nor that they require this or that step for their production. Then there are those who thrive on unreasonable doubts and by this manage to press the proponent of the affirmative position into the most severe difficulties. But all this does not prove that the task is impossible, even where borderline cases emerge. (In fact these presuppose the possibility of definition.)

We do, as a matter of plain, everyday fact, encounter many things— relationships, events, actions, complex matters of a large variety—that appear and are similar and/or distinguishable from others. We can, for example, understand the idea that anything that exists must be something and cannot both be and not be what it is. This is plainly basic to anything we think or do. Nor can something just up and change without cause or purpose in any way we might imagine or fantasize, Walt Disney-style (or along lines of various types of "philosophical imagination"). Drastic things *can* happen, but we have no justification for accepting that nature itself is somehow intrinsically, inherently irrational or mysterious—only that much is new and will forever be new to man in an on-going world.

None of this counts against what in fact we do each day, each minute, in science, law, technology, education, recreation, personal relationships, as well as morality—sometimes better and sometimes worse: we come to justified definitions of our ideas or terms in accordance with what we have detected, within the range of our awareness of what there is in the universe. The idea that this is impossible, despite its often respectable sources, is absurd. Moreover, to do so is indispensible for human (personal as well as cultural) survival, not to mention for purposes of living a decent, meaningful, and *good* human life.

Space has been taken to make these points because so many people undercut our confidence (not just in ourselves but in human nature itself) by constantly referring to wide-scale disagreements, conflicts, and contradictions within mankind's store of ideas, especially about matters related to values, including morality and politics. Yet this reference and criticism is itself futile without the possibility of truth. Nor could the advice stemming from it make much sense, granted it may be *bad* advice in the final analysis, if we cannot tell the difference between what is right and wrong in the advice we receive.

But the above does not mean we always need to know the precise, exact, up-to-date definitions of our ideas. Things can be sufficiently understood without much reflection on the constituents of that understanding. Most of the time, hopefully more often than not, little need for definitional inquiries exists. Much of our studies, research, and work in general concern these issues, but we certainly have other interests not related to these.

Difficulties in our search for understanding can and do emerge. This could prompt efforts to justify how we make sense of the world. Why is that object better classified as a table than as a stool? Why call this a kitten instead of a cub? Why that a tree and not a bush? In science, where precision and accuracy become systematic goals, such efforts to justify classification are almost all-pervasive. Electrons and positrons must be identified and differentiated so as to preclude blunders in both theoretical and applied physics. Bees and wasps should not be mixed up if we are after a good honey supply.

We now reach our present concern. We *are* capable of focusing on our world—and on its people in order to understand how they differ from, or are similar to, the rest of what exists. In that way we can discover their nature; we can identify, to the best of our present abilities but still with great reliability if we keep matters well integrated, what it is to be a *human* being as such.

We are involved with the issue of man's nature day in and day out just through our encounters with people. We certainly do not need to be told that people differ from dogs; that they are unique among animals and living beings in general, because, for instance, they theorize about their lives, write books, build libraries, travel to the moon, and compose symphonies. Anyone past the age of two begins to realize this much.

Sometimes we meet with problems that are not solely within the realm of ethics or politics. These can require more precise and self-conscious understanding than what will accommodate us in everyday, ordinary cases. The issues of abortion and euthanasia, of the treatment of children, of organ transplants, of the consideration given to so-called human vegetables, as well as of the problem of what difference in people are simply acceptable and which, if any, should not be tolerated—all these require deeper than average reflection about the nature of man and his relationship to reality.

We need to know what we are dealing with. The question is: What will give us clear grounds for considering someone a human being, especially when we try to build on those grounds in order to explain human actions and institutions?

The relationship between an understanding of human nature, to the best of our present ability, and the kind of society we would work for should be evident. Serious disregard of the best we can do to date can harm us immensely, perhaps irreparably, in both personal and community contexts. The errors and evasions of people in these matters have been drastic. We need to know what things are required for people in order to live well, to lead successful human lives! So what answer is viable?

Human nature

What distinguishes people for what they are is their capacity to choose to conceptualize within their own individual range of intellectual abilities and circumstances, to initiate rational thought, to reason at will—to attend to the world via their specific kind of consciousness. Other living entities can be understood by reference to the conscious capacities they possess. We cannot say with certainty that no animal other than man can choose, since some animals, at least on some occasions, exhibit conscious conceptual capacities. But most, if not all, do so only when human beings prompt them to. Thus apes and porpoises have been taught to act in ways we know of only in connection with the specifically human faculties familiar to us. In these we must consider that man's interference prompted the relevant sort of behavior. But in man we can only invoke the idea of choice to account for these sort of actions. (To invoke God so as to explain matters here would lead to another form of determinism. And surely one could not consider that a significant alternative to Skinnerism.)

A feature of the argument against denying freedom indicates that choice is located in man's capacity to think. That argument hinges on our responsibility to *choose* between alternative accounts of human behavior. That responsibility, presupposed in the determinist's advocacy of his account, is meaningless unless we are free to assume it. Even Skinner's denial of consciousness, intention, purpose, and other mental capacities at a conceptual level points to what must be focused on in connection with human beings and affairs. Psychology in general, where people consult it in their personal or professional lives, points to man's involvement with matters that require thinking, planning, analyzing, valuation, appraisal, and the related emotions (remorse, regret, guilt, fear, etc.).

In the argument for human freedom what stood out was that denying freedom leads to the inconceivability of a differentiation between good and bad judgments, between objectivity and bias, honesty and prejudice—in short, the rationality of decisions and choices as well as the point of all these in human communication. One may object that "perhaps we cannot conceive of this; so what? That may well be the case." But to this, too, the answer must be that from within the framework of determinism not even such a hedging consideration could be rationally assented to; both assent and dissent would be equally justified. And that must lead to nonsense.

Perhaps we are free in the respect in which this analysis implies. But could we not be free in other respects also? Why restrict human freedom to man's rational capacity? The most direct answer is that actions, which are candidates for being considered free, presuppose judgment, planning, intention, purpose, and a host of other *mental* activities. For we are required to trace the freedom of an action to whatever feature distinguishes it from movement (behavior), namely that it involves the use of conceptualization at its inception (whether now or at an earlier time).

Branden puts this result very clearly:

> Man's greatest distinction from all other living species is the capacity to originate an action of his consciousness—the capacity to originate a process of abstract thought. (XXXI/59)

And he adds to this what amounts to a logical tie between the nature of man's mind and his unique stature as a moral agent, a living being with the capacity to choose between what is right and what is wrong:

> Man's unique responsibility lies in the fact that this process of thought, which is man's basic means of survival, must be originated volitionally. In man, there exists the power of *choice,* choice in the primary sense, choice as a psychologically irreducible natural fact.

> This freedom of choice is not a negation of causality, but a category of it, a category that pertains to man. A process of thought is not causeless, it is caused by a man. The actions possible to an entity are determined by the entity that acts—and the nature of man (and of man's mind) is such that it necessitates the choice between focusing and nonfocusing, between thinking and nonthinking. Man's nature does not allow him to escape this choice . . . (XXXI/59)

Science and human nature

Perhaps the above is still too much of a philosophical consideration of the issue of human choice and its relationship to man's place in nature, the realm of the special sciences. We ought to consider, incidentally, that the study of man's psychology is not in such a state of development that we can deny it certain excursions into philosophy. Perhaps such a study is more closely tied to philosophy than those carried out in other fields. (In a sense everything else man studies is either smaller or larger than human beings, so the units of measurement and vocabulary appropriate to studying man could turn out to be those we use in prescientific terminology, in everyday discourse. That is, provided we are careful and observant.)

But others than openly philosophically oriented psychologists have found the above to be a sensible, *scientifically* respectable account of the nature of the case under scrutiny. Roger W. Sperry, the renowned psycho-physicist and researcher of split-brain phenomena, provides us with additional observations that support the present line of argument. He notes that "Attempts to restore free will to the human brain by recourse to various forms of indeterminacy—physical, logical, emergent, or otherwise—have failed so far . . ." (XXV/86) He thus accepts Skinner's point against that theory of human freedom which argues for a capricious or spontaneous agent. But he adds that although, e.g., in his studies of the brain, some interpretations would conclude with a kind of determinism,

> . . . before we start drawing gloomy humanist deductions from this apparent inevitability [of a kind of determinism], concluding that moral responsibility is thereby removed or, on the other hand, simply rejecting science and determinism on emotional grounds, we should bear in mind a few additional points. In the present scheme, these points add up to the conclusion that if we really did have freedom of choice we might well prefer . . . to leave determinism in control, exactly as science postulates. It should be clear by now that in the brain model described [in Sperry's paper], man is provided in large measure with the mental forces and the mental ability to determine his own actions. This scheme thus allows a high degree of freedom from outside forces as well as mastery over the inner cellular, molecular, and atomic aspects of brain activity. Depending on the state of one's will power, the model also allows considerable freedom from lower-level natural impulses and even from occasional thoughts, beliefs, and the like, though not of course, from the whole complex. In other words, the kind of brain visualized here does indeed give man plenty of free will, provided we think of free will as self-determination. (XXV/87)

It will be recalled that Skinner rejects self-determination, yet never considers the evidence for it. From what Sperry (among others) has found, however, we get a scientifically coherent picture of man as a free agent yet a physical, psychological organism. No inconsistency between science and human freedom arises. Nor is an exclusion of human dignity, the moral element of man's life, required. Sperry is, without a doubt, an experimental scientist who deals with the behavior of human beings, including their brains. But of course this does not force him to accept Skinner's assumptions and limit himself in what he may conclude. (We may suppose that Skinner would therefore deny Sperry's qualifications.) Thus Sperry is not outside his scientific structures when he tells us

> This does not mean . . . that [man] is free from the forces of his own decision-making machinery. In particular, what this present model does not do is to free a person from the combined effects of his own thoughts, his own reasoning, his own feeling, his own beliefs, ideals, and hopes, nor does it free him from his inherited makeup or his lifetime memories. (XXV/87)

Contrary to Skinner and his school, as well as to the majority of so-called social scientists, science rightly understood (i.e., unrestricted by a false philosophy) advances a view of man in terms of which people can be free, can have the capacity to initiate action. Add to this the philosophical argu-

165

ment presented earlier *against* the position that denies human freedom, and the conclusion is obvious.

Mind, nature and science

To complete the picture we set out to paint in contrast to Skinner's "image of man," we need to return briefly to the mind/body (brain) identity theory. Earlier we offered critical comments only; we must now indicate the compatibility of the reality of mind, the unity of nature, and the possibility of a scientific study of man. The topic is a rich one and we shall only summarize it to provide the basis for rejecting Skinner's requirements before proceeding to a constructive view of human political affairs.

> The crucial question for mind/body theories is that of the materiality or immateriality of man's mind. A case could be made for saying that the mind is "material" if one means by "material": "that which is possessed by a material entity." On the other hand, if one means that to be "material" means to be "composed of atoms," then mind definitely is not, on this [non-Skinnerian] view, "material." It is not "composed of atoms," but rather [it is] the capacity of a particular living entity whose body is composed of atoms. (XXVI/26)

Bissell, whom we have quoted above, continues to outline the alternative theory in a later paper:

> The dual-aspect theory [of mind/body relation] holds that mental processes are actually certain physical brain processes *as we are aware of them introspectively*—that "mental" refers to the introspectable *aspects* of those particular brain processes. The mental aspects which are the object of introspection, are fully real, and not merely an illusion. (Our awareness of them is the form in which we are aware of certain brain processes extrospectively [i.e., when we examine with our senses that may be focused on the world outside ourselves] . . . And just as both visual perception and tactual perception are different but equally valid forms of apprehending real aspects of entities (such as their length or their surface), which can be correlated with one another; so, too, the dual-aspect theory maintains, are extrospection and introspection different but equally valid forms of apprehending real aspects of brain processes.) (XXIX/9)

In short, the mind is an aspect of man's organism, more specifically an aspect of the brain, which has correlated physical aspects as well. But the two cannot be reduced to one without losing sight of something that exists and may play a significant part in our understanding of the entity in question—in this case, man.

Skinner, basing his analysis on the empiricist theory of knowledge, cannot allow the reality of anything that is apprehended by way of introspection. So he denies the existence of mental life. Thereby behaviorism loses the capacity to deal not just with thinking, believing, theorizing, and other active intellectual pursuits, but with dreams and more subtle and equally psychologically significant aspects of human life as well.

166

In all this we must remember that the major alternative to Skinnerism appears to be the view that the human mind is outside the natural realm. And, if so, it is clearly inaccessible to scientific study. (For Skinner, however, more seems to be at stake. He does not like the fact of mental life because this puts man outside physical control by environmental contingencies, and therefore outside the control of behavioral technologists.) So to be scientific, most concerned are eventually led to reductive materialism. But, as Bissell remarks,

> Since a capacity is not "material" (in the sense of being composed of atoms), the alternative obviously is that it is "immaterial," although this in no way necessarily implies the view that the conscious capacities (mind) are somehow "supernaturally spiritual." (XXVI/27)

There is therefore no need to deny the fact that there is "only one inclusive and consistent over-all order of law," as Chein put it earlier, or the position of the monist who accepts the unity of nature, including the physical and the mental aspects of it. For these do not require that the multitudinous forms in which reality emerges and may be apprehended must be blocked out of view, and all that exists must be called physical or material. The latter rests on the assumption that the only way we may legitimately understand the many-faceted, multiaspectival reality which we encounter is by observation as taken in the narrow, Humean/Skinnerian sense of that term.

We could now go on to the problem of how the mind and the body relate to one another in such matters as wishing, feeling, and intending. But first we must consider one clue, provided by Bissell:

> . . . Now, with regard to volition, man's capacity for "free will" is merely the highest, most complex manifestation of a principle which can be *empirically* observed at all evolutionary levels: namely, the capacity for living organisms to *self-regulate their natural life processes.* Volition is, then, the capacity of human beings to regulate their consciousness. (XXVI/27)

None of this presupposes that nothing *more* can be learned about the nature of man. Obviously work has just begun toward a more precise conceptualization of how mind and brain as well as the nervous system and the rest of the human organism all relate to each other.

Nor is it easy sailing toward the desired discoveries, since it would be in violation of the best strictures of science to compel man to submit to experimentation. That would gain little of the needed understanding—only vicarious desires can be satisfied by learning of man's state in total compulsion, under constraints by others, with all the artificiality that produces. Science itself would be endangered if scientists could simply *compel* people to submit to tests; soon the biologists would subjugate the physicists, while the sociologists would put all of us in experimental cages. Skinner's idea that "A culture is very much like the experimental space used in the analysis of behavior" (I/145) comes close to conflicting with the requirements of science itself. But then morality applies to scientists, and when advice by a member of the scientific community contradicts morality, it is no wonder that his own best practices are threatened.

What the above discussion of the nature of human consciousness offers is not a closed story, but an emerging picture that will continually be filled in. A final drawing is not desired. We need the most consistent, up-to-date information, even about the areas that are still under dispute and those that are just coming into focus. So far we can conclude that the human mind is free to be used or neglected by the person, but details are still forthcoming.

This is where the present approach to the issue of human freedom and dignity adheres to science *and* naturalism in full. Despite Skinner's (as well as some of his opponents') constant allusions to the contrary, freedom does not imply something mysterious, unexplainable, incomprehensible, or supernatural. We need not rip man out of nature in order to accept something we can observe about him every day—that he makes choices, runs his life, makes blunders, succeeds, takes responsibility for his acts, or defaults on his capacity to do so in all the millions of variations we find everywhere there is human life. This neo-Aristotelian, dual-aspect (not simply dual-stuff) theory of the relationship between man's mind and the rest of his organism cannot be reconciled with Skinnerism. But neither does it require abandoning science. Man can act freely and responsibly, possess what Skinner calls "autonomy," and we can make perfectly good sense of the widespread, "prescientific" contention that he has a mind and can think, choose, believe, intend, and want—all with the sanction, even support, of science and philosophy.

Our presentation has not been all-inclusive. Many questions could be raised, objections countered, and arguments elaborated. But the aim has been to argue with and offer a viable alternative to Skinnerism. The questioning and the debate won't end here or elsewhere. In this and all other fields that are closely related to what we think of ourselves, our conduct, the society in which we live, and our prospects in all these areas, there will never be the universal peace and agreement some people long for regarding such matters. In a dynamic world—where time simply won't stand still to allow us to conclude the search for what we have *not* discovered and what is just emerging *to be* discovered—the utopian vision of a finally closed theory of anything, human behavior or metaphysics, can only misguide.

Some areas, for instance, which are still in the process of being developed are the fields of psychophysics and neurophysiology. Specifically, what is it by which the properties of mind might be measured? As Efron puts it in his discussion of measurement and perception:

> It is often claimed that consciousness is unmeasurable because it has no attributes such as mass, extension, charge, etc. which can be quantified in physical units. For this reason some philosophers have referred to it, pejoratively, as "the ghost in the machine." (XXXII/550)

168

Efron continues: "If it can be demonstrated that at least *one* attribute of mind *can* be measured in terms of the units used by physicists, then one of the more persistent attacks on the concept of mind can be definitively discredited." He then proceeds to outline the "series of experiments the purpose of which was to measure the duration of the perceptions of brief light flashes and tone bursts." By these experiments Efron demonstrates that he has "measured the duration of a perception," that is, "the duration of a mental event."

No doubt all sorts of work will ensue in the wake of this achievement. No doubt, also, some Skinnerians will conclude that it must be simply the fanatical responses of the defenders of freedom and dignity. These are the people with emotional instabilities and the like, who might best be shut off from society and exposed to some hearty schedules of (un)reinforcement to make them behave well.

But we need not pay much attention to what Skinnerians might *wish* to do, so long as we do not allow their "science" to become the official science of any government, on the model of Marxist-Leninist "science" that keeps recurring in the USSR whenever it is diplomatically feasible. (What with the renewed attack on intellectual liberty, as evidenced by the cries of help from Russian physicist Sakharov, American liberals have lost all support for their idea that cultural exchange is a sure way to loosening the dictatorial grip of the Party over the lives of the Russian people.) The fact that Skinner's ideas accommodate just the sort of planned society the Soviets are running will serve to combat any charge of "right-wing lunacy" concerning these matters.

Fortunately, in our society there is still some serious concern for freedom and dignity, including the right to free expression (however obnoxious the results may be for some to witness). Skinnerians as well as others are free to attempt to gain scientific respectability. (In fact, what with the government's program of funding selected scientific research, the Skinnerian establishment is now the beneficiary of a subtle form of censorship that tends to exclude support for work that would challenge Skinner's theories and proposals.) To the extent that it is a real possibility that Skinnerism becomes official science, the remaining protection of free (scientific) expression is threatened.

From science to freedom: Contra Skinner

What then is the result of our investigation into the relationship between freedom of choice and the view of man advanced by some of the scientists and philosophers who are at odds with Skinnerism?

In our overview of the nature of science and the concept of man consonant with it, we have arrived at important conclusions that plainly contradict what Skinner advocates. In contrast to his belief that man is passive, a mere reactor or respondent to stimuli, incapable of choice, we have seen that the opposite is consistent with the facts. Man is a being that can act, even though he has the choice to refrain from doing so and maybe *react* only. Human beings are capable of choice, even if they do not always exercise this capability. And the basic choice, one which each person with a relatively healthy brain can make, consists of the position one might take on the continuum between a full *conceptual* mental focus and total inattention to the world.

The emphasis on "conceptual" is important since people can be *made* to focus on the world perceptually and by way of their senses. Stimuli do produce or evoke sensory and perceptual responses without the need for a conscious choice. Moreover, once a person has learned to master certain forms of conceptual awareness as a well-developed skill, it is possible for him to be prompted to think about something. We can all observe how we keep thinking of something even though in some respect we would rather put the matter out of our minds. Our thinking of the past, or our failure to have thought about some issues that in fact concern us, can determine what we will think and do later on. But the point is that certain basic mental processes must be initiated: the function of the initiation is to activate these processes and to prepare them to operate in certain circumstances. At the sign of danger most people, even the most thoughtless, will respond with some degree of attention. But earlier one had to learn of danger, to gain an understanding of its nature, so as to recognize it as such in some particular case. Branden states the general point clearly:

> The process by which sensations are integrated into percepts is automatic; the integration of percepts into concepts is not. It is a volitional process that man must initiate, sustain and regulate. (XXXI/34)

We have seen also that this contention is consistent with a scientific approach to the study of human consciousness. That approach is not what Skinner believes it to be. According to Skinner we must start with the assumption that man is unfree, that all things can engage in only one type of causation, and that there is only one kind of thing in the universe, namely, matter in motion.

In the present view we are not justified in making such assumptions and in fact the evidence conflicts with them. Rocks, flowers, worms, dogs, and human beings are all part of nature, but that does not lead to the conclusion that they are all one type and kind of thing which simply *appear* to be different. In the study of human affairs we must recognize man's distinction in nature, just as in botany we must acknowledge what makes plants what they are. This helps avoid many confusions, among which are the mixup of zoos and botanical gardens!

The Skinnerian and other reductionist "scientific" approaches to human affairs have led many students astray. Efron puts it like this:

> . . . . The phenomena of consciousness must be understood *before* one can hope to 'explain' them in terms of neural action. The attempt by many neurophysiologists to reverse this order—to study the neural mechanisms underlying

170

perception prior to any adequate definition or conceptualization of perception—is doomed to failure. (XXXIV/171)

And we can add that without an understanding that we possess our type of consciousness we cannot comprehend the bulk of man's behavioral mechanism, especially where verbal communication, planning and the most important as well as the problematic features of human life are concerned.

The widely held fear that free will contradicts the possibility of a science of psychology is unwarranted. That fear stems not from any actual practical difficulties in dealing with people by accepting them as capable of choice— even the most ardent behaviorist does that, despite all his theoretical lip service to the contrary. There are hundreds of behaviorists and determinists who still engage in moral rebuke, blaming, and punishment despite what their "science" requires. Rather, the fear is part and parcel to the acceptance of the reductive materialist philosophical doctrine, that normative enterprise where, if you do not deny free will, you should not consider yourself within the scientifically respectable domain.

But consciousness, free or not, can be studied. "Its manner of function exhibits specific principles or laws which it is the task of psychology to discover and identify. None of this is contradicted by the fact that the exercise of man's reason is volitional." (XXXI/62) Branden continues:

> Just as the driver of an automobile can steer the car in a chosen direction, but cannot alter or infringe the mechanical laws by which the car functions— so man can choose to focus, to aim his cognitive faculty in a given direction, but cannot alter or infringe the psychological laws by which his mind functions. If a man does not steer his car properly, he has no choice about the fact that he will end in a smash-up; neither has the man who does not steer his mind properly. (XXXI/62)

The fear that free will prevents prediction is also unwarranted. We do not deny that someone is free just to be able to justify our prediction that at parties he is very likely to be withdrawn. It is because of what he has chosen to do, to think, to value, that he will act in certain ways in certain circumstances.

> . . . to the extent that one understands the principles by which man's mind operates, one can predict the psychological consequences of given ideas, values, conclusions, attitudes and thinking policies. One can predict, for example, that a man of authentic self-esteem will find intellectual stagnation intolerable; that a man who regards sex, life and himself as evil will not be attracted to a woman of intelligence, independence and guiltless self-confidence, will not feel at ease and "at home" with her romantically; that a man whose guiding policy is "Don't antagonize anyone," will not be the first to stand up for and champion a radical new idea or theory.

One cannot predict with certainty that these men will not change their thinking. Therefore, one's predictions must take the form of "all other things being equal," or "Assuming no new factors enter the situation." But this is true of prediction in the physical sciences also. (XXXI/63)

What emerges then may be summarized as follows: in line with the broader-than-Skinnerian conception of the character of science and causality, we are entitled to conclude that human beings by their nature can choose freely. This they are able to do in their capacity to initiate the functions of their distinctive type of consciousness; they can choose to think or they can refrain from thinking; this choice is open to them within the limitations of their biological organism (e.g., while not experiencing total fatigue), barring brain or equally relevant organic damage. It is this fact that defines people as the kind of living being that they are. The phenomenon of borderline cases—e.g., people in very bad shape either physically or mentally (or both)—is not denied, just as one need not deny borderline cases in other areas where definitions, i.e., the knowledge of the nature of something, is required.

First, we developed the case for a certain definition of man—i.e., that any individual with the capacity for volitional consciousness is properly said to have a human nature; next we advanced toward a consideration of some of the central ethical and political issues touched on by Skinner in the works under consideration. I have avoided most distinctively psychological issues. I noted earlier that what psychologists are called upon to do in applying their knowledge and skill—to help people with their problems in connection with their conscious and emotional capacities—points to the need to reject Skinner's view of *what* it is that this admittedly infant science *must* study to be scientific. Whatever a particular theorist or therapist may say about his own life, we can all observe, in the broad sense of that term, what it is that generally prompts people to seek psychological or psychiatric help: problems in living, in the most general way that this is meant, arising out of man's specific form of consciousness.

In the main the goal here has been to set the stage. By providing a scientifically supportable, if not conclusively justified, idea of human nature, it is now possible to investigate whether freedom and dignity can thus be made sense of. The next task will be to see what follows from the above for morality and politics, the realms of human life in which freedom and dignity make their appearance.

7

In Defense of
Political Liberty

SKINNER'S ATTACK ON political liberty is no secret to anyone. Although there are some who would interpret him as a defender of freedom, this is not possible. His advocacy of expert human engineering, even if only through benevolent direction, i.e., positive reinforcement, makes his stand on this issue quite clear. (V/52)

What exactly *is* political liberty and how can we show that it is something best suited to human community life? What are the connections between man's nature and the value of political liberty?

We have seen that there is *nothing unscientific* about man's capacity for choice, and we have also noted that the most basic, irreducible choice a man can make is to activate his conceptual consciousness. Based on this consideration we will outline a theory of human rights. Such a theory is needed to establish that man should live in a free society where his rights are protected and preserved. In presenting this theory we can rely on some work in the field of political philosophy well known to anyone familiar with the American political tradition. The present argument will not be quite the same as John Locke's, primarily because Locke's idea of what it is to have a nature—as in human nature—requires some modification. We will nevertheless conclude with a reasonably complete defense of Locke's belief that political liberty is indeed right for people, certainly more so than the survival of some unspecified culture with Skinnerians at the helm.

Freedom and Morality

We come now to the idea that human beings are morally responsible, certainly a notion as alien to Skinnerians as possible. The idea of moral

173

responsibility means that while each person is free to choose between various alternative courses of action, there are among these ones he *ought to* select and others he *ought to* avoid. Precisely because man is the distinctive kind of entity he is and not one that is infinitely malleable, not all actions are right for him to engage in. Morality investigates and defines the principles of conduct by which human beings, just by virtue of their humanity, ought to live. It is the field of study that seeks to identify the most basic values of human life, those pertinent to all people at all times; thus morality seeks to identify the virtues, what is right and wrong for people to do in any situation and epoch, by reference to certain basic values.

Skinner has chosen the survival of the culture as the highest value by which all people ought to guide their lives. He asks that all of us be induced, conditioned, and controlled to promote that goal. It is this that Skinner counts as the central moral goal and value. It is his highest value for all human beings. This reveals his moral point of view, his ethics. It does not, by any means, reveal the validity and truth of the ethics of culturalism. (We have seen that he provides no justification for his selection.)

Man's capacity for choice has been seen to be consistent with good scientific procedures. Science as such cannot speak against volition—although some philosophies of science seem to demand that scientists reject its very possibility. And *science* cannot deny that some choices can be right and others wrong for human beings as such. The possibility of morality then is left wide open by science per se. Psychology must accept this, although it does not mean that a psychologist may not at times conclude that a specific person's capacity to choose has been damaged or even destroyed. That however must always be a discovery, not a dogma.

The above leads us to take a different view of explanations of human behavior, of answers to the question "Why did he do that?" If reference to reinforcing stimuli, genetic make-up, and antecedent factors of the environment will not suffice (and in Skinner they do not) then where do we seek explanations? Not in the case of the sick, the retarded, or the physically impaired, but in the case of the healthy person with no organic brain disease and no entrenched psychological dysfunction.

The point of view adopted here will be that which has been defended and explained so well by A. R. Louch. Louch's treatment of these issues (without recourse to mysticism or antiscience) establishes the following conclusion concerning our questions:

> . . . when we offer explanations of human behavior, we are seeing that behavior as justified by the circumstances in which it occurs. Explanation of human action is moral explanation. In appealing to reasons for acting, motives, purposes, intentions, desires and their cognates, which occur in both ordinary and technical discussions of human doings, we exhibit an action in the light of circumstances that are taken to entitle or warrant a person to act as he does. (XXXV/4)

This is consistent with our view that people are conscious, rational agents whose capacity to initiate action consists in their generating judgments, including the understanding of circumstances, in the light of purposes, including what they ought to do as persons. To explain human behavior then, requires reference to both the circumstances in which people live, their histories, the possibilities available to them, and what they have done with all these. Their doings are a crucial aspect of understanding their own lives, and their mental actions—reasoning, judgments, evaluations, cultivation of desires, styles, and habits—constitute a central factor in answering the question "Why?" concerning anything they do.

Since this is the respect in which they are free and responsible to act as human beings should, it is evident that our explanation of human action will be morally significant. It will be necessary to view what people do in the light of certain standards of conduct. A moral point of view will either be implicit or explicit in considering why people do what they do. Even those who deny that people should be evaluated morally and who treat man as a passive entity—with no responsibility for what he does—cannot help but implicate some and commend others as they discuss human conduct. (Skinner's references to some people as emotionally unstable and to others as capable of advancing the survival of the culture carry moral implications strong enough for any country preacher.)

The implications of these contentions and conclusions are many. We find that such fields as sociology, economics, and especially history, would have to undergo serious changes in order to live up to the view of man advanced here. (Locke once noted that ". . . with the reading of history, I think the study of morality should be joined. I mean not the ethics of the Schools . . . but such as . . . the New Testament teaches, wherein a man may learn how to live, which is the business of ethics" [XXXVI/899].) If what has been said is correct, and it certainly seems reasonable to believe so, those who advocate matters of concern to people ought to at least be aware of this frame of reference. It makes no difference for its validity whether or not they refuse to accept it. The mere existence of disagreement about what is right and wrong, good and evil does not prove the absence of truth; it even presupposes possible agreement although it can point up that such matters are not always agreed upon. (For example, in science there is ample disagreement also. No realm of existence escapes the fate of people disputing its true nature. Morality, which is perhaps the closest topic to the inquirer himself, has the best chance of being widely disputed.)

What we are concerned with is: What relevance does the image of man here advanced have for the findings of political theory? What does political theory try to understand and explain? What questions does it try to answer?

We contend that Skinner rests his condemnation of the ideas of freedom and dignity on a supposed scientific analysis, but that was no more scientific than it was an analysis. We have presented a critique of Skinner but

175

we are now considering whether an alternative approach can be found—what it is and what are its implications concerning such matters as freedom and dignity. Our conclusions thus far have certainly left room for free will and morality within a scientifically respectable framework. But we must now ask how this bears upon politics—the design of a culture, to use Skinner's own phrase. Skinner gives us plenty of hints, so let us follow them up.

Human rights and morality

Skinner notes that the libertarian is concerned with human rights. He tells us that "Life, liberty, and the pursuit of happiness are basic rights. But they are the rights of the individual and were listed as such at a time when the literatures of freedom and dignity were concerned with the aggrandizement of the individual. They have only a minor bearing on the survival of a culture." (I/172) And he is partially correct. He seems to have a clear enough idea of what he is opposing, even though he does not really contend with any of the better arguments in its support. The individual has only recently come to center stage in political theory. Emphasizing his importance within the organized political community seemed to be important to those who realized that man is the most vulnerable of the real, living, existing beings on whom a political/legal system has a direct effect. In some sense of course the survival of a certain *kind* of culture is also connected with these rights, namely the kind that concerns itself with the protection of the life and liberty of people. But the survival of such a culture is valuable only because the individuals within it can flourish. Cultures have existed throughout human history, but fortunately only a few of the worst kind have lasted very long. Nonetheless, even today there are cultures whose existence is of no value to the people, except perhaps to some groups, and only at a great cost to others who should not have to shoulder it. (It is not at all apparent that one class of people that keeps another class in subservience is even a beneficiary in anything but comparative terms. One wonders if oppressors, such as members of fascist or communist hierarchies, would be better off if all people could enjoy their rights without fear of them—and without keeping them in fear.)

But aside from these points against Skinner, we have already seen that he never bothers to justify the survival of a culture as the primary value. He simply asserts it and declares that no explanation is needed for why this ought to be everyone's "pure concern." Nor does he *prove* that concern with human rights really expresses an aggrandizement of the individual. In fact it need not do this at all. Human rights simply provide the intellectual justification for protecting the individual's moral autonomy in a social context; as Rand points out,

> "Rights" are a moral concept—the concept that provides a logical transition from the principles guiding an individual's actions to the principles guiding his relationship with others—the concept that preserves and protects individual

morality in a social context—the link between the moral code of a man and the legal code of a society, between ethics and politics. *Individual rights are the means of subordinating society to moral law.* (IX/92)

The idea of natural rights or individual human rights is now in total disrepute in our world. Skinner is not the first to have cast aspersions, just as freedom and dignity did not suffer attack at his hands only. Leo Strauss made this clear in his *Natural Right and History:*

Whatever might be true of the thought of the American people, certainly American social science has adopted the very attitude toward natural right which, a generation ago, could still be described, with some plausibility, as characteristic of German thought. The majority among the learned who still adhere to the principles of the Declaration of Independence interpret these principles not as expressions of natural right but as an ideal, if not as an ideology or a myth. Present-day American social science . . . is dedicated to the proposition that all men are endowed by the evolutionary process or by a mysterious fate with many kinds of urges and aspirations, but certainly with no natural right. (XXXVII/2)

These words were uttered in 1953. Since that time, in the intellectual atmosphere the idea of natural human rights has been abandoned to an even greater extent.

Yet no one can doubt the impact of the partial implementation of human rights in America's legal system. That America's geographical, climatic, or other humanly unrelated conditions cannot explain its development both in power and economic strength has been demonstrated by many. Numbers of places enjoy similar conditions with people starving and economies faltering. The American economy is still the lifeblood of most of the world's industry and commerce, even though it has been crippled by decades of bureaucratic meddling. And while problems abound in the U.S. to almost the same extent as they do elsewhere—and in some aspects of people's lives even more—the question as to where a good man would make out better, in the U.S. or elsewhere (provided his adjustment to the culture would not stand in his way) would have to be answered "In the United States." This does not deny that other cultures have values which may not be found in the American one. In the main, however, the political system which has at least given lip service to human rights, and has actually implemented the provisions that follow from recognizing them in many cases (especially in the criminal courts and the market place), has flourished in one respect better than any other: the moral excellence of each individual has been for him alone to achieve in the majority of cases, at least where human rights have been recognized.

Of course the United States' legal system is not consistently guided by consideration of man's rights. This is one reason why Skinner's emphasis on the literature of freedom is both crucial and unfair. Skinner does not mention that the culture no longer emphasizes freedom and dignity. But he seems to realize that they are powerful ideas: to make any more headway toward destroying people's insistence on at least some measure of freedom, these ideas must be made to look completely invalid, useless, disreputable.

But in spite of their being ignored in academia and inconsistently implemented by government, why are human rights so important? A legal system's basic features are much like the basic principles of any system of thought and action: *all* aspects of a given field are or should be (depending on the nature of the system) organized in line with its basic principles. Inquiries, calculations, corrections, speculations, research, development, revisions, and many other activities of the people involved are guided by those principles, or paradigms, as one philosopher of science calls them.

Human rights are candidates for the position of fundamental political principles, for organizing the actions of mankind within a human community: *if the people accept that human rights are best suited for this position, the field of politics is most likely to be adjusted accordingly.*

Whatever human rights may be, they are politically, *not* ethically, fundamental. They pertain to human *interactions,* whereas ethics pertains to human conduct in *or* outside the social context. To expect considered agreement with claims about human rights requires the understanding and acceptance of an ethical viewpoint. Ethics is more basic than politics, and a political principle requires, ultimately, an ethical justification.

In the present discussion this last point must be considered understood. Unfortunately too many thinkers have politicized ethics enormously; this is the result of those views of morality in terms of which only *interaction* is ethically relevant. Human rights pertain only to what ought or ought not to be done in social/political circumstances. Moral principles can also cover conduct that is socially irrelevant.

At this stage we need first to explain where we now stand with human rights—"we" being the prevailing academic/political climate, left and right. Next, the reasons why human rights are so unacceptable to people in relevant fields—philosophy, political science, legal theory, and so on must be explored.

Against human rights

Since its recognition the concept of natural rights has been under severe criticism. Many political theorists from Jeremy Bentham on have held natural rights to be mythical in one way or another. Bentham argued that the idea of absolute natural rights, the sort John Locke and the U.S. Declaration of Independence referred to, stultifies legal reform. Marx maintained that such rights are disguised privileges of the capitalist or bourgeois class. Legal positivists from John Austin to Alf Ross have argued that since no statements about what is morally or politically right or good could be derived from facts of nature, there could be no natural rights. More recently such philosophers as Kai Nielsen (XXXIX/594) and Gregory

Vlastos[13] have called natural rights into question, the former claiming that in no sense can we make the idea intelligible, the latter arguing merely that we must substitute *prima facie* for natural/human rights. (*Prima facie* rights are supposed to be in effect so long as no stronger moral considerations present themselves, in which case the claim that one has a right must be considered untrue.)

The traditional natural rights theory is not one that can be completely defended with success. We will see later why this is so. Nevertheless it has provided the most prominent support for man's rights. The gist of the theory is that *people in a social/political context, simply because they are people, are entitled to certain actions or restraints from one another.* These entitlements are morally justifiable. They ought to obtain in society! They warrant action that will ensure that everyone receives them—that is, they warrant the construction of a legal system in accordance with them. *Therefore, we* ought to *institute such a system!*

But let's first consider the case against *natural* rights and how well it does. It started within the philosophy of David Hume, although earlier thinkers, e.g., Machiavelli, had suggested it. All subsequent arguments against human rights rest, however, pretty much on what Hume said.

Hume, the absolute skeptic, held the view that nothing about the world can be known and only our subjective sensory experiences are valid. But he forgot that a total skeptic need not bother to justify moral skepticism also. So he advanced a famous argument for this position: since all statements of fact contain the copula "is" and all valuations (moral, political, and aesthetic judgments) contain the copula "ought to," the latter could surely not be derived from the former. It would be logically improper to do that. But since only "is" statements can be used to refer to *nature,* natural rights —i.e., moral or political judgments which are right by virtue of a justification based on nature—are impossible. That, in essence, is the argument against not only natural rights but all attempts to prove moral or political principles.

Hume did not argue against human rights *per se* but against all moral judgments allegedly justified on rational grounds. All major moral skeptics or critics of moral knowledge have relied on some feature of Hume's skeptical philosophy. Consider G. E. Moore[14] who gave us the famous naturalistic fallacy that is supposed to underlie all attempts to prove what is right or wrong, good or bad. Or consider Bertrand Russell who once viewed ethics and politics as necessarily entirely outside the realm of philosophy or science—despite his concommittant fervent political activism (or maybe because of it). For Russell, as for A. J. Ayer and many other well-known contemporary philosophers, our judgments about whether this or that is the right thing to do, or whether Joe or Harry is the more deserving human being, can only be expressions of feelings, sentiments, attitudes—expressions that have such purposes as goading people.

Among these emotivists Margaret Macdonald,[15] who wrote on human rights specifically, claimed that these rights are mere expressions of our favorable sentiments for equality, justice, freedom, and so on. And they have no prospects of being true or right, merely more or less well supported, somewhat as our taste in wines or pop songs might be. A few philosophers and people concerned with political theory have supported human rights, but they have been in a meager minority.

In the main, human rights are now generally regarded as pragmatic metaphors or accidental ingredients (ideals) of America's political history. The exception, interestingly, is that when people want something very badly they contend that they have an inalienable, absolute, universal human right to it. But few prominent political theorists conceive of human rights as principles that are even in a remote sense inalienable, absolute, and universal. As Kai Nielsen puts it in his paper "Skepticism and Human Rights":

> As much as I value a respect for human beings, all human beings great and small, good and bad, stupid and reflective . . . it seems to me quite evident that we do not know that there are any universal human rights. (XXXIX/594)

How to establish human rights

In a recent work, however, M. P. Golding spells out clearly what would need to be accomplished in order to establish the existence of human rights. He says that

> For someone to ask me to concede something to him as a human right is implicitly to ask whether I admit the notion of a human community at large, which transcends the various special communities of which I am a member; whether I admit him as a member of this large community; and whether I admit a conception of a good life for this community. Without these admissions on my part I will not allow the pertinence of his claiming; once I make these admissions I must allow the pertinence of his claiming. (XXXIX/549)

Golding's requests are the traditional ones, of course: he asks for a *definition* of the concept human being—"a notion of a human community" amounts to just that; he wants to have it spelled out *how* one might ascertain if someone or other actually belongs to this community, i.e., whether he is a human being; and he wants a *standard* for judging some human community as good, which means he wants a moral standard by which to judge people and their communities.

When Golding talks of "admission," he is not talking about his own particular, individual, and subjective admission of course. He means "admission" in the sense of "admissible on rationally defensible, justifiable grounds." That and nothing else will do the job. (Of course, not even reason *will work with everyone.*)

Now, one problem with *natural* rights theory is that it does not escape the skeptics' wrath; natural rights and law theories are characteristically *closed* systems. Propositions or doctrines based on them cannot admit the *possibility* of revision—all past, present, *and* future circumstances must be accountable in terms of them. And this is impossible because it requires that such theories should treat problems in all conceivable *and* possibly conceivable cases; it requires the point of view of omniscience. No human being could succeed in developing such a point of view—and since natural rights and law theorists have traditionally aimed at that, they must fail.

Initially these views damage any attempt to develop a viable natural or human rights theory by making it impossible to *define* anything. The definition of "human being" is impossible if it has to state the eternal, final, unchangeable nature of man. Thus the first requirement Golding poses cannot be met within the framework of traditional naturalist political theory. That failure undercuts the prospect of satisfying his other requirements via that point of view. If we cannot define man we certainly cannot make use of the definition in particular cases. Nor can we ascertain what is right or good for people *as human beings* since we cannot know what is characteristic about being human and, therefore, what is characteristically right or good for people as such and for their communities.

The alternative, however, need not be abandonment of our program. The underlying theory of knowledge is at fault, actually. Any view of knowledge that demands of people that they know *all* before they make reliable judgments about the finite amount that they must manage in their lives, needs to be questioned. And for several decades philosophers *have* questioned these demands. (But they have not gone much beyond the groundwork; they have not revised normative theory.) The result of the constant and ensuing effort is a contextual view of knowledge. Briefly, it holds that to know something is to identify it in terms of the context, i.e. the best evidence and information available to mankind. Later it might be important to update or revise what was once said about some aspect of the world, but at any time the best we can do is all we can be asked to do. Definitions by this view, as Barry Stroud suggests, may be conceived on the model of "rails that . . . we have traveled . . . and we can extend them beyond the present point by depending on those that already exist." These rails, however, do not "stretch into infinity and compel us always to go in one and only one way; but neither is it the case that we are not compelled at all. . . . In order for the rails to be navigable they must be extended in smooth and natural ways; how they are to be continued is to that extent determined by the route of those rails which are already there. . . ." (XL/496) In other words, how we define a concept is neither arbitrary nor unchangeable. So the skeptic's most powerful objection against definitions, namely that they simply cannot be expected to hold forever—not, that is, on any rational basis—is overcome.

181

Before moving on to the issue of how people make use of definitions, let us recall the definition of "man" (the concept "human being") we provided earlier in this work. Although many people *will disagree* with such a definition, *that* is not enough to knock it down. A well-defended definition isn't hurt by blindly stubborn opposition, except socially.

People are most parsimoniously characterized, we noted before, as rational living beings who can choose some of what they will do. What we know about people is intelligible *in terms* of such a definition. Language, creativity, originality, complexity, evaluation, responsibility, remorse, failure, pride, criticism, error, judgment, self-consciousness, freedom, dignity, and the rest all presuppose the existence of man's basic characteristics of choice and rational capacity. We need not argue the point further; it is philosophically, scientifically, and common-sensically justified (aside from being obvious).

This definition of man is not *static* or timelessly *fixed*. This is why most of us are willing to consider alternative definitions. Many books, philosophical theories, anthropological treatises, even science fiction stories ask us to take seriously the possibility, although not quite the probability, that human nature has changed.

The above would have to satisfy Golding's first point: the human community consists of those who are members of the class designated by the concept "human being," defined as "living beings capable of choice and rationality." This would seem to hold, to the best of our knowledge. Let us leave the issue of borderline cases for later.

Now to Golding's request for an account of *how we* must go about identifying members of the class of human beings. Our discussion of man's nature and consciousness should help to answer this point. To identify anything, including membership in some class, requires rational thought, differentiation, integration. This, in turn, must be something that a person does *on his own*. That, again, is the focal point of his freedom, his nature as a choosing, acting *agent*. All intentional action depends on judgments made either implicitly or explicitly, rapidly or via painful deliberation. Free judgment *must* lie at the source of intentional, free action. Thus, in order to organize our activities vis-a-vis what there is in our world, we must judge. And some of our judgments will concern people—including whether this or that entity we come across is a human being.

Usually we handle the problem of identification in a relatively routine fashion. Only when complex issues need treatment does it arise whether someone is doing all that he can to succeed—or at least to do his best. In difficult cases of identification, as with borderline cases, we may not have at just that time precise rules or exact criteria. Yet we need not accept the skeptic's view that there is no way to handle these cases. Anyone who commits himself to the task of solving problems, and thus to the underlying view that *the world is coherent,* can generate the knowledge and understanding needed to make the best possible decisions! This could involve, for example, whether some strange entity is to be judged a human

182

being or an alien; or in different kinds of cases, a deceased or a fetus. Unless we assume the necessary irrationality of either ouselves or the world, the basic method can always be appealed to: logic. But the *effort* of making decisions is the individual's own.

One answer to Golding then is that *the means* of reaching an answer to the question "Is this a human being?"—should this question arise (and it does only rarely)—is *thinking*, rational conceptualization. It is not a formula, of course, but a practice or skill that people must undertake by choice.

Golding's last request is the most difficult. He asks for an entire moral theory—a rationally justified moral point of view, a standard of conduct for human beings. We shall outline such a theory and this should indicate that such a program may be manageable. Later we shall consider it in greater detail, when we examine the nature of human dignity.

The question of morality involves what criterion of truth we must appeal to in order to justify such claims as "A is a good man," "B is an evil man," "X is the right way to act," "Y is the wrong thing to do." (Such judgments, too, may be implicit when made by acting individuals, or explicit when offered as a considered assessment of someone else.)

With respect to other matters we make judgments as to excellence, worthiness, failure, and such by reference to some *purpose* or goal we take such things to serve. A good knife cuts well, a bad engine burns up oil, and a mediocre dancer occasionally steps on his partner's feet. But what can be construed as man's purpose so we can judge whether A does well and B poorly at it? What is a human being's central goal?

The Aristotelian notion of success at living *as a human being* is the most sensible candidate. Each man's goal is to live both as his humanity *and* his own individuality indicate will suit him best. That, if achieved, may be considered living a *good* human life. And if done on one's own, by choice, then one has done an excellent job of being a human being. *A good man does the best he can with his life as a human being.*

Spelled out this means that living one's life rationally and by one's own choice makes a man good. Clearly, living requires the use of one's reason, since knowledge is necessary for even the barest survival and since learning requires thought. Living *well*, then, requires a good deal of the same. And the purpose of man is to succeed at life, to be happy. This must mean—alternatives having had to rely on less than reasonable notions—that for each person his moral excellence consists of his putting forth *his best possible effort* toward living his (human) life well, i.e., to learn how best he can succeed in life. More than this need not be said at this point (since that would prejudge the specific circumstances of people) except for the spelling out of some general virtues that tie in with one's humanity. But these we will not go into; most of us know them as honesty, integrity, and the like (although arguments would be needed to work them out in detail). It bears noting that much of this has been worked on by Aristotelians and Objectivists.

If the above is right, we have gone some distance toward satisfying

183

Golding's last request. But we must go further. Thus far we have discussed individual excellence only, and Golding asks us to spell out the good life for a human community.

It would appear that any community that will enhance to the maximum the likelihood of its members aspiring to and achieving success in living, i.e., moral excellence, may be considered a good human community. The alternative, again, would seem absurd—hindering the moral growth of its members cannot render a community worth much. It is at this point that we can detect the emergence of human rights; a human right connects what is morally good with what is politically right. As Ayn Rand put it, *"Individual rights are the means of subordinating society to moral law."* (IX/92)

What this means is that human rights are *the* social conditions that when established *can/will* (and do) enable people to go about the business of living a good life. These social conditions, however, require the actions or sanctions of people. (One cannot have the human right to something or to do something which is outside of human control to provide, establish, or maintain.) Golding is correct in suspecting that without some idea of the good life for a human community there cannot be an intelligible notion of human rights. Conditions must be *right for* something, *good for* someone. And human rights are those social conditions that are right for people just because they are people.[16] The actions or abstentions of others establish them as principles *in practice*. This, in turn, is done through a legal system— and the criterion by which such a system must be judged or evaluated is how well it protects and perserves human rights.

Liberty and rights

Freedom of the sort Skinner attacks (or maintains is at best an illusion in the face of man's total lack of autonomy) includes the sort referred to with the idea of political liberty. He does use the term to mean free will as well, but that is not our concern now. Political liberty is the type of freedom we have a human right to.

An important element of being free in this sense is that no one is justified in treating you as if you were his property. People as such, persons, are not the property of anyone or anything. People may be owners of various *things* but not of other people; if it is tried it is unjustified and should be prevented or even punished.

The right to life means that the life one has is one's own to be governed; that one is, at some point of maturity, an end in oneself and should not be used by others without one's permission. To have a right to something is to have authority over its use and disposal. Thus one's life cannot be conceived of as being owned by someone else without some imagined conception of the innate superiority of a certain group of others. The others we are concerned with are people. (If God could exist, his superiority may

184

or may not entitle some to act toward others by using them. But if God exists, then that still must be proven, and no proof exists that God's words are best interpreted to mean that *some* people should use *other people*. What is required is proof—good reasons, not claims.)

Skinner's god is the survival of the culture. That is what he invokes to justify some people's claims to exercise control over others. But the idea of freedom stands in the way of such claims. If Skinner could justify either his attribution of supreme value to the survival of the culture or that that superior value entitles anyone to impose himself and his ideas on others by force, then perhaps some attention to his political/social proposals would be warranted.

No one can own another, whether in the name of God or of science, culture, art, or ecology. Yet so many try over and over again to invoke such supposedly superior values on behalf of their violation of other people's rights! It is difficult enough to make sure that this or that action does not involve limiting another's liberty; to also have to battle against those who want to deny its existence is unfortunate.

Yet the libertarian has to recognize that people often want solutions to problems without considering the consequences these have on areas such as human liberty. Even when people would never consider it a solution to overpopulation to kill off fifty million people, they do consider related and not so dissimilar means of producing "solutions" quite valid.

From the fact, however, that people must *make* a good life for themselves in whatever circumstances (which can be filled with contingencies, complicated factors, etc.), it follows that Skinner's notion is confused. Indeed there *is* good reason "why progress toward a world in which people may be automatically good should be impeded." (I/63) It is that such "progress" goes nowhere. The goal is illusory and its pursuit can and often does have disastrous results.

If the philosophy of science does not lead us to accept that people are impotent reactors, and if science itself seems to require just the opposite possibility as a good one to work with, then we have nothing even close to a justification for interfering with people's lives against their will when they have done no demonstrable wrong to others. (In case of the latter we design a legal system to protect and preserve human rights, including the right to liberty.)

There are many ways in which people can be influenced, even to do something that is bad for them. Selling, advising, suggesting, persuading, convincing, proving, cajoling are indeed sometimes misused by people for purposes of getting others to do what can turn out to be wrong. Sometimes it is done intentionally. But none of these compare with enforcement by law, i.e., legalized use of force, for getting people to go against their interests. It is the worst means by which to "get people to be good." Psychologists of the clinical variety have supplied some evidence for this: the nature of a free economy and the entire atmosphere of a free society versus one that practices oppression, arbitrary power, and so on indicate that human freedom is what makes human excellence possible. This can vary, and sometimes the snobbish will despair of what the middle class or the lower class or whatnot *value*. Marxists are appalled that individual judgment not *social* use is what governs supply and demand. But they cannot make sense of social use without taking into account, first and foremost, what people want and judge to be good for themselves.

Skinner worries about punishment as a concommittant to freedom and responsibility. And no doubt there is a good deal of question about the consequences of punishment. Sometimes, in some circumstances, punishment is meted out with no justification. Even when it is justified it can be entirely unproductive of anything detectably worthwhile. It is obvious that where it does not belong it should not be used.

But one must go on record to members of a community intent on fostering liberty and virtue that when some people obstruct others in their attempts to live by their own judgment, they should not profit from this. A legal system should serve to protect against this happening. The idea of punishment here is that doing wrong to another against his will and consent is contrary to membership in a *free* community of human beings. It is destructive of it. Showing that this is important and *intolerable* is part of what punishment should achieve. Thus being punished is being limited in one's actions within a community but by one's own *consent*—implicit in what one has done in violating another's right. Herbert Morris, professor of philosophy and law at UCLA, has argued eloquently that punishment is the right of someone who has violated other's rights. (XXXIX/475-501)

What the specific nature of punishment must be and where it is due are separate issues, more the purview of legal theory than political philosophy. Suffice it to conclude for now that the right to liberty is not violated by punishing someone when that person has voluntarily broken a law which serves to protect people's rights. That is important to remember, since Skinner trades a lot on the fact that punishment can be abused, misapplied, and that sometimes innocent people, doing something no one should be punished for, receive "punishment." The line between punishment and brutality must be clearly identified before condemning or defending either.

Political liberty is a human right that Skinner attacks without justification. It is also a human right that has reasonably sound support within political thought. We are justified in our belief that human beings, by their nature, have the right to life, liberty, and the pursuit of happiness (including ownership). Here we have argued that liberty is clearly the cardinal political value to be guarded.

But liberty cannot exist without the right to make use of parts of reality so as to exercise it. If one is free, one must be free someplace, with some things, i.e., in some sphere of reality. The idea of the human right to property catches the importance of ownership in relation to life and liberty. Skinner does not attack private property and this is not the place to consider the problem.

Skinner opposes the free market, of course, This is natural, inasmuch as he rejects the basis of that market, the political theory of human rights. Freedom, not just efficiency and competition, is the central ingredient of such a market. Because Skinner thinks that political liberty is a nonsensical goal and its propagation an obstacle to his own aims, he derides its economic corallary in several places in his books. The idea of a free market depends on the view that every individual has the human right to acquire items for uses judged by him to be valuable. This, basically, is the idea of private property. Only a viewpoint that acknowledges the capacity of individuals to choose between different courses of conduct can take such an idea seriously. And Skinner's view contradicts this viewpoint at every turn.

8

Dignity—
Its Best Chance
in Freedom

No one can deny that Skinner attacks human dignity without doing justice to the arguments that might give this idea support. *Beyond Freedom and Dignity* is a polemic, filled with assertions, ramblings, hints, dubious ("casual") English usage, equivocations, nasty charges against an opposition whose views are ill- or not at all represented, and so forth and so on—generally a very bad book, considering its avowed purpose.

Yet Skinner has "good reasons" for objecting to human dignity, just as he has for rejecting free will and political liberty. That is, if by "good" we mean simply "suited to Skinner's purposes." He tells us that if a culture

> . . . continues to take freedom or dignity, rather than its own survival, as its principal value, then it is possible that some other culture will make a greater contribution to the future . . . (I/173)

It is unclear what "a great contribution to the future" means to Skinner; he never illuminates this. But whatever it is, to him it relates closely to the survival of a culture—its sheer, unqualified longevity. And he considers this the "principal value" which people should be induced to promote.

According to Skinner freedom and dignity conflict with this goal. The reason is that as long as man has or is capable of having dignity, man himself is important. The significance of the individual in society, manifest in practices (admittedly scarce anywhere) that protect his rights and justified interests, is an obstacle to Skinner's purpose, which is to control others. If human dignity does not exist, then the objection to control amounts only to something like: controlling Harry Smith does not contribute to the survival of the culture, so let's not do it. And since the designers of the culture, behavioral technologists themselves, *will* determine what promotes its survival, this objection to control can only come from Skinnerians. In effect, without reference to human dignity (the personal worth of individual human beings) there is nothing that stands between Skinnerians and their control of anyone. Even though Skinner never justifies the value of the survival of the culture, by eliminating human dignity as an objection to controlling people, he renders his own chosen value more respectable. But we will have to conclude that it stands without proof *and* against powerful opposition based on human dignity.

Whenever some goal is cited that supposedly justifies *using* people, depriving them of their liberty and property, it is helpful to denigrate the importance of people (individuals) per se. National destiny, society, the race, or the culture—all have been alleged to justify forcing some to do what others want to have done. Virtually all public-works projects, goals supported by taxation, ad infinitum, require this sort of justification, since leaving it to rational persuasion might not accomplish the task. There has never been a political theory that gave a sound justification for using individual human beings without their consent to achieve such goals.

Abolishing human dignity is helpful to those who want to control others to achieve their own desires. (Not that the survival of a worthwhile culture could really be enhanced by centralized expert conditioning. But Skinnerians might gain legitimate use of controlling mechanisms, just as other political ideologues have managed to ascend to power, never mind their subsequent failures. Today's federal regulatory agencies do more harm than good and yet are legally entitled to regulate people's lives.) When people begin to have doubts about their own dignity, their own worth, they are more likely to tolerate abuses and controls. One might say that we need studies to support the last claim; it does not, however, require systematic research to learn some facts of life. Undercutting people's convictions in their own worth and dignity *does* contribute to their submissiveness or malleability.

So we see that despite insufficient arguments to prove that human dignity is a myth, Skinner has reasons, suited to his particular purpose, for opposing human dignity. In our own investigation we have noted that neither philosophy nor science supports Skinner. This leaves the possibility for human dignity wide open.

What is it then to possess dignity? What follows from the fact of its attainability? What impact does human dignity have on the sort of political system suited for people? These are the questions to which we must find answers.

Moral worth and dignity

The idea of dignity indicates that a person possesses, or is capable of possessing, moral worth. To deprive a person of his dignity is to rob him of the opportunity to excel as a human being. To offend someone's dignity is to treat or consider him incapable of moral worth.

There are other related senses in which this idea can be used. Anyone whose apparel and looks match those who have rank or status is assumed to have a dignified appearance. Not that rank or status necessarily imply this, but without some actual worth and achievement the idea of rank or status would mean nothing. Thus a dignitary could in fact be less than worthy of the rank he holds. It is the relationship between worth and status that renders the notion "dignitary" meaningful.

When human dignity is at stake however we are definitely considering moral worth. So whatever the latter idea expresses, it can make clear how we might best identify the nature of human dignity. Skinner himself sees the close connection between giving credit (acknowledging achievement, accomplishment and worthiness) and human dignity. He is correct in making these connections. Basically, it is the capacity to achieve moral worthiness that provides any human life with some measure of dignity.

For purposes of organizing a society and for designing a culture's legal system, recognition of human dignity means the realization that every person has the capacity to be morally good. He must, therefore, be left undeprived of what is most important to exercise this potential. That is to say, the political circumstances suited to human beings must involve the protection and preservation of human liberty. (When it comes to choices which force themselves on others, the latter may respond with punishment. When the choices pertain to oneself and to those consenting to follow them, the consequences will be the only measure of whether good or bad choices were made. Presumably doing wrong in one's own life, within one's own sphere, has a direct payoff *to* oneself. Thus no outside interference is justified.)

What then is moral worth? Before this can be answered we need to have some idea as to whether it is possible to make judgments about human life and conduct that have universal validity. To speak of moral worth when it means no more than what some people might *feel* is morally good, right, or virtuous simply will not suffice. That is not what "moral" means—for morality is precisely the set of standards of conduct that apply to *all* human beings—simply because they are *human*. There can be variations depending on various special circumstances—e.g., age, culture, epoch, wealth, even climate. But at the basis of all variations some principle must pull the entire picture together. Unless some basic standard of conduct can be identified as applicable to all human beings of reasonable maturity, such notions as dignity, virtue, morality, and goodness make no sense. And even without Skinner's attack, the idea of dignity would have to be declared meaningless if no common standard of conduct can be found for human beings.

Man, virtues, and liberty

Trying to identify a moral code for man is taking on an enormous task. Yet in some way every person must be expected to shoulder it. While

190

philosophers, theologians, psychologists, and others debate whether this or that moral point of view is best suited to human nature, *all* people are faced with important choices, decisions, conflicts, dilemmas, and the ordinary problems which fall within the purview of morality. What is the right thing to do, was this wrong, should we do that, is this justified, and similar questions—with the specifics filled in—confront people everywhere every day.

The answers to those questions, those categories of issues which are specifically unique in human life, are treated in a system of ethics, a moral code. For human beings some ways of approaching life are right, others wrong. Which particular manifestation of right and wrong will apply in individual situations is sometimes very difficult to identify. One may know that he should be honest and yet find it hard to identify what counts as honesty in some situation. Integrity, courage, honor, justice, and other virtues may all indeed apply universally; but their specific manifestations can vary. (This is what a number of people misinterpret as implying moral relativism. Cross cultural evaluations of conduct must take into account the difficulties of identifying virtues and vices in entirely unfamiliar and diverse circumstances. Yet difficulties are not impossibilities. The trouble is that when things are difficult, it may seem that they can be made easy by denying that they exist.)

But all this still does not identify any specific moral code that is right for mankind. The reason for this lengthy introduction to the topic is that disagreements about moral codes are so numerous, such an evident aspect of human history and life, that to just come right out and announce what is *the* right moral code simply amounts to arrogance. Certain obviously sincere objections would have to be overcome before anyone could be expected to deal with the matter openly. Moreover, it may seem odd for the libertarian to make claims to universal moral knowledge since he is the one political theorist who entitles no one to *impose* any moral judgments on others by force. Knowing what is right however does not entitle anyone, just on that ground, to *force* others to live up to this knowledge. There is absolutely no logic in the move from knowing *right* to forcing others to act on such knowledge.

On the other hand libertarians are often mistakenly grouped with moral agnostics and skeptics. Their advocacy of political liberty has been taken by some to be a rejection of the possibility of moral knowledge. Some classical liberals have in fact shown such an inclination. David Hume, certainly the most noted moral skeptic, was himself an advocate of greater political liberty than what had been enjoyed by people up to his time. However it is not necessary to deny the possibility of moral knowledge so as to advocate political liberty. Quite the contrary. Because knowledge of what is good and bad, right and wrong is possible, people require freedom to discover it. Liberty is not a substitute for virtue. But in a human community without liberty, virtue has no prospect of flourishing; it will be

political purposes it must be assumed that everyone would choose to make the most of his life, no obstacle should stand in the way of his doing so.

Nevertheless, Skinner is right to claim that with the expectation of moral achievement we must leave open the possibility of failure as well. Indeed, too many impatient people want to limit everyone's liberty so as to prevent such failure on the part of some. Vice squads, censorship and other legal measures designed to prevent personal corruption and moral degradation are expressions of this impatience. Yet the willingness to limit liberty in order to improve others—something Skinner wishes to accomplish on a grand scale by denying that people are or could be responsible for themselves—leads to greater evil. Meddling with others' lives cannot be excused by reference to supposedly noble goals of "preventing people from ruining their lives." The fact is that no one is really improved when he is forcibly kept from degrading himself. All the energy spent on that fruitless task could go into making the enforcer's own life a better one.

The good of man and America's political tradition

There has been much complaint about the American political tradition of human rights because it caters to an egoistic ethics. Skinner himself charges that individualism encourages the pursuit of happiness. And indeed this is true. Egoism is often confused with egotism or lack of benevolence, kindness, or generosity toward others. But to view it as such is to accept a rather dubious assumption, namely that it is really in one's interest to be hostile, unkind, greedy, cruel, or brutal. Can it be seriously maintained that someone's self-interest would in fact be enhanced by such a style of life? Egoism, in the sense in which most of the great thinkers have taken it, from Plato and Aristotle to Spencer and Rand, means a rational, sensible concern for one's life. This includes a full realization of one's humanity, one's place in a human community, the enormous joy of human company and peace among people. It does also include a certain degree of independence and unwillingness to compromise one's values when pressured by others.

It is this independence in egoism that is resented by many who try to smear the doctrine so as to deprive it of its possible appeal. Parasitical people, especially those intent on controlling others, need to demean the significance of the individual, the ego. Skinner is quite open about this and, considering his wishes, this is understandable. Most dictators make attempts to convince the people that *individually* no one means too much, only the race, the future society, the survival of the culture, the nation, or whatever matters.

America's political tradition has suffered somewhat from finding itself grafted onto a culture that embodies, in the main, a self-denying moral code, thus showing veritable national schizophrenia. The rights to life, liberty, and pursuit of happiness make little sense if everyone believes

194

that people should live, work, and show regard primarily for others. The moral and the political have been and still are at odds in our culture—although these days both morality and politics seem to be leaning away from individualism, from regard for the importance of the life, liberty, and happiness of each person. This is evidenced both in the provisions of the legal system, which is now definitely oriented toward collectivism and statism, and as implemented by members of the culture in their own personal lives.

Today the main advocate of the politics of a free society and the ethics of egoism is Ayn Rand. Although her polemic sometimes detracts from her substance, in point of fact her ideas have managed to make clear that a sensible, active, rational concern with one's own life as a human being is the moral responsibility of everyone. This has nothing to do with the "Me only, damn everyone else" caricature of egoism depicted in movies, literature, politics and even philosophy. Rather it is the classical recognition that a good human life *means* the good life of a given individual human being. Every individual must realize it for himself. The guidance for that is provided by an understanding of what *kind* of being every individual is, namely a human being. But the implementation of goodness must be on the individual's particular level.

Unless a person appreciates the value of his life, it makes no sense to expect from him benevolence, kindness, not to mention love, toward others. To advocate, as Skinner does, some sort of high regard for humanity —or culture—while rejecting the primary significance of the individual's freedom and dignity is to forget that "humanity," "society," "nation," or "culture" have their "cash value," concrete manifestation, or reality, in the lives of the individuals of every moment or epoch. There is no way to pay heed to the former unless the latter are closely attended to, cared for, and valued. And who should care, attend to, and value a person if he himself should not? The answer must be plain.

The individual vs. others

What of the widely held conviction, shared by Skinner, that there must be conflicts between society (the group, the country, the culture) and the individual? It is commonly believed that there can be and are genuine clashes between what is of value, good or right for individuals and what is the collective, common, general, or social good. Yet little agreement exists as to the precise sense or meaning of "good," "value," and "right" in the contexts of these supposed conflicts.

Today there is widescale profession of relativism about what these terms mean—even when preferences are held in common quite firmly. Yet people do use these terms continually; moreover, it is not as if they relied on them in situations where the terms have no practical, real significance. Major political decisions, legal reforms, diplomatic missions, and the like are justified, explained, and promoted by their use. In these and similar contexts and terms "good," "interest," and so on are combined with "collective," "social," or "common." The point that now bears some discussion is whether, in the light of what we have said thus far, such expressions have a consistent meaning and, if so, what that meaning might be.

The following statements offer a sample of their use:

1. Every statesman has the duty to preserve the public good.
2. Sometimes the common good requires that the private interest of people be sacrificed.
3. Government exists in order to secure (through courts, militia, regulatory agencies, etc.) at all costs the good of the society.
4. This governmental agency is designed to secure the public interest, necessity, and convenience.
5. Censorship conflicts with (or enhances) the common good.
6. Water and air pollution are detrimental to the public good.
7. In times of national emergency the rights of individual citizens must be sacrificed for the benefit of the society, for the common welfare.
8. Political liberty is a common good.

Quite a long list of similar claims with identical content and intent could of course be cited. Some of those above may have an odd ring about them in their present form. This is due, primarily, to the absence of the usual context in which references to or mention of the common good occur. When considering examples of expressions or utterances of any type it is always useful to remember that they occur within highly complex contexts, in the main, and stand on their own infrequently. But the above list contains familiar enough cases so that an appropriate context should be easy to imagine.

The purpose of citing these examples is to investigate whether any factor is central to whatever is at least nominally identical in each case before us. In all, the idea of the "common good" or one of its synonyms is significant. (It might be objected that calling some notions synonyms for others in this case is to prejudice our inquiries. The expressions cited, however, do have essentially the same *usage,* at least within the arena of politics. Admittedly, this does not necessarily tell us whether the application itself is consistent or wise.)

By taking the examples in turn, we can get a reasonably good idea of what is often intended by their employment within the contexts they most often occur. That is to say, we shall see what people believe they mean when they use the ideas under investigation. And it will be apparent that in most cases the meaning they *believe* the idea has simply will not be found. (Which is not surprising—words, terms, concepts, expressions are often misused, sometimes through honest error, other times as expressions of protest, and still other times as intentional deception. But the fact is that in using ideas we must refer to a fairly specificable range of what there is in the world, however complicated it might be to identify the boundaries of this range. Denying that this is so is simply to deny the very possibility of knowledge or communication.)

Identifying the public good

Starting with the first example, if every statesman has the duty to preserve the public good, presumably every statesman must know what that is. What might the public good be so that a statesman could, in fact, keep it alive? For if it is something that statesmen could not preserve, they surely would have no such duty.

The public good would have to be something that is good for the public, something from which benefit would accrue to *everyone.* "The public" refers to all and every member of the community, otherwise one ought to say "some people" and not others, the majority, the bulk of people, or something else that would certainly be a less powerful commitment. So before we can tell what this duty of statesmen amounts to, we would have to know what could constitute living up to it. Is there anything that is to everyone's benefit?

If we take as examples certain legislative measures that a statesman might support, the question becomes, what kind of measures could be of benefit to *everyone?* Unless we think that "the public" or "collective" transcend everyone, we are faced with the responsibility of having to identify what, if anything, does actually serve every person in a human community. This would require an investigation. We would have to note at the outset that citizens of a community differ in innumerable respects; we must also acknowledge that, to the degree that they differ, the things of benefit to each will also differ in many respects. We need, therefore, to ask if there is anything that is universally possessed by the citizens of a country, any respect in which everyone is the same, so as to identify what there might be that can clearly be advantageous to all. Only after something of this sort is determined can we rest assured that the claim we are examining could be meaningful, i.e., used successfully to convey what statesmen are dutybound to carry out.

At this point we will not consider whether there is, in fact, something that is to everyone's benefit; we have only to make note of the need for utmost care for certain considerations when we investigate the claim at hand.

Clashing of interests

In the second example we are told that the common good sometimes requires disregarding or sacrificing the private interest of individuals. Here we encounter a difficulty not found before. It appears that there can be a dichotomy between the interest or good of the public and that of some members of the public. Is this implication acceptable? What about some specific examples often cited? One of these is a highway designated "to serve the public," but its construction is held up by the fact that a private citizen owns a piece of land which lies just where the engineers assure us the highway could best serve its desired purpose. This is not unlike the cases covered in current law under the heading of "eminent domain." But are we confronted with a genuine case of public versus private interest?

In one sense of the idea of public interest, this example is markedly different from the first one. Where the statesman had a duty to preserve the public good, namely the good of everyone included in "the public," here the owner of the land has been definitely excluded from such membership. That is, unless we want to argue that although the individual does not want to relinquish his land (on terms set by those who maintain *they* represent the *public*), his real interest lies in accepting the conditions put to him. By arguing this we commit ourselves to having to demonstrate that the highway will in fact benefit the stubborn landowner over and above any advantage he might reap from staying put. This demonstration would once again involve proving what is or is not of benefit to some particular person. We would have to judge *for this person* the kind of life he ought to lead, goals he should pursue, and so on. His attachment to his property would have to be evaluated, the consequences of forcing him to yield would have to be estimated and compared to leaving him be. If he puts a value on his land beyond what the public officials would be willing to compensate him for in other goods (e.g., money), our claim that he benefits more from the highway than by keeping his land would require a lot of argument. Even if we could establish without a doubt that the public authority's goals (unbeknownst to him) are going to benefit the owner far more than his own plans, there is a further question: does knowing what is profitable to someone entitle us to *impose* it on him? (In the case of parent and child there is some defense for such imposition only because we understand the relevant distinctions between adults and children, on the average at least.)

But the example specifies that the public good goes contrary to the private, in which case talking about the benefit which accrues to the stubborn landowner simply does not concern us. What remains is this: the public has become "the public *minus one person,*" namely the private citizen who finds himself in conflict with the goals of *the rest of the* public. So the central problem is that there is a conflict between the claims as to what is of benefit or interest to everyone except the landowner, and the landowner himself. In short, it is not the public which clashes with the private interest, the interests of *some* seem to conflict with those of *others*. (The "seem" here indicates that we are only dealing with claims. It could turn out that conflicts of interest are really no more, at least in the bulk of cases we know of, than misunderstandings or deceptive claims as to what is to someone's *best* interest.)

The problem is once again that some meanings are not clear in the statement. Do we mean by "interest" anything which in fact benefits someone, or whatever he desires or wants? If we admit that the landowner has a true, valid, justifiable interest in keeping his land, can we also accept that others have a true, valid, justifiable interest in depriving him of it? The issue is not whether others have an interest in acquiring the land—if that is all that were at stake, the case would be simple: others could buy the land. There is no conflict between the interests of buyer and seller— theirs is a mutual interest when exchanging goods (e.g., money for land); both would gain from the trade if their decision to engage in it was justified. (Of course, people can make mistakes—but so can planners, with far greater impact.)

But the claim under inspection alleges that the interest of the private citizen ought to be sacrificed for the public good; in fact what the example shows is that the term "the public" simply masks the fact that what is being talked about is the sacrifice of the expressed interest of one (or some) person(s) to the expressed interest or desires of other persons. The public, since it includes all people, *cannot* be involved in such conflicts. Skinner might have considered this when he presented his polemic against individualism, human rights, and human dignity.

But clearly Skinner is not alone in using a term such as "the public," in his case "the culture," to disguise the fact that opposing *wishes* of different people are at stake. In line with this the claim under inspection would have to read: Sometimes the desires, wishes, goals, purposes, etc., of a certain segment of the public conflict with those of another, and one ought to be sacrificed to the other. This in turn pushes the discussion to ask again whether anything at all follows from this as to what *ought to be* done.

Is this a democratic justification for recourse to eminent domain, for the use of behavioral technology in the services of one or another faction, and so forth? Is this something that obliterates human dignity and everyone's right to its free pursuit? What grounds are there for favoring the preferences of majorities in these cases? By what right, it may be asked, do people who find themselves in larger groups and in company foist their wishes on those who are either alone or enjoy smaller numbers? There does not seem to be any good reason for supposing that such a right exists— although all indications are that such imposition is rampant. (From all circles there seems to be some evidence for a willingness to make such impositions. The liberal virtue of equality would seem to be violated just as much as the conservative virtue of free enterprise when the practices of each aim at reform.)

States and the public interest

The third example states that government exists to secure at all cost the good of society. This case is similar to that of the duties of the statesman. To determine what the government exists for requires knowledge of what the good of society is in this example. And unless we artificially narrow "society" to "the majority" or "those with wisdom" or the like, the "good of society" could mean only "that which is good for every member of society."

The same points hold for example four where we are dealing with some governmental branch or administrative body. The only difference is that an agency such as the Federal Communications Commission (FCC) is consigned to some specific sphere of human activities, in that case virtually all telecommunication. The regulation of these types of activity cannot involve consideration for the public at large since not everyone has an interest in such specific areas. (This accounts for why, once the state assumes control of some aspect of even one industry, there is sufficient precedent to move into any others. Certainly no reference to the right to liberty of action could have force once one such agency is legally tolerated. Even nationalization is merely a further step along the same lines as regulation. No legal objections can exist, at least with consistency, to such a step once the initial intervention has been tolerated.)

Nevertheless the statement at issue does refer to the public interest, necessity, and convenience. And it is an exact rendition of the text stating the purposes of the FCC. Despite limited application and limited benefits (if any at all), its operations are financed out of general taxes. It is clear then, that here again the expression "to secure the public interest, etc." hides from us the fact that what is being made fast are the goals, interests, or wants of *some* people. That this *should* be done by governments would require justification in its own right; but by referring to the *public* interest the need for that is evaded. (And here what we are talking about is the confusions perpetrated by those hired to secure the public interest. One need only think of the compromises, evasions, concessions, and similar abridgments of good judgment and sound principle that ensue in committees of government. That there is corruption in such circles is virtually a foregone conclusion—just in case anyone is truly surprised at the likes of Watergate.)

When another proposed governmental agency attempts to woo the people with such terms, not only is it impossible to understand by "public interest" the rightful interest of every citizen, but even the majority's interest is missing. It is obviously rare to find a governmental agency that serves the interest of even *most* of the people. Instead, the goals and wishes—who knows about interests?—of certain groups of lawyers, engineers, military officers, industrialists, artists, professors, religious leaders, and housewives are served—while *everyone* is taxed to support them.

The Public and censorship

Can we make better sense of the claim that censorship (the legal prohibition of the sale of specified printed matter—books, magazines, films, photos) works against (or for) the common good? Here the phrase seems intended to mean an overall condition of harm or benefit that allegedly affects everyone in society. But that would be begging the issue: If a book is forcibly kept off the market, it is only a few people (author, publisher, and potential readers) who suffer as a result. Just taking the book off the market may indeed have this limited effect. But keeping it off forcibly could institutionalize the practice and lead to widescale censorship. Even then, only so many people in any society care to express themselves and receive the benefits of others' self-expression. In the case of those who argue that censorship is in the public interest, e.g., members of the League of Decency, the claim is often that the smut and obscenity can affect the "moral fiber" of society. Others argue that unless broadcasters are forced to cut down violent scenes or commercialism, the society will suffer cultural damage. (Skinner would not endorse the idea of forcing any of these matters; he would insist that they be handled by elaborate schedules of positive reinforcement—meaning that these goals should be achieved by inducing people to accomplish them on their own—perhaps by some tax benefit program.)

The issue of censorship is no different from any other, although some people really think that reading dirty books can have permanent, widescale and harmful effects. Instead only a few people may be ill-affected from reading smut, just as some people have allergies, aversions, dislikes, and hates and when they encounter whatever provokes these reactions they can be hurt. Other people eat too much, stay up too late, or exercise too strenuously. But none of this has established that the forbidding of such activities is in the public interest; and we are concerned with the forbidding part as well as with what is being forbidden. The question is always whether legal prohibition of certain actions, the control of human beings under threat of legal repercussions (even if this may turn out to mean behavioral modification therapy or psychosurgery), is justified. The concept of human dignity is the strongest obstacle to such theories and practices.

Pollution vs. public good

In example five it is noted that pollution is detrimental to those who are themselves not polluting but must carry the burden of cleaning things up or living with dirty water and air. Ecologists have drawn rather dismal pictures about the total interdependence of all portions of the universe—or at least the biosphere: what happens in Lake Erie is necessarily going to effect Arizona's environment. There is only lately, finally, an ounce of sanity in the ecology literature.

In our example, reference to the public good obliterates the real issue: whose pollution, at what and whose expense? Some people stand to gain from virtually any kind of pollutants; the sanitation workers would not object to a gradual increase of garbage; the recently emerging smog-control industry can only regard smog emission as profitable; even the individual citizen who pollutes would not likely continue to do so unless the consumption that produces waste benefited him in some measure. The question of what kind of pollution is appropriate for people with different purposes and goals is obscured by declaring the problem of pollution to be universal and a danger to the public interest.

Many economists have provided answers to the more substantive issues that arise in connection with pollution. According to some, its worst cause and the biggest hindrance to its solution is that too many items of value are considered to be "free goods." The national parks, lakes, beaches, public roads, and buildings—even the air and water—are all treated as if they were free, as if no cost accrued from using them. But costs do exist. And these will not disappear by way of wishful thinking and federal regulation. The problems of pollution imperialism are best handled when the polluters can be identified as individuals or groups and when property can be tied clearly—even if by court action—to owners who use it unobstructively. Hiding these and related problems under the label of "public interest" leads quite simply to the unchecked evasion of who must be held responsible for any actual, identifiable harm caused by pollution.

National emergency vs. you

We come now to the most appealing reference to the idea of the public or common good. Does a national emergency require abridgment of individual rights in behalf of the public good? Skinner opens *Beyond Freedom and Dignity* by announcing that he is working "to solve the terrifying problems that face us in the world today." (I/1) By casting his mission in such a light he appeals to something like a national emergency or, even more, a world crisis. We need not go that far to appreciate the impact this kind of situation can have on those concerned with designing a political system. Floods, tornadoes, earthquakes, and similar massive natural disasters are often invoked in order to justify overriding the individual's right to pursue his own existence in peace. Virtually all advocates of a relatively free society hedge when it comes to a consideration of these kind of circumstances. So when national emergencies and world crises come into focus, one of the more troublesome matters arises for the libertarian who insists on the inviolability of individual rights and human dignity.

John Locke, the founder of modern natural rights theory, seemed to feel that famines and other disasters should be excluded from circumstances in which every individual's right to property must be protected and preserved. In line with such exceptions some people have suggested that human rights are not absolute but only *prima facie*. This means that standing by one's human rights will not do when overriding moral considerations arise. Yet there is danger if we allow one emergency to encroach upon human rights; why not another and another, so that in the end simply *calling* something an emergency will suffice to march in and take over control. This is not an exaggeration these days when shortages of beef, grapes, or gasoline, as well as many matters that came out of the Watergate hearings, are all treated as national emergencies (instead of the occasional, even if serious, inconveniences that arise in people's lives in any age), thus bringing in their wake apparently called-for control of people's lives. If "emergency" cries are to be used as grounds for action, careful consideration and selective use of that term are required. Emergencies are cases where something very harmful and quite unexpected occurs. A community, like a person, may experience an emergency. The problem is that in emergencies, it is *impossible* to utilize principles of organization designed to accommodate normality. So the idea of human rights cannot apply in such cases since the conditions for organized human community living—where they should function—are not present. When this occurs, reliance on ready-made legal measures is simply impossible. If and when we confront conditions in which the ordinary precautions involved in dealing with people are not even open to us, there really *cannot* be any meaningful regard for human rights; people will have to be on their own, struggling for the bare minimum of prospects for life and well-being.

In more massive cases, such as foreign aggression against one's community, there does not appear to be any conflict between what is good for the community and what is good for its individual members. Granted: to abstain from defending one's land or country may involve an individual in a situation where he becomes a free rider, inasmuch as self-defense on the part of another person or the community could serve to repel the aggression that otherwise could have hurt the person who refused to participate. Yet this is not unique to emergency cases. Presuming that people have an interest in self-defense and that, as with all forms of insurance, they recognize the value of planning ahead, there is no special ground for concern in terms of political theory. In such a climate, where solutions are reached without shortcuts—i.e., it is illegal to use other people as means to one's own ends without their consent—, there is no reason to believe that left to their cooperative, noncoerced efforts, individuals will not make preparations for defense. The free rider is only a problem in terms of certain assumptions, namely that people are unaware of the possibility or that they are fully determined to avoid short term costs. If they realize that the free rider is likely to appear in any community, they will have to choose whether risking no defense or high expenditures is wiser. The free-rider problem can also be forestalled by means of effective boycotts, persuasion, or payoffs. (The famous "prisoner-dilemma" type of puzzle, with everyone trying to calculate in total ignorance of what others want, would obtain only if people were *obsessed* with trying to get away with free riding. Such obsession is not justifiably considered a general human condition. That would not be greed but plain stupidity in most circumstances where communities exist.)

Aside from some of the practical objections to this example, in response to the emotional content of "emergency" situations, there is the question of what would justify imposing on anyone a burden, such as military service, if he refuses to "help himself?" Mankind has enough alternative means by which to cope with disastrous circumstances, provided coping is an option in the first place. In a truly free community, where no short-cuts are legally tolerated, these alternatives would most likely emerge. ("Most likely" because no *guarantee* exists as to what people *will* do. But we can see what would be the most sensible, rational, and morally appropriate approach to all kinds of eventualities. We need a theoretical inquiry—which is not helped by some pure laboratory model, only by common sense—and historical studies of what people did in periods of relative political liberty.)

In general the emergency-case argument in support of imposing on individuals the wishes, wants, or purposes of others, even when of them-selves these wishes, wants, and purposes are justified, does not carry force. Argument from the will of the majority—even the needs of the majority—begs the question: why is that any justification at all? The majority must fetch for itself if the minority will not help; this has to be understood along the same lines as the population problem, which can-not be *solved* by murdering people.

If the emergency is so severe that a society has broken up and no legal framework exists, there simply is no general, political guideline con-cerning what may or may not go on between people. Here we have to accept the fact that people are responsible for creating solutions where none exist and it won't do to pretend that such solutions can be invented ahead of time. In emergency situations it becomes ever so important that each person be prepared to think quickly, with a cool head, and adjust himself to the conditions in such a fashion that the maximum possible degree of morality and civilized life is retained. To presume that in such cases people must or will lose their sense of decency and humanity is to ignore evidence to the contrary and to give up on people altogether; yet to expect them to be as capable of living in terms of the ethics that should ordinarily govern their lives is to obscure the context entirely.

Liberty as the good of all people

In the final example to be considered we are left with the claim that political liberty is the common or general good. We have already identified the nature of political liberty: the condition people enjoy in a human community where no one is legally entitled to impose his values, goals, and purposes on another. In such a community the purpose of organizing a system of laws is to protect and preserve the freedom of each person to aspire to dignity, to moral worthiness. It is accepted as a fact that each person is capable, within his unique or shared circumstance, of making the effort to that end. Political liberty is therefore the organized expres-sion of the dignity of each individual capable of moral worth.

Thus it is clear that political liberty is indeed a possible *universal* value for man in the community of others. It is the absence of interference with one's life and with one's efforts to lead it *in peace*. It is not, however, a condition of license to interfere with the rights of others, for *all* possess the right to life, liberty, and the pursuit of happiness. Thus the claim at hand means that freedom from aggression is something of value, benefit, and interest to every person, even to someone who would not acknowledge it.

A person who might prefer slavery either for himself or for others has no "freedom" to implement his wish, for slavery is the denial of human autonomy and dignity; it is not a genuine consensual or contractual relationship since the slave is forced to abandon his humanity by serving another's purposes; even where some might be willing slaves, the wish is impossible to fulfill since only by death can someone escape his nature, his humanity. A free society, mindful of the nature of man as capable of dignity and responsible to achieve it (or carry the burden of its neglect) himself, should not tolerate even a masochistic wish some might have for total subjugation. That wish must either go unsatisfied or lead one to secede from the community that has as its purpose the possibility for each person to lead a morally worthy life. (Of course anyone is free, also, to submit himself to virtual serfdom. But the option to reconsider the matter, to renegotiate his terms with another, must always exist. Everyone must be regarded, even against his own wishes, as a person capable of choice where the legal system is concerned. Unless, of course, by disease or deformity of one or another kind it is *impossible* that he could exercise choice, in which case special provisions are made within the legal system. But these are outside the present scope.)

Skinner's proposal that people be induced to give up their claim to freedom and dignity might succeed. Many may wish to commit themselves to Skinnerian control systems and schedules. But the provisions of a free legal system can consider this only a case of contractual agreement that may be challenged. The kind of voluntary slavery Skinner asks for, however benevolently it is intended—or might even turn out—contradicts human nature and the kind of human community suited to people. A good legal system could not tolerate it as a *legalized* condition of any person. (Which is not to say that *voluntary* submission to behavior modification therapy is anything resembling this.)

The existence of human dignity implies that the common good to be secured by means of politics—law, legislation, enforcement, protection, preservation, defense, or adjudication—is political liberty. This is because *in fact* the appropriate condition of social existence for everyone is political liberty; it is something that should be and can be secured for everyone without discrimination. All people have an implicit or explicit stake in it for purposes of conducting their lives. While bread, butter, cars, golf courses, parks, fine art, education, and the myriad services now promised but rarely provided by governmental edict are *not good for everyone,* political liberty is the condition that enables each member of a community to pursue some or all these goods to the best of his will and ability. This condition is a real possibility, not a utopian ideal, because people can in fact choose to refrain from interfering with each other's lives. Since what ought to be achieved within both the moral and political sphere must be possible to achieve, and what cannot be achieved should not be considered a moral imperative, political liberty is a real ideal. When legally instituted it makes possible the flourishing of each individual as a self-responsible, dignified person; this renders it of value to everyone within a human community.

If we now return to our examples of the statesman and the government, we can make better sense of the idea that each is responsible to secure and protect the public or collective good; since political liberty is the only value that is universally applicable, those in the service of a community (the public, the collective, the people in common) are duty-bound, by their very occupation, to strive for it.

Thus far we have considered the nature of human dignity and, in terms of it, the meaning of such well-worn phrases as "the public interest" and the "common good." We have seen why placing the good of society or the value of the survival of the culture in opposition to human dignity cannot be defended. We have seen also that Skinner's idea that *a culture* ought to work for its survival makes no sense except insofar as this means that *people* ought to work for the protection and preservation of the kind of political system that is good for them as individuals.

The public good of different ideologies

Before summarizing our conclusions a few considerations must be given to the suggestion that we have dealt with an artificially restricted sense of such phrases as the "public good." It is not infrequently proposed that the various senses in which such notions are used cannot be so wrong-headed. Perhaps there is something to going beyond the meaning delineated here. These terms are part of common political parlance after all and their meaning must have some foundation that allows for greater variation than tolerated here. Perhaps Skinner's own idea of the "culture" has some meaning such that its good or interest might be put in competition with the good of individual human beings. Admittedly Skinner himself has so far refused to supply us with any clues. But as in other matters he touches on, there have been more elaborate and formidable suggestions as to what we should understand by such notions.

So to examine the suggestion introduced here, let us discuss a few candidates for what such ideas as the common good might mean. We shall consider five well-known examples. The phrase or idea in question then might be taken to mean:

(a) That which is wanted by most of the people

(b) That which experts believe people ought to do or have

(c) That which the ideology of a given political faction dictates

(d) That which God has decreed through representatives

(e) That which benefits the species or culture as an organism or organic whole, that transcends each person (akin to the way one's fingers or elbow is transcended by himself as an organic whole)

Some of these examples come close to what we have already considered but the present challenge calls for different responses.

In (a) surely what most people want could very easily be not only bad for *some* but for *all* members of society. Majority want is perhaps a minor clue to what is right and good. And for particular purposes, e.g., in the running of a corporation, polling what people want can help to decide on a course of procedure, even on the goals to be pursued. But such a method is valid only when what is morally good and politically right are considered as basic guidelines that no majority may abridge. A constitution, for example, functions on these basic guidelines.

(b) What experts prescribe is very often of immense benefit to someone. But there is no reason to believe that experts can prescribe what anyone should do with *his* own life. Obviously once a person has decided to become an architect, or a doctor, or a tool-and-die maker, it is expected that experts will advise and direct him in the acquisition of these skills. It is for such purposes that the experts of Skinner's trade, the technology of behavior, may be employed. But there can be no experts on what the good life is for an individual—unless each of us becomes an expert, subsequent to careful consideration of what and who we are. The individuality of every person lies in just this need for self-expertise in his own life. Wise men can tell us some of the basic guidelines, virtues, moral or political principles to observe as we attempt to carry out our purposes. But there simply cannot be experts for deciding what people ought to live for, what purposes they should have. (Most professional psychologists, even the clergy concerned with guiding people, realize that prescribing purposes to people is impossible; these purposes would be someone else's.)

Whether or not the ideology of some political group can define the public good depends on the specific content of that ideology. An ideology is a political doctrine that implies a fairly concrete course of conduct. To consider whether (c) is correct we need to distinguish between the sensible, correct doctrine and just any doctrine. If the former is meant, then the statement is true but not very useful. If the latter, then it is clearly false. Since there are many ideologies, there would be contradictory meanings of the idea of the common good and its synonyms. And that cannot be without making all discourse about politics useless and meaningless.

(d) Decrees of God come in many forms and in the final analysis it is dubious whether accepting one or another purported version is better. The difficulty in making out God's will or message, and of identifying what it would be *to know* these, is so evident that counting on an understanding of the concept of "common good" by reference to religion seems entirely fruitless. Whatever religion is, it must be a strictly private matter since it is, by definition, ineffable. The most significant aspect of any religion escapes communicability. Thus to organize a human community by reference to the content of religions would amount to relying not on reaching an understanding but on achieving some mystical inspiration—something that is rare if not illusionary.

Finally we come to what is the closest to Skinner's idea of what should be preferred to freedom and dignity. This involves a theory of human community life as constituting an epoch or period in the life of a greater, more superior, transcendent entity, the Species or Culture. He tells us that "A culture corresponds to a species . . . [but] . . . the parallel between biological and cultural evolution breaks down at the point of transmission." (I/124) This is because "There is nothing like the chromosome-gene mechanism in the transmission of cultural practice . . . But a culture . . . can transmit [a] practice not only to new members but to contemporaries or to surviving members of an earlier generation." (I/124)

As with those who take Plato out of context and attribute to him a personification of society, and with the orthodox Marxists who see only social groups, never individuals, as significant elements of political discourse, so Skinner finds the culture to be *the* active agent of interest to political theory. Cultures carry on in all kinds of fashions—they transmit, diffuse, induce, convince, and so on. Yet the only explanation we are given as to how this can happen is that "A culture evolves when new practices further the survival of those who practice them." (I/127) This points right back to people and robs culture of any transcendent identity.

Others who have proposed the idea of a species-personality have gone so far as to argue for the literal, strict validity of such concepts as "social consciousness," "the general will," and "national purpose," ascribing to the various groupings of people or communities features and capacities that are dependent for their existence on the organic constitution of individual human beings. But society or culture has no brain, not to mention a mind. It cannot feel sorrow, or pride, or be depressed—except in a statistical sense, meaning that the bulk of the people feel such emotions. It cannot intend or will anything, or have a purpose, because it does not have what individuals have—a human biological organism.

Theories that make more out of society or culture than what it is have given rise to some of the most destructive and horrible social and political conditions encountered throughout human history. Should Skinner's doctrine catch on, this will be repeated. The illusion that man is more than what he is, an individual, is comforting to some. Being part of a great race, the surviving culture, even some profession, and thereby acquiring noble traits, even dignity, is an appealing fiction. Certainly it contributes to the appeal of racism, chauvinism, nationalism, and other obstacles to

208

open human relationships. For some people these may supply the avenue of escape from self-responsibility.

The most indiscriminate among us, interestingly enough, are those who judge others by racial, national, or other irrelevant distinctions. Politicians find it convenient to couch their wishes in such phrases as "the national purpose," making it appear that not their own but their nation's wishes (whatever that might mean, but it sounds respectable) are at stake. The familiar reference to "we" in articles and books—as in this one!—and the more common reference to collective guilt in connection with ecology, war, and other harmful circumstances point to how convenient an escape such theories provide to some people.

But whether our society is populated by those who incline toward escapism or not, the fact remains that there is no escape from individual responsibility. The dignity that is possible to man cannot be achieved through fraud, evasion, or complex rationalization. The onslaught against human dignity is dangerous and wrong—more often evil.

Although more could be said about each of the considerations undertaken, it should be evident that man needs his freedom and should aspire to his own dignity as a man. This could take many forms and so long as it is guided by sound principles of conduct, suited to the kind of being we are, it ought to be diverse. No one can assume the task for anyone else. There is no guarantee of success. But in a climate of greater political liberty, with the realization of each man's responsibility to make his own life a good one, the good of every person as well as the kind of culture in which that good is respected can be advanced.

The dignity of each person as an entity capable of striving for excellence as a human being in his own life requires a free society. Man's right to life, liberty, and property are the social conditions that accommodate his moral nature. This is the only nonutopian conception of the good society—it acknowledges both the possibility of human excellence and the impossibility of guaranteeing its achievement by some formula akin to Skinner's pseudoscience.

This book aims merely at an outline of a system that stands in complete opposition to Skinner's own; few of the *details* of the conception of human affairs summarized here will be evident. (I have edited *The Libertarian Alternative*[17] in which many authors with views similar to what is being outlined here discuss the many crucial aspects of a social and political philosophy suited to human nature.) The task of this section has been to make an effort toward the development of a theory of human dignity, to explain what it is for people to possess dignity. The major requirement of that task has been the discussion of a rational moral point of view[18]—the justification of the idea that everyone ought to strive for happiness and that only by abiding by certain standards, starting with that of full rational focus on life and including such virtues as honesty, integrity, independence, etc., will that moral goal be achievable. The rest of the section concerned the relationship of this idea of the moral life with the prominent notion of the "common good" or "public interest." The conclusion arrived at shows that political liberty is the one good that everyone in a human community shares as a matter of course. Not the survival of culture, but of liberty, should then be our central political goal.

Conclusion

The story of B. F. Skinner told in this work has not been a pretty one. But it is not an unusual story. Any time when answers are sought not only to important personal and political questions, but also to those concerning what to do with the answers that have been provided, Skinner's point of view is not unusual. In the final analysis his thesis is familiar from even the most cursory knowledge of the history of ideas: when you believe you know the answers to some important questions, make every effort to *impose* your answers on everyone's life in reach. In short, coercive approaches to implementing solutions to the problems of mankind are by no means new. Skinnerism is, therefore, just the latest of many attempts to force humanity into shape, to make people behave well.

But it is important that Skinner be answered. The philosophy of human freedom is constantly in need of support—reinforcement—lest human beings forget that life is for them to govern, that they are the ultimate agents of their actions, policies, institutions, and governments. The mere fact that this is so is not widely acknowledged. When Skinner argues against human freedom and dignity he, as many others, counts on the uncertainty most people feel about their capacity to govern their own lives. By reinforcing this uncertainty, by making it appear that it is par for the course, he paves a less troublesome way toward the ultimate goal of assuming control over people's lives. And this kind of bamboozlement requires a response. Such a response has been the goal of this work.

Many may believe that the proposals offered in this response—the unqualified support of a free society in which human beings are fully entitled to and responsible for self-government—could only constitute a hopeless ideal, a form of utopia no better than Skinner's and those of others who have promised a final solution to mankind's problems. When we consider how remote any existing social arrangement is from the one proposed herein, the charge of utopianism seems entirely justified.

Yet to be utopian may be understood in two significantly different ways. For some, like Plato, an ideal political system was required in order to provide standards the satisfaction of which should provide guidelines to actual community life. Plato's *Republic,* when taken literally, is a utopia of the highest order. But even when taken symbolically, as some philosophers understand it to have been meant, it provides serious problems. The main one is that when an ideal is inherently impossible to achieve—and considering that Plato believed that the ideal form of anything, including human communities, lies outside the reach of earthly life, this is how we must view his proposed ideal—to be guided by it can only lead to disastrous results. The means to achieve impossible ends must misguide us in our attempts to reach goals that are viable in reality. So the utopianism of a Plato, however well intentioned, is indeed dangerous, even when proposed merely as a standard toward which people ought to aspire with no real anticipation of reaching it.

A second type of approach to human conduct, personal or political, may be thought to involve utopianism. This is the attempt to achieve the *best possible* understanding of what could guide human life toward its proper fulfillment. If this be utopianism, so much the better for it. But in fact this is not quite in the tradition of utopian thinking. This is because aiming for the best *as we now understand things* does not assume that no improvement can be made on life *in the future*, when our knowledge of reality expands. Nor does this sort of idealism promise any final, un-alterable formula for universal, personal happiness. Here the idea is that personal happiness is an achievement of *a person*. It is an achievement that a person must initiate and carry forth mainly on his own, with a little help from his friends—not necessarily to be confused with Federal or state governments.

As such the point of view proposed in the second part of this book cannot justifiably be considered utopian, in the sense of that term that we are familiar with in connection with political philosophy. But the view *is* idealistic. And many want to sell us on the idea that ideals are at best myths that soothe our sense of insecurity—and at worst are dangerous illusions. That charge is based on the very same view of human nature that Skinner has tried to sell us. It rests on the belief, unjustified but favored by many people in "high places," that all there is to life is what *happens* to us, and that we are impotent to make improvements. All we may count on is luck and empty chance. Ideals must then be irrelevant to any attempt to cope with reality honestly, candidly, and with some justi-fiable hope for success.

This view of man has been countered in the pages of this work. With it we are now entitled to scrutinize ideals without prejudice. We need not apologize for such labors (in response to the charge that we "should know" that no ideals can have meaning outside of the illusionary, the ultimately insane). Instead we are justified in our search for an ideal (or ideals) that is proper to mankind. We are justified because man is the kind of entity that must choose between the right and wrong ways of doing things. And although the consequences of past wrongs may not make it possible to implement immediately our ideas of how to conduct either personal or political matters correctly, knowledge of what constitutes a correct approach to such matters can gradually guide us toward the avoid-ance of previous errors, even if only in the far-off future. There is nothing utopian, dreamy, blindly visionary about efforts that aim at discovering the ideals that can improve human life, provided that the scrutiny invested in identifying the best of the suggested ideals is carried out conscientiously.

There is an additional oddity about the need to respond to a Skinnerian type of attack on the ideals of human freedom and dignity. This is that freedom and human dignity *have to be* the natural forms of human existence, not the sort which require some form of special justification. It is an infringement on human freedom and a denial of a person's dignity that must be provided with justification—as when in a court of law the verdict commands that a person be incarcerated, or when a mental patient is sent to an asylum. In these cases the prosecution has to prove the case, while the defendant need do nothing at all but wait to see whether the proof is valid. In the larger arena of attacks the burden of proof should fall, no less naturally and sensibly, upon the shoulders of those who want to deny the reality of man's freedom and dignity.

Unfortunately arguments and good sense do not always reign in the halls of intellect. The realization of the natural right of each man to life, liberty, and property came only after centuries of systematic enslavement of millions of people who had done no harm to anyone. The doctrine of human rights is still a *radical* doctrine. It has not had a good press nor a sustained tradition. Despite the fact that most modern constitutions make reference to human rights—with the United Nations at the top—there is very little hope at present for the wide-scale adoption of this doctrine by individuals or communities throughout the world. Mention of man's rights is very far from an understanding of them. As with all basically sound notions, human rights are now on the lips of even the most brutal despots. (As an illustration of the violence done to the concept "human rights," in some communities human rights commissioners have been selected whose function is to make people help each other in the attainment of such "rights" as a yearly vacation, good housing, proper education, U.S.D.A. choice beef, etc.—all of which must, of course, be provided by others whose actual human rights will necessarily fall by the wayside in the process.)

With the low status of human liberty and dignity in the intellectual arena as well as the legal systems of most nations, it is no wonder that the defenders of human rights must try to make the case for what would ordinarily be the most natural, sensible, state of affairs humankind should enjoy. True, the burden of proof does not rest on the defense—where the logic of the argument is concerned. But when we face literal lynch-mob conditions, with no attempt to follow logic and strictures of justice, the defendant must go out to fight, on all fronts, to defend his natural rights. Indeed, as much as one might wish to eschew sloganizing in a work that aims to confront issues impassionately, the final point is still made best by the exclamation: "Eternal vigilance is the price of liberty." Or to bring the full weight of that remark to bear upon our task:

It is the common fate of the indolent to see their rights become a prey to the active. The condition upon which God hath given liberty to man is eternal vigilance; which condition if he break, servitude is at once the consequence of his crime and the punishment of his guilt.

—John Philpot Curran (1790)

Notes

1. All references are to works listed in front of text by roman numerals. These indicate titles of books and periodicals throughout the book, with date of publication and/or volume, number, year, page numbers, as appropriate. Important works that are only mentioned in the text are footnoted and listed in the bibliography. Skinner's own works are sometimes mentioned in abbreviation.

2. Cf., Science and Subjectivity (Indianapolis: Bobbs-Merrill Co., 1967).

3. Cf., The Philosophy of Science (New York: Humanities Press, 1953); The Uses of Argument (New York: Cambridge University Press, 1966); Human Understanding (Princeton: Princeton University Press, 1972).

4. Cf., Objective Knowledge (New York: Oxford University Press, 1971); The Logic of Scientific Discovery (New York: Harper and Row, 1965).

5. Cf., Criticism and the Growth of Knowledge (New York: Cambridge University Press, 1970).

6. The Structure of Scientific Revolutions (Chicago: University of Chicago Press, 1970).

7. The Justification of Scientific Change (Dordrecht, Holland: D. Reidel Publishing Co., 1971).

8. Thematic Origins of Scientific Thought (Cambridge: Harvard University Press, 1973).

9. Error and Deception in Science (New York: Harper and Row, 1960).

10. Pense, Vol. 1, Nos. 1 and 2.

11. Cf., Richard Taylor, Action and Purpose (Englewood Cliffs, N. J.: Prentice-Hall, 1966); Edward H. Madden, "The Third View of Causality," The Review of Metaphysics, September 1969, pp. 67-84; John Yolton, "Action: Metaphysics and Modality," American Philosophical Quarterly, Vol. 10, No. 2, pp. 71-85; Fanny L. Epstein, "The Metaphysics of Mind-Body Identity Theories," APQ, Vol. 10, No. 2, 111-121; Rom Harre and E. H. Madden, "Natural Powers and Powerful Natures," Philosophy, Vol. 48, No. 185, pp. 209-232; D. O. Hebb, The Organization of Behavior (New York: Wiley, 1949), "The semi-autonomous process: Its nature and nurture," American Psychologist, Vol. 18, No. 1, 1963, pp. 16-27.

12. Douglas Rasmussen, "Aristotle and the Defense of the Law of Contradiction," The Personalist, Spring 1973, pp. 149-162.

13. A. I. Melden, Human Rights (Belmont, California: Wadsworth Publishing Company, 1970, pp. 75-95.

14. G. E. Moore, Principia Ethica (New York: Cambridge University Press, 1903, passim).

15. Op. cit., Melden, pp. 40-60.

16. Cf., Eric Mack, "Egoism and Rights," *The Personalist,* Winter 1973, pp. 5-33; Tibor R. Machan, "On Rejecting Human Rights," *Reason,* May 1973, pp. 26-28; "A Rationale for Human Rights," *The Personalist,* Spring 1971, pp. 216-235.

17. (Chicago: Nelson-Hall Co., 1974) In this work the authors present essays that aim at a fully integrated, non-utopian development and analysis of a free human community. While all of the contributors do not approach their topics from the same philosophical framework, their political conclusions and elaborations—on topics ranging from the nature of liberty, theories of punishment, critiques of contemporary statism to considerations of the prospects of a fully free society—offer a clear alternative to dominant statist currents which prevail throughout the intellectual and political communities of the world.

18. It should be noted that many defenders of the free society tend to deemphasize that such a society best accommodates the moral elements of human nature. As Milton Friedman recently put it, if one *knows* that another is sinning, he is obligated to stop him. To defend individual liberty, then, those who follow Friedman's approach deny that moral principles can be known and that one can ever identify their violation in particular instances. Yet from the fact that someone is acting immorally nothing follows about what another ought to do about it. Additional facts need to be known to support that conclusion—e.g., that the immorality unavoidably affects someone other than the person acting immorally. (See my article "The Moral Imperative of the Free Market," *New Guard,* April 1974, pp. 17-20, for a criticism of the value free defense of human liberty.) Several collectivist as well as conservative thinkers have made note of the dominant anti-moralism in classical liberal and libertarian social and political philosophies. (See, e.g., Irving Kristol's criticism of libertarian moral theory in his "Capitalism, Socialism, and Nihilism," *Public Interest,* No. 31, Spring 1973, pp. 3-16.) Nevertheless, the charge levelled at advocates of the free society is not entirely fair. Among those who have offered powerful philosophical/ethical defenses of the fully free society are Ayn Rand, Murray N. Rothbard, John Hospers, H. B. Acton and others. Unfortunately most of these defenses do not get consideration in intellectual circles, so the wider public is indeed left with the impression that capitalism can only be defended from the framework of some crude theory of psychological egoism, the idea that everyone necessarily pursues his own best interest. (See Richard Schmitt's "The Desire for Private Gain," *Inquiry,* Summer 1973, pp. 149-167, for yet another demolition of this weak defense of the free society. My response to Schmitt, "Selfishness and Capitalism," is forthcoming in *Inquiry.*) I should mention at this point also that the political philosophy sketched in this work and in the several essays published in various journals (and forthcoming) will be defended in detail in my book *Human Rights and Human Liberties,* to be published by Nelson-Hall Co. in 1975.

Bibliography

Acton, H. B., *The Morals of the Markets*. London: Longman, 1971.

Adler, Mortimer J., *The Difference of Man and the Difference it Makes*. New York: World Publishing Co., 1968.

Anderson, A. R. (ed.), *Minds and Machines*. Englewood Cliffs, N.J.: Prentice-Hall, 1964.

Aristotle, *Metaphysics*. Bloomington, Ind.: Indiana University Press, 1966 (H. Apostle, trns.)

Ashcraft, Richard, "Locke's State of Nature: Historical Fact or Moral Fiction?" *The American Political Science Review*, Vol. 62, No. 3, September 1968, pp. 898-915.

Ayer, A. J. (ed.), *Logical Positivism*. New York: Macmillan, 1959.

Beardsmore, R. W., *Moral Reasoning*. New York: Schocken Books, 1969.

Bissell, R., "Dual-aspect Theory of Agency," Unublished paper (to appear, revised, in *Reason Papers*, No. 1, Fall 1974).

———, "Volition and Mind as Natural, Non-material Phenomena," *Invictus*, No. 10, pp. 25-28.

Borger, R., and Cioffi, Frank (eds.), *Explanation in the Behavioural Sciences*. New York: Cambridge University Press, 1970.

Bottomore, Tom, "Is there a Totalitarian View of Human Nature?" *Social Research*, Summer 1973, pp. 429-442.

Boyle, J. M., Jr., G. Grisez, and O. Tollefsen, "Determinism, Freedom, and Self-Referential Arguments," *The Review of Metaphysics*, September 1972, pp. 3-37.

Branden, Nathaniel, *The Psychology of Self-Esteem*. Los Angeles: Nash Publishing Company, 1969.

Braybrook, David and Rosenberg, A., "Antibehaviorism in the Hour of its Disintegration," *Philosophy of Social Sciences*, 2 (1972), pp. 355-363.

Breggin, Peter, "Is Psychosurgery on the Upswing?" *Human Events*, May 5, 1973.

216

Chappell, V. C. (ed.), *The Philosophy of Mind.* Englewood Cliffs, N.J.: Prentice-hall, 1962.

Chein, Isidor, *The Science of Behavior and the Image of Man.* New York: Basic Books, 1972.

Chomsky, Noam, "Review of Skinner's *Verbal Behavior*," *Language,* Vol. 35, No. 1, 1959, pp. 26-58.

———, "The Case Against B. F. Skinner," *The New York Review of Books,* December 30, 1971.

Day, Willard F., "Radical Behaviorism in Reconciliation with Phenomenology," *Journal of the Experimental Analysis of Behavior,* Vol. 12, No. 2, 1969, pp. 315-328.

Delgado, Jose M. R., *Physical Control of the Mind.* New York: Harper & Row, 1969.

De Mille, R., "Review of The Imperial Animal," *Reason,* Vol. 5, No. 8, pp. 29-30.

van Den Haag, E., *Political Violence and Civil Disobedience.* New York: Harper & Row, 1972.

Efron, Robert, "An Invariant Characteristic of Perceptual Systems in the Time Domain," in S. Kornblum (ed.), *Attention and Performance IV.* New York: Academic Press, 1973, pp. 713-736.

———, "Biology Without Consciousness—And its Consequences," *Perspectives in Biology and Medicine,* Vol. 11, No. 1, Autumn 1967, pp. 9-36.

———, "The Conditioned Reflex: A Meaningless Concept," *Perspectives in Biology and Medicine,* Vol. IX, No. 4, Summer 1966, pp. 487-514.

———, "The Measurement of Perceptual Duration," *Studium Generale* 23 (1970), pp. 550-561.

———, "What is Perception?" *Boston Studies in the Philosophy of Science,* Cohen, R. S. & Wartofsky, M. W. (eds.), New York: Humanities Press, 1969.

Epstein, Fanny L., "The Metaphysics of Mind-Body Identity Theories," *American Philosophical Quarterly,* April 1973, pp. 111-121.

Evans, R., *The Man and His Ideas.* New York: E. P. Dutton & Co., 1968.

Feigl, H. & Brodbeck, M. (eds.), *Readings in the Philosophy of Science.* New York: Appleton-Century-Crofts, 1953.

Feinberg, J., "What Kinds of Beings Can Have Rights?" in Blackstone, Wm. (ed.) *Philosophy and Environmental Crisis.* Athens: University of Georgia Press, 1974.

Fienberg, G., "Physics and the Thales Problem," *The Journal of Philosophy,* Vol. 63, No. 1, January 6, 1966, pp. 5-16.

Fields, Wm. S. (ed.), *The Neural Bases of Violence and Aggression.* Proceedings of the Houston Neurological Symposium, 1972.

Gendin, Sidney, "Insanity and Criminal Responsibility," *American Philosophical Quarterly,* April 1973.

Gluckman, Max, "A Band Wagonland of Monkeys," *The New York Review of Books,* November 16, 1972.

Gustafson, D. F. (ed.), *Essays in Philosophical Psychology.* Garden City, N.Y.: Anchor Books, 1964.

Hacker, Edward A., "Rationality versus Dehumanization," *Philosophy and Phenomenological Research,* December 1972, pp. 259-267.

Hare, R. M., "Rawls' Theory of Justice," *The Philosophical Quarterly,* April/July 1973, pp. 144-155/241-252.

Harre, R., *The Philosophies of Science.* New York: Oxford University Press, 1972.

217

Hayek, F. A., *Studies in Philosophy, Politics and Economics*. New York: Simon and Schuster, 1967.

Hospers, John, *Libertarianism*. Los Angeles: Nash Publishing Co., 1971.

Hume, David, *A Treatise of Human Nature*. Garden City, N. Y.: Dolphin Books, 1961.

Joseph, H. W. B., *An Introduction to Logic*. New York: Oxford University Press, 1961.

Jeffres, L. A. (ed.), *Cerebral Mechanism of Behavior*. London: Chapman Hall, 1951.

Keat, Russell, "Positivism, Naturalism, and Anti-Naturalism in the Social Sciences," *Journal for the Theory of Social Behaviour*, Vol. I, No. 1., pp. 3-18.

Keller, F. S., "Engineered Personalized Instruction in the Classroom," *Revista Interamericana de Psicologia*, 1 (1967), pp. 189-197.

———, "A Personalized System of Instruction," Institute for Behavioral Research (Silver Springs, Md.), 1968.

Kelley, David, "The Necessity of Government," *The Freeman*, April 1974, pp. 243-248.

Koestler, Arthur, *The Act of Creation*. New York: Dell Publishing Co., Inc., 1964.

Kordig, Carl R., *The Justification of Scientific Change*. Dordecht, Holland: D. Reidel Co., 1971.

Kuhn, Thomas S., *The Structure of Scientific Revolutions*. Chicago: University of Chicago Press, 1970.

Langer, Susanne K., *Mind: An Essay on Human Feeling I & II*. Baltimore: John Hopkins University Press, 1967/1972.

Lefcourt, Hebert, "The Function of the Illusions of Control and Freedom," *American Psychologist*, May 1973, pp. 417-425.

Louch, A. R., *Explanation and Human Action*. Berkeley, California: University of California Press, 1966.

Machan, T. R., "A Rationale for Human Rights," *The Personalist*, Spring 1971, pp. 216-235.

———, "Education and the Philosophy of Knowledge," *Educational Theory*, Summer 1970, pp. 253-268.

———, "For Moral Growth," *The Freeman*, October 1970, pp. 620-622.

———, "Has the Skeptic Won?" *Individualist*, May 1971, pp. 14-17.

———, "Kuhn's Impossibility Proof and the Moral Element in Scientific Explanations," *Theory and Decision* (forthcoming)

———, "Liberty: Economic versus Moral Justification," *The Occasional Review* (forthcoming)

———, "Politics: A Sometimes Personal Matter," *New Guard*, April 1973, pp. 13-14.

———, "On Selfishness and Capitalism," *Inquiry* (forthcoming)

———, "Prima Facie versus Natural (human) Rights," *The Journal of Value Inquiry* (forthcoming)

——— (ed.), *The Libertarian Alternative*. Chicago: Nelson-Hall Co., 1974.

———, "The Moral Imperative of the Free Market," *New Guard*, April 1974, pp. 17-20.

———, "TV Violence: An Analysis," *Human Events*, December 16, 1972, p. 23.

Madden, Edward H., "A Third View of Causality," *The Review of Metaphysics*, Sept. 1969, pp. 67-84.

——— and Harre, R., "In Defense of Natural Agents," *The Philosophical Quarterly*, Vol. 23, April 1973, pp. 117-132.

Madden, E. H. (ed.), *The Structure of Scientific Thought.* Boston: Houghton Mifflin, 1960.

Malott, Richard W., *Contingency Management in Education.* Kalamazoo, Mich.: Behaviordelia, 1972.

Malott, Richard (ed.), *An Introduction to Behavior Modification.* Kalamazoo, Mich.: Behaviordelia, 1972.

——— and Svinicki, J. G., "Contingency Management in an Introductory Psychology Course for One Thousand Students," *The Psychological Record,* L9 (1969), pp. 545-556.

Melden, A. I. (ed.), *Human Rights.* Belmont, California: Wadsworth Publishing Co., 1970.

Miller, Eugene F., "Hume's Contribution to Behavioral Science," *Journal of the History of the Behavioral Sciences,* April 1971, pp. 154-168.

———, "Positivism, Historicism, and Politicl Inquiry," *The American Political Science Review,* Vol. 66, pp. 796-817.

Miller, Fred D., "A Refutation of Anarchism," *New Guard,* September 1973, pp. 7-10.

Mischel, Theodore (ed.), *Human Action.* New York: Academic Press, 1969.

Nozick, Robert, "Distributive Justice," *Philosophy and Public Affairs,* Fall 1973, pp. 45-126.

———, *Anarchy, State and Utopia.* New York: Basic Books, 1974.

Pitcher, G. (ed.), *Wittgenstein.* Garden City, New York: Anchor Books, 1966.

Pitkin, H. F., *Wittgenstein and Justice.* Berkeley, California: University of California Press, 1972.

Polanyi, Michael, *The Study of Man.* Chicago: University of Chicago Press, 1963.

———, *Knowing and Being.* Chicago: University of Chicago Press, 1969.

Quine, W. V. N., *The Ways of Paradox.* N.Y.: Random House, 1966.

Rand, Ayn, *Introduction to Objectivist Epistemology.* New York: The Objectivist Inc., 1970.

———, "The Stimulus . . . and The Response," *The Ayn Rand Letter,* Vol. 1, Nos. 8-11.

———, *The Virtue of Selfishness.* New York: Signet Books, 1965.

Rasmussen, Douglas B., "Aristotle and the Defense of the Law of Contradiction," *The Personalist,* Spring 1973, pp. 149-162.

Rawls, John, *A Theory of Justice.* Cambridge: Harvard University Press, 1971.

Reiman, Jeffrey, *In Defense of Political Philosophy.* New York: Harper & Row, 1972.

Riley, G. (ed.), *Values, Objectivity and the Social Sciences.* Menlo Park, California: Addison-Wesley Publishing Co., 1974.

Roberts, Paul C., "Politics and Science: A Critique of Buchanan's Assessment of Polanyi," *Ethics,* April 1969, pp. 235-241.

Ryle, Gilbert, *The Concept of Mind.* New York: Barnes & Noble, 1949.

Schmitt, Richard, "The Desire for Private Gain," *Inquiry,* Summer 1973, pp. 149-167.

Selsam, Howard, and Martel, Harry, *Reader in Marxist Philosophy.* New York: International Publishers, 1963.

Sheppard, W. C., and MacDermot, H. G., "Design and Evaluation of a Programmed Course in Introductory Psychology," *Journal of Applied Behavioral Analysis,* Spring 1970, pp. 5-11.

Skinner, B. F., *Beyond Freedom and Dignity.* New York: Bantam/Vintage Books, 1972.

————, Cummulative Record. NY: Appleton-Century-Crofts, 1961.

————, Science and Human Behavior. New York: Macmillan, 1953.

————, The Behavior of Organisms. New York: Appleton-Century-Crofts, 1938.

————, Verbal Behavior. New York: Appleton-Century-Crofts, 1957.

————, "The Concept of the Reflex in the Description of Behavior," Journal of General Psychology, Vol. 5 (1931), pp. 427-458.

————, "Freedom and the Control of Man," American Scholar, Vol. 25, 1955, 47-65.

————, "The Design of Cultures," Daedalus, Summer 1961.

Sperry, Roger W., "Mind, Brain, and Humanist Values," in John R. Platt (ed.) New Views of the Nature of Man. Chicago: University of Chicago Press, 1965, pp. 71-92.

————, "Neurology and the Mind-Brain Problem," American Scientist, XL (1952), pp. 291-312.

————, "The Great Cerebral Commissure," Scientific American, CCX (1964), pp. 42-52.

Stough, Charlotte L., Greek Skepticism. Berkeley, California: University of California Press, 1969.

Strauss, Leo, Natural Right and History. Chicago: University of Chicago Press, 1953.

Taube, Mortimer, Computers and Common Sense. New York: McGraw-Hill, 1963.

Toulmin, Stephen, The Uses of Argument. New York: Cambridge University Press, 1969.

Trigg, Roger, Reason and Commitment. New York: Cambridge University Press, 1973.

Walker, E. L., Psychology as a Natural and Social Science. Belmont, California: Brooks/Cole Publishing Co., 1970.

Walter, Edward, "Empiricism and Ethical Reasoning," American Philosophical Quarterly, October 1970, pp. 364-369.

Wann, T. W. (ed.), Behaviorism and Phenomenology. Chicago: University of Chicago Press, 1964.

Watts, Meredith W., "B. F. Skinner and the Language of Technological Control," The American Political Science Review (forthcoming).

Wheeler, Harvey (ed.), Beyond the Punitive Society. San Francisco: W. H. Freeman & Co., 1973.

Windelband, Wilhelm, A History of Philosophy I & II. New York: Harper Torchbooks, 1958.

Yolton, John, "Action, Metaphysics and Modality," American Philosophical Quarterly, April 1973, pp. 71-85.

Young, Robert, "A Sound Self-Referential Argument?" The Review of Metaphysics, September 1973, pp. 112-119.

Ziedins, Rudi, "Identification of Characteristics of Mental Events with Characteristics of Brain Events," American Philosophical Quarterly, January 1971, pp. 13-23.

Zupan, M. L., "The Conceptual Development of Quantification in Experimental Psychology," Journal of the History of the Behavioral Sciences (forthcoming).

————, "Is Mental Illness a Myth?" Reason, August 1973, pp. 4-11.

Index

221

222

Kristol, Irving, 153, 215n
Krutch, Joseph Wood, 37
Kuhn, Thomas S., 54, 67, 148
Lakatos, Imre, 54
Lashley, Karl, quoted, 89, 107
legal system, and human rights, 184, 185-186, 204
Leucippus, 24, 59
Lewis, C. S., 37
libertarian, defined, 38
liberty. *See* political liberty
Locke, John, and human rights, 13, 153, 173, 178, 202; and literature of freedom, 36; an empiricist, 75; quoted, 175
logic, Skinner's rejection of, 30, 84-85; fundamental, 149-150
logical atomists, 77
logical empiricism, 75
logical positivists, 77
Louch, A. R., 148; quoted, 174
Lucretius, 62
Macdonald, Margaret, 180
Mach, Ernst, 72, 87
Machiavelli, 50, 179
man, natural vs. divine, 100, 103, 167, 168; active vs. passive, 169-170; goal of, 183, 193. *See also* human nature
Manne, Henry, 50
Marx, Karl, 15, 45, 50; utopian, 40; empiricist, 72; materialist, 110; view of human nature of, 132, 159; and human rights, 178
Marxism/Marxists, 44, 77, 150, 186, 208
Maslow, Abraham, 37
materialism, in Skinner, 15, 59, 97-102, 139; ancient, 59; and causality, 97; defined, 103, 104-106; and mind/body identity, 106-113
mechanism, in Skinner, 15, 59, 104, 139; defined, 104; in psychology, 104-105
mentalism, 78
metaphysics, 71, 105, 144
Mill, John Stuart, 33, 36, 37, 72, 153
mind, and rationalism, 73-75; scientific study of, 104-105, 167-172
mind/body, dualism, 74-75, 103; identity theory, 106, 107-113, 166; dual-aspect theory, 166-168
mind/mirror, identity theory, 110-111
moral excellence, 183-184, 193
moral good, and nonnaturalism, 154
morality, in classical liberalism, 152-153; a field of study, 174; and freedom (choice), 174-176; and politics, 178, 184; criterion of judgment, 183-184; purpose of, 193; and rationality, 192-193; and happiness. *See also* dignity
moral skepticism, 14, 153-156, 179, 191, 215n
moral standards, universality of, 190
Moore, George Edward, 154-155, 179
Moore, Thomas, 40
Morris, Herbert, 186
Musgrave, Alan, 54
national emergency, 202-204

national purpose, 208, 209
naturalistic fallacy, 179
natural rights, 179-181. *See also* Locke, John, and human rights
natural selection, 91
nature, and man, 100, 103, 167, 168
natures, 158-159
need-deprivation, 26, 91, 93
Newton, Isaac, 59
Nielsen, Kai, 178; quoted, 180
nominalists, 159
Objectivists, 183
objectivity, and determinism, 28-29; and neutrality, 130, 155-156; and observation, 144-145; and value-free science, 155
observation, and empiricism, 71-72, 78-79, 81; and description, 90, 155; and objectivity, 144-145
operant, the, 26, 27
operant behavior, and freedom, 27, 92-94; defined by Skinner, 92
operationalism, 68-69, 75; defined, 68; in Skinner, 85, 87-88; and descriptivism, 90; and empiricism, 118
"ought," Skinner's analysis of, 115-119
pain, and reductionism, 106-110
Peltzman, Sam, 153
perception, Skinner's analysis of, 79, 86; measurement of, 168-169
philosophy, scope of, 70; and science, 145-150; methods of, 148
philosophy of science, 71
physicalism, 15, 104
physiology, 64, 101
Place, U. T., 106
Plato, 60, 132, 208; and dualism, 15, 103; utopian, 40, 210, 211; and rationalism, 74; on natures, 159; and egoism, 194
Polanyi, Michael, 122; quoted, 102
political liberty, and freedom (choice), 31, 187, 191-194; and dignity, 13, 189, 193-194, 204-206, 209; a human right, 184-187; and morality, 190-194; a universal value, 205. *See also* Free society
political science, 139-140
politics, purpose of, 143; a field of study, 144; and morality, 178, 184
pollution, 201-202
Popper, Sir Karl, 37, 54, 122
positivists, 50, 144, 147
prediction, and reductionism, 123; and free will, 171-172
prima facie rights, 179, 202
processes, 27, 63, 86, 87, 100. *See also* events
property, human right to, 186-187
psychology, laws of, 113; and political theory, 140-144
psychosurgery, 101, 124, 133
Ptolemy, 145
public good. *See* Common good
public interest. *See* Common good
punishment, and human rights, 186. *See also* aversive control
purpose, and operant behavior, 92-93, 98;

and explanation of action, 174-175; and moral judgment, 183
Putnam, Hilary, 106
Quine, W. V. O., quoted, 106
Rand, Ayn, 37, 194, 195, 215n; quoted, 176-177, 184
Randell, John H., 100
rationalism, 14, 73-75
rationality. *See* consciousness
Rawls, John, 153
reductionism, as a faith, 27-28, 89, 142; in Skinner, 61, 85-96; linguistic, 87; mind/behavior, 97; appeal of, 103-104; in psychology, 104-105; mind/body, 105-113; in idealism, 112; alternative to, 141-144. *See also* reductive materialism
reductive materialism, 81, 171; defined, 27, 85; in Skinner, 85-86, 94; versions of 105-106, 112; and design of culture, 123
Reich, Charles, 149
reinforcement, negative, 35-36; positive, 38, 39, 40; defined by Skinner, 91; and operant behavior, 92-93, 95; and values, 115-116; *passim. See also* behavioral technology
Relativism, ethical, 116-117, 191
Republic (Plato), 40, 210
response, reduction to in Skinner, 92, 94-95
rights. *See* human rights
Rogers, Carl, 62
Ross, Alf, 178
Rostand, Jean, 54
Roszak, Theodore, 149
Russell, Bertrand, 72, 86, 179
Ryle, Gilbert, 74
Sakharov, A., 169
Scheffler, Israel, 54, 148
science, appeal of, 14-15, 17, 48-51, 124-125; and human freedom, 14-15, 57, 61-62, 65, 165-172 *passim;* importance for Skinner, 23, 48-49, 54, 60, 86; Skinner's view of, 55-56; cumulative development of, 56-61, 101; Skinner's view of criticized, 56-70; and humanities, 59-61, 144-145; traditional view of, 62-63; and the planned society, 122; without reductionism, 141-148; and philosophy, 145-150; controversy in, 146-147; value-free, 149, 153; and mysticism, 149-150; and morality, 174
sciences, physical vs. humane, 14, 101, 58
scientific approach, 14, 48, 51, 144-146; field-specific, 27, 148
scientific language, and everyday language, 67-68, 116; and contingencies of reinforcement, 68
scientific laws, generation of, 65-66, 127; psychological, 113
sense-impressions, 75-76, 78, 79
self-determination, attributed to culture, 44-

45; denied by Skinner, 45, 62; and self-regulation, 165-167
skepticism, 76. *See also* moral skepticism
Skinner, applications and contributions of, 18, 40, 129-132, 134; claim to novelty, 23-24, 59, 100-101; political implications of, 38-42, 43, 44, 123-134, 140-141; and nonscientific conclusions, 39, 64-65, 80-81, *passim;* and "God's-eye view," 42-45; and empiricist tradition, 78-80, 86; and causality, 97-100; reductionism in, 83-104; materialism in, 97-103; and other schools of psychology, 140-141; quoted, 23, 27, 28, 32, 33, 35, 36, 37, 38, 40-49 *passim,* 55, 56, 60, 61-62, 63, 64, 74, 78, 79, 80, 82, 84, 85, 86, 87, 89, 91, 92, 94, 95, 96, 97, 98, 99, 100, *passim,* 115, 119-120, 121, 122, 123, 124, 125, 126 *passim,* 128, 167, 176, 185, 188, 202, 208
slavery, 205
Smart, J. J. C., 106
Smith, Adam, 152
social consciousness, 208
Socialists, Utopian, 40
Socrates, 40
Spencer, 194
Sperry, Roger W., quoted, 165
Spinoza, 103
stimulus, unexplained in Skinner, 94
Strauss, Leo, 37; quoted 177
Stroud, Barry, quoted, 181
subjectivism, and antiscience, 15; and values, 140
Szasz, Thomas S., 132
Taube, Mortimer, 57
Thorndike, Edward L., 75
totalitarianism, 30, 40, 43, 44
Toulmin, Stephen, 54, 148; quoted, 111
utopianism, 18, 40-41, 121, 122, 210-211
utilitarianism, 153
value-free science, 140, 149, 153, 155
values, 114; Skinner's analysis of, 115-119; Skinner's identified, 119-123, 127-129; subjective, 140; in social sciences, 140, 155; emotive, 155, 179-180. *See also* moral skepticism
van den Haag, Ernest, 159
variables, vs. causes, 97
Velikovsky, Immanuel, 146
Vienna Circle, the, 72
Vlastos, Gregory, 178-179
volition. *See* free will
von Mises, Ludwig, 153
Walden II (Skinner), 43, 54
Weaver, Richard M., 132
Weber, Max, 50
Whitehead, Alred North, 27, 86, 87
Windelband, Wilhelm, quoted, 100
Wittgenstein, Ludwig, 72, 159
Ziedins, Rudi, quoted, 108-109